THE LAST BATTLE STATION:

The Story of the USS *Houston*

THE LAST BATTLE STATION:

The Story of the USS *Houston*

DUANE SCHULTZ

St. Martin's Press/New York

Library of Congress Cataloging in Publication Data

Schultz, Duane P.
  The last battle station.
  1. Houston (Cruiser : CA-30)   2. Java Sea, Battle
of the, 1942.   3. Sunda Strait, Battle of, 1942.
4. World War, 1939–1945—Naval operations, American.
I. Title.
VA65.H66S38   1985   359.3'253   84–24970
ISBN 0-312-46973-X

First Edition

10 9 8 7 6 5 4 3 2 1

To those who stand watch in Sunda Strait

Contents

Contents

Houston's great fight, the last half-hour of it waged singly against overwhelming odds, is one of the most gallant in American naval annals.

—Samuel Eliot Morison

I knew that ship and loved her. Her officers and men were my friends. . . . They sold their liberty and their lives most dearly.

—Franklin Delano Roosevelt

The full story of the mysterious disappearance of the USS *Houston* was revealed last night, four years to the day after she went down fighting.

—*The Washington Post*
March 3, 1946

THE LAST BATTLE STATION:

The Story of the USS *Houston*

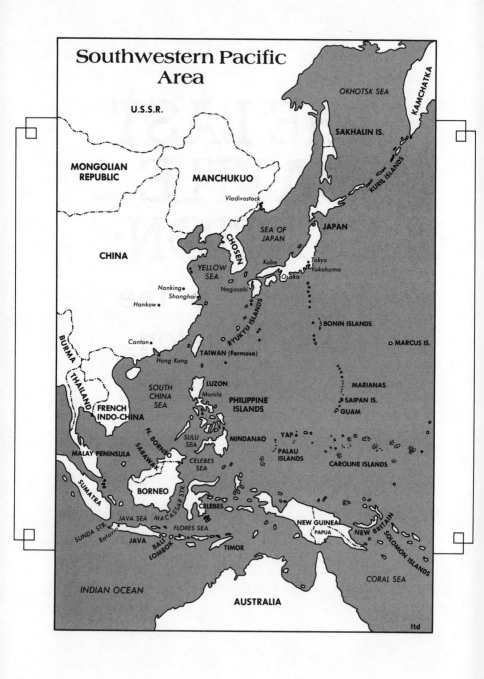

Southwestern Pacific Area

1

Overdue and Presumed Lost

Major Robert Bartlett was a long way from his home in Los Angeles, California. With a handful of other American OSS men, he was crouched by a small campfire deep in the steamy jungle of Thailand. It was August 1945, and the war against Japan would not end for two more weeks. It was not a time for Bartlett to let down his guard, not in that part of the world, where the Japanese could sneak up on you before you knew it. Bartlett and his men were tense and watchful.

Suddenly a prearranged signal overrode the raucous jungle cries. The men grabbed their carbines and spread out. After several agonizing moments, a line of Thai guerrillas—the men Bartlett and his group were there to train—broke into the clearing. With them were two white men, and to Bartlett they were the most pitiful sight he had ever seen. Dirty and emaciated, their hair plastered to their heads, their bodies shining with sweat, these ghostlike figures wore only meager scraps of clothing.

Bartlett hurried over to them. "Who are you?" he asked.

"Jap prisoners," one said. It was a great effort for him to talk, but he took a deep breath and went on. "We got away four days ago. We're Navy men, sir. Survivors of the *Houston*."

The *Houston!* These men were like voices from the dead. Bartlett knew that the cruiser *Houston* was a mystery ship, vanished three and a half years ago. She had sailed from the harbor at

Batavia in the Dutch East Indies at 7:30 on the evening of February 28, 1942. At 11:30 that night, a cryptic message had been received at the naval radio station on Corregidor in the Philippines: "Enemy forces engaged." Nothing more was heard.

For nine months a curtain of silence cloaked the fate of the crew. Had they all gone down with the ship? Had some been captured? Were they hiding out on the Japanese-occupied island of Java? Some high officers in the U.S. Navy conjectured that the ship had been trapped and captured intact.

Then, slowly, bits of information filtered back to the United States about some of the men, but there was no word on the whereabouts of the ship itself. On November 18, 1942, ham radio operators on the west coast of the United States picked up a shortwave broadcast from one of the *Houston*'s pilots, Lieutenant (jg) Walter "Windy" Winslow. It was a brief personal message to his wife in Stamford, Connecticut. Two months later, on January 25, 1943, another broadcast was detected, this one from Seaman First Class Joseph L. Bingham.

Tokyo's official propaganda broadcasts said that some *Houston* survivors were safe in an internment camp in Batavia, and finally, on February 9, 1943, almost one year after the *Houston* disappeared, the International Red Cross announced that the Japanese government had informed them that four members of the *Houston* crew were being held as prisoners of war. Four! Out of 1,064 men who had been aboard the night the ship sailed from Batavia.

The U.S. Navy high command was perplexed. It did not feel there was sufficient evidence to alter the status of the men of the *Houston* from "missing in action" to "prisoner of war," but as more months passed with no word about their fate, their status was changed to "believe killed in action." Their families could only wait and wonder. As to the ship itself, the official report continued to be "overdue and presumed lost."

Now, in August of 1945, the two seamen who had stumbled into Major Bartlett's OSS camp would begin to clear up one of the great mysteries of the war. They reported that about 300 of the crew were being held by the Japanese. Over the next several weeks, as these prisoners were discovered in camps in Thailand and Japan, the fate of the ship became known. But there were not many left to tell the tale. Only 292 survived the ordeal of the flagship of the Asiatic Fleet, one of the best-known and loved ships of the prewar Navy.

The story of the *Houston* and her crew is a microcosm of the early grim and desperate days and weeks of the war in the Pacific, a time when defeat screamed from every headline, and when Japan seemed invincible. Like all American forces caught in the Pacific by the Japanese onslaught—the marines on Wake and Guam, the soldiers and airmen on Bataan and Corregidor—the Asiatic Fleet was doomed the moment the first enemy bombs fell on Pearl Harbor. From that instant, all the carefully laid prewar plans became obsolete and the fate of the little fleet was sealed.

With no possibility of relief or reinforcement and little hope of survival against such overwhelming superiority, the *Houston* and the other antiquated ships of the Asiatic Fleet, together with the equally frail British, Dutch, and Australian naval forces, had just one mission: to hold on as long as they possibly could. Every day they could keep the Japanese from advancing farther south toward Australia was another day of grace in which America and her allies could build their strength. But these sailors had to do it alone. "We finally got the feeling," one seaman said, "that we were going to be left there, that nothing or nobody was going to come, and that we were there as a sacrifice."

They were truly expendable, the *Houston* and the other ships of that ragtag outfit, and they were expected to hold the line or die trying. As it turned out, they couldn't hold the line, but they did die trying. Admiral Samuel Eliot Morison wrote that the Asiatic Fleet "drank the cup of defeat to the bitter dregs." The *Houston*, once the favorite ship of President Franklin D. Roosevelt, died along with the fleet, and did so gloriously, in one of the fiercest sea battles of World War II, surrounded by five enemy cruisers, eleven destroyers, and an uncounted number of torpedo boats.

But the *Houston* died alone, with only the enemy as witness, with only a fraction of the crew, swimming for their lives, knowing what she had endured and accomplished in her last hours. To the rest of the world, the *Houston* had disappeared.

The memory of the ship did not easily fade. She was too well known for that to happen. Most Americans knew the ship from prewar photographs and newsreels, had read about the magnificent cruiser, gleaming white and spotless from stem to stern, and knew that every man aboard felt honored to serve on the naval vessel that had transported a U.S. President more frequently than any other in history.

In those balmy prewar days, the ship had been called the "Little White House," in recognition of Roosevelt's frequent vacation cruises. No other ship received so much favorable publicity during the peaceful 1930s.

The *Houston* was sleek and beautiful and she made good copy for the press and the newsreel photographers who clambered after the President. The ship was as long as two football fields and capable of slicing through the seas at a speed of over 32 knots. Her nine eight-inch guns could hurl shells more than 31,000 yards, nearly 18 miles. In addition, she bristled with antiaircraft guns and .50-caliber machine guns.

Although the *Houston* looked like a formidable warship, there were weaknesses beneath the impressive exterior. Like all the armed services, the Navy was operating on a cut-rate budget in the years between the wars, with never enough money to prepare for the conflict that was coming, as a stunned American public would soon learn.

The peacetime Navy of the 1930s also suffered from the naval limitation treaty America had signed in 1921. This disarmament agreement seriously impaired the Navy's ability to fight in the early days of World War II. Morison referred to it as a "crime against American defense," and it was particularly disastrous with regard to cruisers, limiting not only their size but also their firepower and armor plating.

The *Houston* was one of these treaty-class cruisers, built according to the restrictive guidelines imposed by the government's decision to pull back from the arms race. Some called the ship a "paper cruiser," because the armor plating was so thin.

There were other weaknesses as well. By the time war came, the *Houston* was 12 years old and overdue for modernization, but there were no funds available. She had no radar; there was no money for that. Indeed, most of the crew had never even heard of radar. Her fire-control equipment was antiquated, and there was no budget allotment for its modernization.

The gunners had had no target practice with live ammunition. Shells cost money. Not until their first enemy engagement, when the *Houston* was being attacked by 54 enemy airplanes, did the crew learn that most of their antiaircraft ammunition was worthless. "It was like throwing spitballs," one said. "Those guns were pumping it out," another remembered, "but they were absolutely useless." Forty-eight men died that day.

The physical condition of the *Houston* reflected that of the rest of the American forces in the Far East as Japan was preparing to launch a war. Too little, too old, too late. But there was nothing wrong with the crew. They were prepared, well trained, and confident.

A gunnery officer said, "I've never in my naval career seen a ship that was so well trained. Everybody knew his job and the next man's, too." Another survivor, an engineering officer, recalled the *Houston* as "one of the best-maintained ships I've ever been on, before or since. The morale of the crew—officers and men—was extremely high. They were proud of their ship.

"It was largely a volunteer crew that had wanted to go to China that had brought her out, and the personnel on board were a cut above what the rest of the Navy was experiencing as they were building up under the threat of war. The personnel of the *Houston* were very truly an exceptional group of people."

All during the closing days of peacetime in the Pacific, the men of the *Houston* drilled and trained and practiced, then drilled and trained and practiced again. On October 6, 1941, just two months before the attack on Pearl Harbor, a young radioman wrote to his folks back home in North Carolina: "We just got back from another month trip, which was very unpleasant for all hands. Lots of heat and drills. Well, we've got to be ready for those Japs in case they start anything."

The men of the *Houston* were ready. Nothing was lacking in their spirit, their professionalism, their willingness to take on the enemy. It was their government that let them down, that had not been willing to spend the money for an adequate defense. A marine aboard ship summed up their situation. "We worked like

Trojans every day and we had excellent gun crews. We had excellent tracking crews. The only thing we didn't have was modern
equipment."

Nevertheless, the *Houston* was on the firing line, serving as
the flagship for Admiral Thomas C. Hart, commander in chief of
the Asiatic Fleet and the senior U.S. officer in the Far East. She
was not equipped to go to war, but she was there. While America
slept on that fateful Sunday morning in December 1941, the fighting began, and the *Houston* had less than three months to live.

The survivors of the *Houston* have never forgotten the three
months of war aboard their ship, or the three and a half years of
brutal captivity that followed. They cannot forget, and every August they meet in Texas to talk about it, to recall who they were
and what they once did. They echo the past and bring it alive
once again—the final battle in Sunda Strait, the chaos of Java Sea
they miraculously survived, the sights and sounds and terror of
the enemy planes overhead, the burial of shipmates in a Dutch
cemetery on Java, the skill and courage of their captain, the quiet
dignity of their chaplain who gave his life jacket to a seaman and
disappeared beneath the waves, the swift currents driving them
from shore, the hunger and beatings, the malaria and privations
. . . How could they forget such things?

They remember the *Houston*'s wartime nickname, "the gallop-
ing ghost of the Java coast." "I don't know where this name came
from," a seaman explained, "but we would always post on the
bulletin board the messages from Tokyo Rose. She was always
saying, 'Today we sunk the *Houston*.' I think it came out of this
situation, and somebody pinned the title on us. It was very appropriate."

They remember their first experience of death. "We started to
clear the bodies out down below, and I thought there was a couple of them alive. They were bubbling from the nose, like they
were breathing. Two guys were sitting right there by the door. I
reached down to pick one of them up and grabbed a whole handful of flesh. It just came right off. I kind of got a little sick."

"War came to us in a real way. It knocked all the cockiness
out of us, and it didn't take but about three seconds, I guess, to
do it, because we saw what war could be in its real fury in those

few brief moments. So many of these people were dead and many others were wounded."

"All night long the carpenters worked. All sorts of people helped building coffins. All night long there was hammering going on in the hangars and the passageways, and the next morning we went over to the cemetery. I went as pallbearer."

"I can still hear that band playing the funeral dirge."

They remember how their captain took action in their first battle. "Captain Rooks was a hero from then on. That made him right there. He operated that ship like it was a Chris-Craft."

"Of course, everybody wonders what the new skipper is going to be like. Well, the stories went around that he was fresh out of the Naval War College and that he was untried, which we all were. But after our first meeting with the Japanese, then the legends started to go through the ship about this great skipper."

They remember their exhaustion as the weeks of constant strain mounted, when general quarters sounded at all hours and the men slept by their guns—in those short periods when they could get any sleep at all.

"Oh, Lord, we were just dead to the world. We hadn't had any decent food and certainly no rest. We were just staggering around."

"I just figured we had bought it. At that point, we were so exhausted and beyond any more physical endurance that that was it. I mean, we had been at battle stations for months. We'd hardly had any food. We had just fought some fierce battles. There just wasn't another ounce left."

"I needed sleep. I don't think I'd had ten hours' sleep in that week . . . and it just seemed that, well, if I could just lay down here and sleep awhile that when I wake up, everything is going to be all right."

It wasn't all right. When they woke up, the ship was under attack again, for the last time. As tired as they were, when general quarters sounded all the men were ready to give it all they had.

"Even at the last battle station, everybody was gung ho. Our spirits were really high. There was one big rush to the battle stations. In my mind I said, 'Oh boy, we've gone through all these days. We can go through this one.' We never lost our confidence and our feeling of being able to handle whatever came along."

Confidence and spirit were no longer enough. The odds were too high against the men of the *Houston*. They fought to the end, even when all they had left were star shells and the enemy was closing in on all sides.

"I just could not believe that they could ever sink that ship. I was crying. I don't know if from the fear or from seeing that glorious thing go down like that. You know, we'd been on it for a long time. It was our home."

"It was really a beautiful sight. The colors were still flying, flapping in the breeze. I was tempted to go back to the ship, she looked so big and she'd been such a good home so long. She looked so sturdy, compared to being out there in the dark, in the water."

"She was full of holes all through the side. Those close-range destroyer shells had gone right through one side and out the other. . . . Her guns were askew, one turret pointing one way and another the other, and the five-inch guns pointing in all directions.

"There was a big bright flame coming up just about the mainmast and she was listing way over. I couldn't help thinking what she looked like when I first joined her, when she was the President's yacht. She shone from end to end. I think I will always remember that last look, though. And as I watched her, she just lay down to die. She just rolled over on one side and the fire went out with a big hiss."

It was 12:45 on the morning of March 1, 1942. The *Houston* was gone, but the ordeal for her survivors was far from over. They were miles from shore in the middle of the night, battle-weary and covered with oil, surrounded by Japanese ships. Some men were perched in rafts, others clung to debris from the ship. Some had life jackets, others had none.

Some reached shore within three hours, others in three days. They were scattered along 30 miles of coastline. Some were captured immediately, others headed for the jungles. None escaped. The Javanese, extending their hatred of the Dutch to all white men, turned them over to the Japanese.

The men of the *Houston* were kept on Java for six months, in a prisoner-of-war camp they later dubbed the "Hilton," because it was so much better than what came later. Some of the senior officers were sent to a special interrogation camp in Japan. Most of the rest were shipped to Burma to work on the railroad. One of the bridges they built spanned a little river called the Kwai. "I don't know what was so important about the bridge over the Kwai River that rated a book and a movie," a marine sergeant said later. "To us, it was just another stream to be crossed."

Those who survived that hell were sent to Thailand to work on another railroad, and then to Malaya to build an airfield and to lay more track. And then one day it ended.

"One afternoon, a big plane with a white star under each wing came in and made a landing. I was in India a few hours later and, incredibly, a few days later I was in the United States. It was just that easy when it finally came. But those years in Burma, they stretch out to an age. Perhaps, someday, I can forget them entirely."

It was a vain hope. No one has been able to forget them entirely. Each year at the reunion the stories spill out as the survivors purge and renew their memories. They are older now, and many are in poor health. Each year there are fewer of them left. But they stand with pride as they laugh and cry and comfort one another. After all, they served on the *Houston.*

2

We'll Be Shooting
in a Few Days

It was New Year's Eve 1940, the last full year of peace America would know for five long years. In his sumptuously appointed stateroom aboard the USS *Houston*, a 63-year-old admiral with a shock of white hair sat ramrod straight at his desk. Despite the heat and humidity of Manila Bay, he was dressed in his familiar starched high collar, the source of one of his nicknames—"High-Collar Hart." He was also known as "Tough Tommy."

Both suited him well. Admiral Thomas C. Hart was a veteran of 42 years of active duty, an illustrious career now capped by his appointment as commander of the Asiatic Fleet. He bent over the desk and continued with his daily task of confiding his thoughts to his diary in a thin, spidery handwriting.

"The year is ending," he wrote, "*and* the clouds seem to be shutting in on us—out here. There is more and more indication that the Japs are coming south and, for the first time, I really am seeing the loom of WAR, not so far over the horizon. No, I'm not ready, it's impossible to be sufficiently ready, without precipitating something. So of course I am uneasy."

War was coming. Most of the men of the *Houston* were sure of that; you didn't have to be an admiral or have been on the Asiatic station long to know that. A few months later, 23-year-old Radioman First Class Jerry Judson Bunch—"J. J." to his friends—

wrote to his parents in Poplar Branch, North Carolina: "We seem to be getting nearer to war all the time."

In June, a 17-year-old sailor from Newark, New Jersey, joined the crew. Otto Schwarz was a seaman second class—"You can't hardly get any lower than that"—and his battle station was the forward powder magazine, far below the waterline. "You could see that something was building up," he recalls, "and we were being caught in the middle of something big."

Another seaman second, Bill Weissinger, from Waco, Texas, a trainer on an antiaircraft gun, knew it right away. "I hadn't been on the Asiatic station more than a week before I got the feeling that war with Japan was going to happen. It was inevitable."

The men of the *Houston* could also read it in the behavior of the Japanese civilians with whom they came into contact. Lieutenant Robert Fulton, the assistant engineering officer, was impressed with the "aggressiveness and arrogance of the civilian Japanese around Manila. Plain courtesy on the golf course and clubhouse locker room was just nonexistent. They seemed part of the total Japanese effort to take over Asia."

One of the *Houston*'s pilots, Lieutenant Jack Lamade, had noticed the same attitude when the ship was in China. "When we would play golf in Tsingtao, the Japanese were playing right behind us and they would just hit the ball right into you. In Shanghai, walking along the streets, you'd have to get off the sidewalk when Japs came along or they'd walk right through you."

The man sent out from the Naval War College to take command of the *Houston*, 49-year-old Captain Albert Rooks, was convinced there would be war, even before he stepped aboard ship. In the early summer of 1941, he had embarked on the *President Harrison* from San Francisco with a number of other officers headed for the doomed Asiatic Fleet. As they sailed across the Pacific, stopping in Honolulu, Shanghai, and Hong Kong before reaching Manila, he presided over a series of conferences in his stateroom. The officers recall his words well: "The Japanese will make the China Sea a sea of blood in the near future."

As summer turned to fall, Captain Rooks put his thoughts on paper, in one of the most remarkable prewar documents ever produced. He wrote his assessment of the situation while aboard the *Houston*, completing it on November 18, 1941. Entitled "Estimate of the Situation, Far East Area," its 103 pages contain a brilliant summary and evaluation of the military, economic, and social considerations that would have to lead to war.

Rooks catalogued the weaknesses and strengths of the Dutch, British, and Japanese forces, including a list of every Japanese naval vessel by name, and he rated Japan's fighting ability as "excellent." He discussed the hydrography and topography of the entire Southwest Pacific and provided detailed climate conditions in the area that would soon become a battlefield. The Japanese would definitely go to war by means of surprise attacks on bases in the Philippines and on British and Dutch possessions. He did not predict the attack at Pearl Harbor, but by the time his report reached Washington, that event was history, and Captain Rooks and two-thirds of his crew were dead.

So it was easy to predict the war. The problem was in deciding what to do about it, given the meager forces and obsolete equipment. The Asiatic Fleet would have to make do with what it had, and it didn't have very much.

In January of 1941 Admiral Hart had taken the extremely unpopular step of ordering the wives and families of all naval personnel in China and the Philippines to return to the United States. Howls of protest erupted, particularly since the Army dependents were being allowed to stay (they were not ordered home for another four months). There were no *Houston* dependents in the Philippines. Before the ship had left Long Beach in November 1940, the threat of war was considered so great that none had been permitted to go. It would be nearly five years before the *Houston* survivors saw their families again.

Training activities were intensified. Steel helmets were issued to the sailors on the *Houston* and on the other ships of the fleet. The men were told to make their wills.

Hart began to send the ships south for training exercises, allowing them to return to Manila only long enough to refuel and to replenish stores and ammunition. Gone were the weekday training cruises with liberty weekends in Manila. This admiral was not about to lose his ships in a surprise raid on a peaceful Sunday morning while they all lay idly at anchor.

As early as the summer of 1941, *Houston*'s antiaircraft guns were kept manned from before daybreak to after dark, every day of the week. The air defense officer, Lieutenant Commander W. Jackson Galbraith, got the skipper's permission to train the crews of the big eight-inch guns to operate the antiaircraft guns, so they could spell his regular crews during air raids. As a result of his foresight, the *Houston* had more than enough trained personnel to man the AA guns.

The klaxon sounded general quarters at all hours of the day and night, sending men racing to their battle stations in record time. They griped and swore, but they did it again and again, getting better and faster with each drill.

By late November, the crew was informed that if they were attacked, it would likely be from the air; there would be little warning. The next day, the antiaircraft gun captains and the crews of the gun directors were given flash cards containing pictures of Japanese aircraft and told to study them well. The AA crews started sleeping by their guns, to be ready on a moment's notice.

As the situation in the Far East was deteriorating, the *Houston*'s officers and men were doing everything humanly possible to prepare for war. The government in Washington and the Navy at Pearl Harbor may have been caught by surprise, but the Asiatic Fleet was not. Perhaps the men of the *Houston* were even a bit too cocky and confident about being ready for war. Like most Americans, they seriously underestimated the fighting potential of their enemy. A sailor aboard the battleship *California*, moored at Pearl Harbor in 1941, put it this way:

"Our concept of the typical Japanese male was that of an editorial cartoon from a Hearst newspaper: short, nearsighted, bowlegged, and bucktoothed, with a thirty-five-millimeter camera hanging from his neck, smiling falsely and bowing obsequiously. It was a 'known fact' that all Japanese, because of their inadequate diet of rice and fish heads, had to wear thick corrective lenses that unfitted them for flying combat aircraft. It was also thought that they were a nation of slavish imitators, able only to reproduce shoddy replicas of American products, and that they built top-heavy ships that often capsized when launched. The idea that this pitiful island race would dare to challenge the mightiest nation in the world was ludicrous. . . . The consensus among the senior enlisted men, whom I overheard in the petty officers' head, was that it would take about three weeks to sink the entire Japanese navy and steam on into Tokyo Bay with all flags flying."

Lieutenant Thomas B. Payne, the *Houston*'s 32-year-old senior aviator, felt the same way. "I didn't think the war was going to be as tough as it was. We'd been told that they were little bitty guys with funny eyes." Lieutenant Leon Rogers, one of the antiaircraft officers, subscribed to what he called the "conventional wisdom of the day held by young naval officers who believed we could beat any Japs."

To Otto Schwarz, stationed in the forward powder magazine, "a typical Japanese was about four feet tall and wore round glasses and was not too intelligent. When they captured people, they broke their ankles so they couldn't run away. That's the Japanese I looked forward to defeating. A war with them couldn't possibly last more than five or six months."

Bill Weissinger recalled the view of so many of his shipmates among the antiaircraft gun crews: "Our attitude was that we'll rush out on the morning watch and knock hell out of them and be back in Manila Bay in time for liberty. . . . Look at all the bombs they dropped on China and never did hit anything—except the *Panay*."

Seaman Second Class Jack Smith also remembers those thoughts. "I heard all that baloney about the Japs before the war. They can't fly planes and they can't shoot straight. We found out it wasn't quite true."

But in the closing days of 1941, the men of the *Houston* were confident. Marine Corps Pfc Jim Gee, 21 years old and from Howe, Texas, summed up their feelings. "We were as cocky as young men could be, and we were physically ready for battle."

Jim Gee was right. The men were physically ready for battle. They had trained and drilled and could have performed their jobs in their sleep. They swam, climbed ropes, and did calisthenics every morning. They were lean and hard and determined, believing in themselves, in their ship, in their tiny Asiatic Fleet, and in their government. But their ship wasn't ready for battle, nor was the Asiatic Fleet. Nor was their government.

The *Houston* herself greatly needed modernization. The gunnery officer, 40-year-old Lieutenant Commander Arthur L. "Al" Maher, said, "The personnel were prepared for war, but not the materiel. We were long overdue for a complete overhaul. The fire-control equipment for the big eight-inch guns was obsolete, the installation of the new 1.1-inch pom-poms had been a rush job, and we had never been allowed to fire the five-inch ammunition.

"It had been over a year since we had been allowed to fire the eight-inch guns, and that had been short range only. We were once sent south out of Manila for training, but there were no other ships or planes to train with. I drew up plans for long-range practice with live ammunition, but the request was turned down from Washington."

Although the crew had drilled hundreds of times on the technique of firing their five-inch guns, the first opportunity they would have to actually fire them would be at war, against the enemy. Further, only four people aboard the *Houston* knew that the ammunition for those five-inch guns, the prime defense against air attack, was faulty.

A few months earlier, air defense officer Jack Galbraith and his chief enlisted man Gunner James E. Hogan had received disturbing reports from the West Coast Fleet Gunnery School back in the States. A batch of ammunition had been test-fired and was found to be defective; only one shell in four had exploded. Galbraith and Hogan had immediately gone below to the five-inch magazines and had discovered that their ammunition was of the same type tested by the AA school. They informed the gun boss, Al Maher, and Captain Rooks. When the fleet gunnery officer was told, he said, "Oh, that's absolutely impossible." "Yet," said Galbraith, "here was the ammunition the gunnery school had condemned and that was what we had aboard."

The *Houston* ordered replacement ammunition, but it never arrived. They requested permission to test-fire the shells to find out if they were as bad as reported by the gunnery school. Request denied. For reasons of morale, Rooks, Maher, Galbraith, and Hogan agreed to keep the information to themselves. There was nothing else to do but hope that their ammo was not as faulty as the batch tested back home.

The Asiatic Fleet had other problems. The torpedoes carried only 500-pound warheads, half the explosive power of the Japanese weapons, and they were slow, with only one-fifth the range. They ran deeper than they should and many had defective exploders, though no one knew it yet. Many lives would be lost finding out.

The Japanese were superior at night fighting, having trained for years in techniques and tactics not considered worthwhile by American naval experts. They also had some technically superior equipment, including large tripod-mounted binoculars with five-inch lenses that gave unusually good light-gathering power. By comparison, one officer recalled, "the standard U.S. Navy 7 × 50 binoculars looked like bargain basement opera glasses."

America had not chosen to spend money for defense—for binoculars or torpedoes or antiaircraft shells that would explode—but Japan had. While our military power languished because of the disarmament policy, Japan was building the most powerful military machine in the Far East. By 1941, their navy was much stronger and better equipped than the entire Pacific-based American, British, Dutch, and Australian fleets combined.

Although we had little with which to fight the war, we did have a plan, but like most of our equipment it was old, dating from 1921. Called "War Plan Orange," it was based on the assumption that the Japanese would initiate hostilities by means of a surprise attack. The American and Philippine armies would hold Bataan for six months, and the Asiatic Fleet would fight a delaying action until the mighty battleships of the U.S. Pacific Fleet steamed from Pearl Harbor to their rescue, shepherding convoys of troops and supplies.

This official plan for the conduct of the war was fine on paper, but unofficially, military planners had quietly discarded it. They now estimated that it would take two years, not six months, to gather the ships, personnel, and supplies needed to relieve the Philippines. Thus, nearly a year before the Japanese attacked Pearl Harbor, the Philippine Islands had been written off, declared expendable by Washington, along with the Asiatic Fleet.

Still, the fleet's mission was to fight a delaying action against any Japanese invasion, supporting the Army for as long as it could defend the islands. After that, Hart would be free to shift his remaining forces south, to assist the British and Dutch navies in their defense of the Dutch East Indies. Admiral Hart tried desperately to obtain reinforcements. He knew he needed not only more ships to augment his small force, but more modern ones as well. The largest and most powerful of his ships was the *Houston*, the flagship of the fleet, and he was well aware of her deficiencies. Although she was fast, her eight-inch guns powerful, and her crew exceptionally well trained, she was still a treaty-class cruiser with pitifully thin armor plate. The Japanese had battleships.

The Asiatic Fleet also included two light cruisers, the old *Marblehead*, "a ship old enough to vote," and the somewhat newer *Boise*, both with six-inch guns, no match for an enemy cruiser. There were 13 destroyers, but all were old four-stack models from World War I. Like the *Houston*, their crews were willing, eager, and well trained, but their ships were puny and outdated compared to what they would soon be up against. There were 28 submarines, but many were the old-style S-boats. Still, they looked impressive, and no one yet knew about their faulty torpedoes. And there were a number of auxiliary vessels— submarine tenders, rescue boats, minesweepers, and a batch of ancient gunboats just arrived from China. These were flat-bottomed and slow and poorly armed, of no value for action in the open sea. Also unsuited for combat was a squadron of six PT boats.

The Asiatic Fleet had an aircraft carrier. At least to the untrained eye it looked like a carrier, and, at one time, had been one. In fact, the USS *Langley* had been the Navy's first carrier, but now it was a sad sight with one-third of the flight deck lopped off. It was too slow to keep up with the rest of the fleet and had been relegated to service as a seaplane tender.

There were no combat aircraft in the fleet, no fighters, dive bombers, or torpedo planes. A dozen miscellaneous seaplanes were available, along with 28 PBY patrol bombers, the Catalinas, lumbering beasts suitable for rescue and reconnaissance but of limited value against the modern Japanese Navy. To complete the air force were the little SOCs, the wood-and-canvas biplanes carried by the *Houston* and the two other cruisers. In those days before radar they were designed to serve as the eyes of the fleet, to spot for the big guns, but they were no match for any fighter aircraft.

Obviously, this motley collection of ships and planes could not be considered a fighting force. Rather, it was a political creation, designed to show the flag. The fleet's theme song, "We'll All Go Up to China in the Springtime," described their annual sojourns to Chinese ports to escape the heat of Manila Bay. As a result, the officers and men of the Asiatic Fleet were quite familiar with the waters of China, but there had been no opportunity to visit the ports and bases in the southern waters, the area where they would be expected to fight alongside their allies. Captain Rooks and the other skippers had no firsthand experience in sailing the often treacherous seas around the Malay Barrier. Perhaps worse, there had been no opportunity for combined maneuvers with the British and Dutch forces.

The men of the fleet knew their limitations, but it did not dampen their confidence. After all, America had all those battleships, aircraft carriers, and cruisers back at Pearl. All they had to do was fire up their boilers and steam westward. The *Houston* would only have to hold out a week or so before the mighty Pacific Fleet would sail into Manila Bay. In the event of war, said Al Maher, "we thought the battleships would be on their way and we wouldn't be by ourselves. We knew the fleet was coming."

Pilot Windy Winslow agreed. "None of us were afraid of war with Japan . . . we were backed up by the mighty United States Pacific Fleet, based at Pearl Harbor, only a few days steaming time away. If Japan wanted to make trouble, powerful Allied naval forces stood eager to accept the challenge."

On November 27, 1941, Admiral Hart was in his office in the northwest corner of the Marsman Building, located at the end of the gigantic Pier 7 on Manila's waterfront. He had shifted his flag from the *Houston* and had moved ashore in late June. From his windows he looked out over all of Manila Bay, from the Bataan peninsula jutting into the water from the north, to the island of Corregidor at Bataan's tip, to the great Cavite naval base on the southern shore. Cavite was the largest naval base west of Pearl Harbor, the repository of the fleet's supplies and the site of its repair facilities. Admiral Hart stared at Cavite, but his mind was on the top-secret cable he had just received from the Navy Department in Washington:

> This dispatch is considered a war warning. Negotiations with the Japanese looking toward stabilization of conditions in the Pacific have ceased and an aggressive move by Japan is expected within the next few days. The number and equipment of Japanese troops and their organization of naval task forces indicate an amphibious expedition either against the Philippines, Thai or Kra peninsula, or possibly Borneo. Execute an appropriate defensive deployment preparatory to carrying out the tasks assigned in WPL [war plan] 46.

Execute an appropriate defensive deployment. That meant only one thing to Admiral Hart: get his ships out of range of the Japanese land-based bombers on Formosa. The fleet would have to proceed south and lay to in protected anchorages beyond bomber range. He couldn't leave them anchored at Manila, vulnerable to a surprise attack. All he had to do was pick up the phone and issue the orders and the ships would be on their way.

All except one, the one he could see from his window. The *Houston* was tied up at the dock at Cavite, undergoing frantic last-minute attempts at overhaul and modernization. In her present condition, she could not be moved, and the work would not be completed for days. Hart could ill afford to lose the *Houston*. He reached for the phone and asked for Captain Rooks.

Aboard the *Houston*, the already fast-paced work schedule was intensified; Admiral Hart had given Rooks 24 hours to be ready to sail. Civilian workers from the navy yard—called "yardbirds" by the sailors—swarmed over the ship, working around the clock. High-intensity lamps were set up so they could work through the night. The ship was a shambles. The bricks in boiler room number four had been torn out and the rebricking just begun. Down in the two engine rooms, work was being done on the main circulating pumps and the main condenser trunk lines. The main injection valves had been disassembled and some parts had been taken into Cavite's machine shops. Other valves were being packed, and several auxiliary pumps were being over-hauled.

Topside things were equally chaotic. Long cables snaked across the decks and up the mainmast in preparation for a radar set that was supposed to arrive from Pearl Harbor. Men clung to scaffolding over the side welding bolts around every porthole. In the ship's machine shops steel battle plates were being fabricated; these would be installed over the portholes to make the ship lightproof. Teams of men were already conducting drills to see how rapidly they could get the plates in place.

Steel splinter shields were being welded in place around the five-inch antiaircraft guns to give the crews some protection from shrapnel and bullets. New 1.1-inch pom-poms were being hoisted aboard to replace the old three-inch guns. They were welded to the deck as additional protection against low-flying enemy planes. The *Houston*'s searchlights were sitting on the dock; the men hoped to replace them with newer, more powerful ones. And in the midst of all this work and commotion and confusion came the order for the crew to stand gun watches around the clock, four hours on and eight off.

By the following day, Admiral Hart was even more con-cerned about the *Houston*'s fate. His PBY pilots reported that Jap-anese convoys were moving down the Indochina coast. The convoys had strong air cover and included large numbers of cargo ships and troop transports. It was obvious that the Japanese were preparing for an invasion.

Hart notified Captain Rooks that a bombing attack was immi-nent. "Button it up," Hart said. "Put the ship back together as fast as humanly possible and get out of here."

The crew knew that something was up. That night they were watching a movie on deck—though to this day they cannot agree on what they saw—when the marine orderly on duty rushed up to the skipper and the exec with a message. The two men got up and left. The next morning the shore patrol was out on the streets of Manila recalling *Houston* men from liberty.

At Baguio, the Philippines' cool summer capital, three *Houston* officers were enjoying their first leave in months—Al Ma-her, the gunnery officer; Jack Galbraith, the air defense officer; and Richard "Shorty" Gingras, the engineering officer. They were already out on the golf course when a man came running up waving a telegram. They packed up at once and returned to Manila. When they reported to Captain Rooks, they were informed that their orders were to clear Manila Bay as fast as possible. The fleet gunnery officer drew Maher aside. "We'll be shooting in a few days," he said. "I hope your first salvo will be on target."

There was no time to wait for the radar or even for the new searchlights. The old lights were hoisted aboard and put in place. The yardbirds worked alongside the *Houston*'s machinists and engine-room crews to get everything shipshape. By November 30, all civilians were able to leave the ship except for one gang in the engine rooms, but if the *Houston* was to leave Manila Bay in time, the rest of the work would have to be finished at sea.

"We took all the parts off the dock and threw them up on the ship, and we took off," recalled Otto Schwarz. The engine-room crews grabbed the equipment, took it below, and, as the ship sailed out of the bay, got to work rebricking the boiler. Marvin Robinson remembered that "skipper 'busted the mike' and informed us that we would be under way in a very short period of time—a shorter period of time than normally you can get a ship that large under way. The masters-at-arms and the crew whose duty was to see to the workers—the civilians—got them off in record time. And we set out."

The *Houston* got under way on 30 minutes' notice. The prep, a dark blue flag with a lighter blue square in the center, was raised on a signal halyard aft of the bridge to announce to all ships that the *Houston* was ready. The ship's siren pierced the morning stillness twice, followed by the mournful wail of the steam whistle. Her log tells the story:

    0815. Tug *Iloilo* came alongside to starboard for getting underway. Lighted fires under boiler no. 8.

    0900. Underway alongside Machine Wharf in accordance with CINCAF [Commander in Chief, Asiatic Fleet] verbal instructions. Capt., navigator, OOD, and pilot on the bridge. Tugs *Iloilo*, *Vagadapdap*, and *Gama* assisting on towing ship to anchorage.

1009. Released tugs from towing.
1015. Anchored in six fathoms of water with 15 fathoms of chain to the starboard anchor in Cavite Harbor off Sangley Point.
1029. Sounded flight quarters. Hoisted four planes on board.
1045. Cut in boiler no. 8 on main steam line.
1058. Tested main engines. Made daily inspections of magazine and smokeless powder samples. Conditions normal.
1110. Underway in accordance with CINCAF verbal instructions steaming at 10 knots with boilers no. 7 and 8 on main steam line, using main engine combinations.

Not far from Admiral Hart's headquarters in the Marsman Building, sacks of mail sat in the Pan American Airways terminal, waiting for the arrival of the next clipper to transport them to the States. Among the hundreds of letters hastily written the day before was one from J. J. Bunch, the *Houston*'s radioman.

We're leaving the navy yard tomorrow for ? We don't know what's going to happen but the situation is very tense here now. It looks like we may fight. . . . I don't know how long it will be before you hear from me again but don't worry about me if you don't for awhile.

                                    Love to all,
                                    Judson

3

Prepare the Ship
for War

This was not the first time the *Houston* had hurriedly left port to avoid being the target of a Japanese attack. A year earlier in Long Beach, California, the ship lay at anchor with a division of four battleships. Long Beach was then the main West Coast port for the Pacific Fleet.

Lieutenant Commander Al Maher and his wife Bess had gone out for dinner. Walking home, they met the *Houston*'s captain, Jesse B. Oldendorf, who pulled Maher aside. "Al," he said, "I want you back aboard ship by eleven o'clock."

All the senior officers had been ordered back. When they convened in the captain's cabin they learned the reason why. The admiral commanding the battleship group had received a report from naval intelligence: a Japanese Air Force unit based in Mexico planned a surprise bombing run on Long Beach at dawn.

"We believed the story," Maher recalled. "The only surprise was that the attack would come from Mexico. Our feelings toward the Japs then were none too good, therefore we were not skeptical about the suggestion that they would attack us."

The admiral believed the story too and decided to take his battleships out of the harbor at midnight. When Captain Oldendorf asked if the *Houston* should also get under way, the reply was, "We're leaving. You're on your own."

Oldendorf quickly made up his mind and he dispatched the

23

shore patrol to round up the *Houston* sailors who were still on liberty. At dawn, general quarters was sounded and the men raced to their guns. For Lieutenant Commander Jack Galbraith, new to the ship, this was his first opportunity to test the anti-aircraft guns, and he made sure his men had plenty of ammunition in the ready boxes. Lookouts eagerly scanned the sky to the south, watching and listening for the first sign of the raid, but nothing happened. After two hours the captain secured, and that afternoon the *Houston* got under way.

Some years earlier, in January of 1932, the *Houston* had also been forced to leave port on short notice because of the Japanese. The ship was undergoing a routine overhaul at Cavite, and on the night of the 31st, rush orders were received to proceed immediately to Shanghai. Fighting had broken out between China and Japan; American lives and business interests were in jeopardy. The ship was quickly put back together as a force of 250 marines marched aboard; and once at Shanghai, the marines and a detachment of *Houston* sailors went ashore for duty.

One difference between the hasty sailings in 1932 and 1940 and the scramble to leave Cavite the week before Pearl Harbor was the sense of urgency. In those earlier episodes, the crew had not been ordered to write their wills, nor did they wear their steel helmets or keep their kapok life jackets on as protection against shrapnel. Nor did the ship herself appear ready for hostilities.

The hull and superstructure had been painted a white so bright that it hurt the eyes to look at her on a sunny day. The brass gleamed from constant polishing, and the teak decks were bleached almost white from daily scrubbing. The crew was proud of that teak decking. Seaman First Class Leonard "Dutch" Kooper, a loader on the five-inch guns, remembered that if a plane leaked oil or if someone left footprints, the crew would "get a bucket with trisodium phosphate and whitewash, and a wire brush and a scrub brush, and if they caught one of those snipes walking around with his shoes on, they put that bucket in his hand and made him retrace his steps and scrub that whole area down."

The prewar *Houston* was not only spotless, she was also elegant. In officers' country, quarters were fitted with curtains of the finest materials and wooden cabinets with glass panes. The admiral's suite, which President Roosevelt occupied on his cruises, consisted of a luxuriously appointed living room, dining room, bedroom, and private bath. The captain's cabin was equally handsome.

The Navy had supplied some of this luxury, but much of it came from the generous citizens of Houston, Texas. Their donations had purchased, among other things, a Steinway baby grand piano for the wardroom and a magnificent $25,000, 55-piece silver service decorated with traditional Texas themes.

The larger pieces bore the U.S. Navy seal and the seal of the City of Houston. A pair of crossed anchors supporting an 18-carat gold star—the lone star of Texas—ornamented the floral centerpiece. Heads of longhorn cattle supported the bowl, and the sculptured reliefs on the sides depicted the surrender of the Mexican general Santa Ana to General Sam Houston. Two six-prong candelabras with flame-shaped electric light bulbs were surmounted by figures of Sam Houston on horseback.

The matching coffee urn bore the inscription "Presented by the people of the City of Houston in grateful appreciation of the naming of the USS *Houston*," and the remainder of the elaborate service included demitasse cups and saucers, fruit compotes, goblets, dessert plates, and a water pitcher. A seaman aboard in the 1930s recalled that "the silver was on display all the time aboard ship up in officers' country, which was strictly off limits to us sailor boys. All of the fellows on the ship loved that silver, although we only got to look at it from a distance."

The enlisted men had not been ignored by the people of Houston, however. The crew had its own piano, a Gulbransen upright, and a wealth of athletic equipment. In addition, the residents sent fruitcake at Christmastime and opened up their homes to the sailors whenever the ship was in port.

When the *Houston* sailed out of Manila Bay a week before Pearl Harbor, all the finery was gone. The ships of the Asiatic and Pacific fleets had been stripped for action months before. Gray paint now covered the ship, obscuring the teak decks. All fire-prone objects had been removed—curtains, wooden cabinets, even some of the wooden wall paneling. The pianos disappeared, of course, along with the valuable silver service, and none of it was ever seen again. For more than 20 years after the war, the

Navy tried to track it down, but to this day its whereabouts are unknown. A few of the men think the pieces may be sitting in a crate in a warehouse in Manila or Long Beach, but most believe it was long ago melted down.

In the days before the war the *Houston* was known as a lucky ship, a favored ship, often called the "pride of the fleet." The people of Houston laid claim to her even before she was built, largely because of the work of one remarkable citizen, William A. Bernrieder. In 1924, while an assistant to the mayor, Bill Bernrieder began to dream of a ship of the line bearing the name of his city. Three years of concentrated effort culminated in the formation of the Cruiser Houston Committee, a high-powered group of civic leaders. The committee launched a drive that captured the enthusiasm of all segments of the population. Resolutions were passed at local, state, and federal levels to name the next U.S. cruiser—the type of ship traditionally given names of cities—for Houston. The competition was stiff (some 80 other cities wanted the honor), but none of the other cities was able to mount such a well-organized campaign. Even hundreds of Houston schoolchildren had been enlisted to write letters to the Secretary of the Navy, telling him why the new ship should be theirs.

Only eight months after Bernrieder formalized the Cruiser Houston Committee, Navy Secretary Curtis D. Wilbur visited Houston to announce that the Texans had won. He commented that the people of Houston had exerted so much pressure on him that there was really no possibility of choosing any other name!

In 1928, the keel of the $17.5 million ship was laid at the Newport News Shipbuilding and Drydock Company in Newport News, Virginia, and on September 7, 1929, she was launched. The day before, a delegation of 200 prominent Texans descended on Washington, where they were received by President Herbert Hoover, members of his cabinet, and the Texas congressional delegation. They went overnight by steamer to Newport News, where the ship was to be christened by 13-year-old Elizabeth Holcombe, daughter of a former mayor of Houston.

There was a little hitch, however, with the traditional ceremony of breaking a bottle of champagne across the bow. This was the Prohibition era. Not only was champagne illegal, but one of the day's speakers, Texas's senior senator, Morris Sheppard, had written the bill that had become the 18th Amendment. The *Houston* would be launched with a bottle filled with water brought from the Houston ship channel.

The big moment arrived at the stroke of noon. Horns tooted, streamers flapped in the breeze, cannon roared, and the Navy band played "The Eyes of Texas Are Upon You." Elizabeth Holcombe swung the bottle of water at the bow of the ship, and it bounced right back at her. To the sailors, a superstitious lot, this was disastrous, an omen of bad luck. The president of the shipbuilding company, Homer L. Ferguson, quickly grabbed the bottle from Miss Holcombe's hand and swung it at the steel plating of the bow. It shattered as the *Houston* slid down the ways, and the ship was considered properly launched.*

At the reception that followed, the main speaker was Ernest L. Jahncke, Assistant Secretary of the Navy. "The *Houston*," he said, "is not an engine to provoke war, but a symbol to preserve peace. My most fervent hope is that the guns of this ship will never take a man's life."

This symbol of the hope for peace received a long series of choice assignments. Her shakedown cruise across the Atlantic to England, France, and Holland culminated in a tumultuous welcome in Houston when she returned. For ten joyous days the crew was feted, and it was then that Houston presented the ship with the silver service, the pianos, and other mementos.

From Houston there was the long voyage to the Asiatic station to take up position as flagship, showing the flag throughout the Philippines and China. In the fall of 1933 it was home to the States, to be based for a time at Long Beach, then through the Panama Canal to New York as part of an exercise to see how fast ships from the Pacific could reach the East Coast.

From 1934 to 1939, the *Houston* was in the limelight. Presi-

---

*The ship was designated CA-30. An earlier USS *Houston*, AK-1, had been a German cargo ship seized at Charleston at the beginning of World War I. Scuttled by her crew, she was salvaged by the U.S. Navy, renamed, and used as a transport until 1922. The third USS *Houston*, CL-81, was a light cruiser launched in June of 1943 (see Chapter 12). The present USS *Houston*, SSN-713, is a nuclear-powered attack submarine launched in March of 1981.

dent Roosevelt chose her for four separate vacation cruises. Some called her the "President's flagship"; detractors referred to her as "Roosevelt's personal yacht." Adjustments were made to accommodate the President's needs. Some of the ladders, held in place by removable pins, were replaced by a small electric elevator to transport him from one deck to another. Ramps and handholds were installed because he wanted to visit as much of the ship as possible.

A launch was brought aboard, equipped for his fishing excursions, and a boatswain's mate with years of deep-sea fishing experience was assigned to look after it.

Shipboard routine was also altered whenever the President was aboard, lest he be unnecessarily disturbed. It would not do to awaken the Commander in Chief with the sound of sirens or even of paint being chipped away. The Orders for the Day for Tuesday, 19 July 1938, spell out the precautions that were taken:

> Care will be taken by all Heads of Departments to insure that work or repairs required in the vicinity of the President's quarters will be done while the President is off the ship.
>
> Morning cleaning in the area around and above the President's cabin (Communication Deck) will not be started until the President rings for breakfast. The orderly is then to phone the OOD who will make every effort to complete the work by the time breakfast of the President is over.
>
> When at sea, whistle and siren will be tested at 0900 unless the President is still asleep. Do not strike the ship's bell until the President is awake.

The orders also contained instructions for the crew concerning their behavior around the President:

> The utmost personal courtesy will be extended the President and his party. If in his presence, render a cheerful salute and respectfully step aside. If working near stop, remove gear if in the way and continue the work later. If spoken to, remain easily at attention until the conversation is completed.

Although the presidential cruises meant a great deal of extra work for the crew, they were delighted to have Roosevelt aboard. To be selected four times was an honor unique in the history of the U.S. Navy. The President himself got immense satisfaction out of his time aboard. He relaxed much more than he was able to do elsewhere, sat in the sun, joked with the officers and men, and spent many hours fishing, often with considerable success. Harold Ickes, the Secretary of the Interior, who once accompanied him, remembered one incident. "The President himself triumphantly brought in his 134-pounder which was the handsomest sailfish caught by anyone. The fish had taken the President several miles out to sea and it took the President two hours and twenty minutes to land it."

The first presidential cruise got under way on July 1, 1934, at Annapolis, Maryland, and concluded some 11,783 miles later at Portland, Oregon. The ship called at several Caribbean islands, went through the Panama Canal, and stopped at Honolulu. In October of 1935, a three-week cruise aboard the *Houston* took Roosevelt 12,000 miles from Annapolis before concluding at Charleston, South Carolina.

The third trip, in 1938, commenced in San Francisco Bay with a grand review of the entire U.S. fleet. When the President was piped aboard the *Houston*, his greeting was, "It's good to be home again, Captain." The ship slid away from the Oakland pier and headed west into the bay past a four-mile phalanx of warships in straight lines four deep, the largest concentration of American naval vessels ever assembled before the war. The first row contained the battleships, and as the *Houston* passed, each boomed a 21-gun salute.

"Each salute was answered by a salute from our men manning the rail station and by the Presidential Band playing 'The Star-Spangled Banner.' The steady rhythm of a twenty-one-gun salute, playing of the national anthem, salute from the next ship, proceeded at a stately pace. Some twenty-two thousand personnel, officers in their dress uniforms with epaulets, braid, buttons, and swords gleaming, and the men in dress uniforms, stood at rigid attention during the long hour."

After the review, the President left the ship for a tour of Yosemite, Los Angeles, and San Diego, where he reboarded two days later. The *Houston* took him to the fishing grounds off the northern Mexican coast and as far as the Galapagos Islands. They passed through the Panama Canal again and put Roosevelt ashore in Pensacola, Florida. As he prepared to depart, he spoke to the assembled crew.

"I want to take this opportunity to thank the officers and men of the *Houston* for a very wonderful trip. This is the third cruise I have taken in the last four years. Every moment of the trip has been delightful. I feel the *Houston* is home.

"It has been fine to be with you and I want to tell you again that I hope it won't be the last. I want to be with you again next year."

He did join the *Houston* again the following year, boarding at Key West, Florida, for a three-week fishing trip through the Caribbean, ending at Charleston. Although he planned to take a fifth cruise, that was the last time he ever saw the ship. In June of 1939 the *Houston* was alerted to prepare for the President's arrival. They waited in Puget Sound, ready to pick up the President in Seattle and take him to Alaska. All through the summer their departure was postponed. The increasing tension in Europe was demanding the President's attention.

"He was expected each week," recalled Lieutenant Commander Al Maher, "so the ship couldn't go anywhere. We steamed around to Bremerton, Seattle, and Port Angeles. The wives were there and thought it was wonderful. Anyway, that was why there was no training or overhaul that summer. All we could do was spit and polish, keep the ship up."

On September 1, Germany invaded Poland. Europe exploded in war. There was no more time for presidential cruises, but while they lasted, the *Houston* had been a most favored ship.

On December 4, 1941, three days after the hurried departure from Cavite and more than a decade of visiting so many famous and exotic ports, the *Houston* swung at anchor at the city of Iloilo on the island of Panay in the central Philippines. This time the crew was waiting for war. They were beyond the range of Japanese land-based bombers, but the captain kept the AA guns manned around the clock. Japanese carriers might be nearby, and there was another potential danger as well—enemy submarines.

Captain Rooks sent a motor whaleboat out every night to patrol the entrance to the harbor. The men in the boat could not, of course, do battle with a sub—not armed with .45s and Thompson submachine guns—but they could warn the ship. The SOCs were catapulted off the *Houston* every three hours during the day to patrol an area some 50 miles around the anchorage.

The ship was anchored about one and a half miles off the beach, right under the shelter of a high cliff. Several times the sailors were startled to see airplanes suddenly appear overhead. Because of the overhang of the cliff, no one aboard ship could hear or see the planes coming. They turned out to be Ford trimotors from the local airfield, but they were causing quite a bit of tension among the crew.

"I went on gun watch at noon," Bill Weissinger said, "and we were sitting there talking about eating fish heads and rice if we got captured, and all of a sudden we heard the roar of a plane motor and we looked up and there was a plane right over us. Then it occurred to us that they could be Jap bombers. They would just be there before you knew it. If they had been bombers, we would have had it."

The captain sent Lieutenant Commander Jack Galbraith ashore to tell the local authorities that if any more planes flew over the *Houston*, they would be shot at. The warning was effective—no more trimotors surprised them—but the following day the local radio station announced that if any planes flew over the ship they would be shot down. That kind of publicity the *Houston* didn't need! "That just told the Japanese right where we were. But," Galbraith added, "they probably knew anyway."

December 5 was payday, and the men were given liberty. Charley Pryor, at 21 the youngest sergeant in the Marine Corps, remembered that Iloilo wasn't much of a place. "All I did was wander around and watch what all the others were doing. It was just a chance to let your feet feel what dirt's like again." Most of the men had a few beers and returned to the ship. The town had so little to offer that it was hard to get into trouble.

The days at anchor were filled with routine training and shipboard duties. There was always paint to be chipped or something to be polished. There were daily calisthenics and a swim around the ship, with marines in the foretop manning the machine guns in case the sharks came too close. Al Maher, who served as athletic officer, led the crew in the swimming, setting a pace that some men half his age couldn't keep up with. After dinner there was a movie on the quarterdeck. Pilot Windy Winslow recalls the "officers and men sitting in starched white uniforms, contentedly puffing tobacco smoke under the brilliant silvery light of a full moon. A pleasant breeze fanned us and the atmosphere was one of beauty and tranquility. . . . I had a strange feeling that the war we had been expecting for months was now only a matter of days away and soon there would be no more such peaceful nights about *Houston*."

The end of peace was only hours away and it was matched by the last of a unique breed of sailor, the men who had joined when it was still tough to get into the service, when the Navy and Marine Corps were highly selective and took only the best. By 1941, the standards were lowered as the military began its rapid and large-scale expansion, but by that time, most of the men aboard the *Houston* were old-timers. Philip T. "Joe" Gans, a 15-year veteran by 1941, said, "In those days anybody who was in the Navy really liked it. They were all volunteers and they had to like it. If you didn't like the Navy in those days, they'd get rid of you real quick."

Not only were the sailors and marines all volunteers, but they had all opted for duty on the Asiatic station. A spirit of adventure attracted them. "I was a kid," Otto Schwarz recalls, "and it was a great adventure. I think that's what the ship was made up of—a lot of gung-ho kids. Fortunately, we had enough old salts to keep us in tow. It was a ship of people who did what they were told. That's what was necessary to keep it together."

The sense of pride in serving in the Navy and Marine Corps was heightened by service aboard a flagship. "I was proud to go aboard that ship," said Jim Gee, "because I felt that I had been chosen." In the Marine Corps, he added, "They picked out the tall and the strong and the halfway alert, so I did feel that I had been chosen to go aboard the *Houston*, especially since we knew she was to go to Manila to be the flagship of the Asiatic Fleet. Spit-and-polish didn't bother me, because I had been brought up to think that way. Cleanliness is next to Godliness. I respected that and I appreciated that."

His fellow marine Charley Pryor remembered how "all the prewar marines aboard the *Houston* were hand-picked. They didn't send a bunch of mullets to a ship like that. All the uniforms of the marine detachment were specially tailored. All our buttons—seven on the blouse, two on the collar, and three on each sleeve—were gold-plated, not brass. You could just blow your breath on them, rub them with an undershirt, and they'd glitter." And at six feet one, Sergeant Pryor was one of the shortest marines aboard!

The men of the *Houston* joined the service for many reasons. Some enlisted because brothers or friends had already done so. They had swaggered home in their sharp uniforms talking of places most people had only read about, and they didn't fail to mention the girls in every port. Others enlisted because they saw that war was coming and they wanted to be something other than an infantryman. Jack Burge from Beckett, Ohio, joined in 1938 for that reason, though it took seven months before the Navy would accept him. The doctors had found one tooth out of line, an indication of how selective the service was then.

Jim Gee joined the marines after his freshman year at the University of Texas because of all the talk about a draft. Several of his classmates joined with him. "Let's join the Marine Corps," they said. "We'll volunteer and get out in the South Pacific on one of those beautiful islands and just sweat out the war out there."

Jack Smith, also from Texas, joined up because "when you're chopping cotton in the cotton fields, anything looks good. But also I was interested in history and I felt there was a war coming on, and like an idiot I thought if I was already in I'd have a better chance of surviving."

Bill Weissinger, Ray Sparks, and many others joined for a more basic and practical reason. "I needed a job," Charley Pryor said, "and so I joined the marines." Times were tough, and if you could pass the entrance requirements, at least you would be fed and clothed.

"I probably had a typical life, as everyone did during the Depression," Otto Schwarz said. "We didn't have any money, we had holes in our shoes, and I was anxious to have a couple of dollars in my pocket." He joined the Civilian Conservation Corps, which sent him to California. "When I joined the CCC, I had more clothing at one time than I had ever seen in my life. Then I joined the Navy, and of course in the Navy the first thing that happened is that I walk in and they start throwing all kinds of clothing at me. . . . And then to get paid in addition was really great."

"The day I reported to the Navy," said Dutch Kooper, "I had holes that big in both my port and starboard shoes. I had inner tubes in there to keep the water from coming in. After about ten days in the service, the chief told me to fall the men in because we're going to march them to the disbursing office. 'What the hell is the disbursing office, sir?' I asked.

"'You dunderhead. That's where you get paid.'

"'Paid, sir?'

"'Yeah. You're gonna get twenty-one dollars a month.'

"'Sir, you mean we're going to get fed three times a day, a place to sleep, clothes on the deck, and get twenty-one dollars a month on top of it? Wow, I've got it made!'

"That night, I got myself up carefully in my hammock in the barracks and I laid down there and I said my prayers: 'Thank you, God. I've got nineteen years and three hundred and sixty-four more days of duty to go.'"

Regardless of the reason for their enlistment, most of the men quickly adjusted to Navy life and military discipline. This was not a time when young people frequently challenged authority, though some did manage to get into trouble. Consider how Dutch Kooper got his nickname.

"It was kind of hard for me to get adapted to the Navy, being a Chicago hoodlum and born in the slums of Chicago. Every couple of weeks they'd call me up to mast. I'd belt somebody or I'd do something else wrong, and I'd keep seeing the old man, Captain Oldendorf. Finally, about the third or fourth time, Captain Oldendorf looked at my record and said, 'Damn it, Kooper, are you in Dutch again?' That name hung on to me like a tattoo after that."

One day Kooper was put on report for shirking his duty. He had just finished scrubbing down a bulkhead and had been ordered to do it again. When he appeared before Captain Oldendorf he explained, "Sir, I scrubbed that bulkhead the day before and he told me to scrub it again. Captain, I came in this Navy to fight, not to scrub bulkheads."

Captain Oldendorf pondered for a moment and then delivered his judgment. "Well, Dutch, I'll tell you what I'll do. I'll give you five days piss and ponk [bread and water] to plan out your battle tactics!"

The Navy didn't give up on Kooper. His division officer, Lieutenant (jg) J. F. Dalton, ordered "Sampan" Martin, an old China sailor, to teach Dutch the ropes. "Sampan taught me a lot of things about the Navy and he finally got the bit in my mouth and made a sailor out of me. Sampan and Henry Nickel, they were good petty officers. They set the example for the men to follow and they treated the men fairly as long as we did our work. But if you stepped out of line—look out!"

The crew did work hard, but they also knew how to play hard on their liberty. Time ashore had to be earned in those days, and if you were denied a liberty card for some reason, it could be weeks before the ship called at another port. For youngsters who had never been away from home before, liberty was a pretty heady experience. There were plenty of old hands to tell them where to have a good time. Even the ship's newspaper, the *Blue Bonnet* (named for the Texas state flower), offered advice:

> The anchorage the *Houston* will use while in Manila is in Manila Bay, with about a 10-minute ride to the navy landing. This landing is popularly known as the Legaspi landing. Here almost anything can be bought. Meals, drinks, dancing upstairs with dancing partners furnished for 50 centavos (two-bits American). It's a wonderful stopping place for that last drink. From Legaspi, one can get a cab to anywhere in Manila for 25 centavos. . . .
>
> Bachelor's paradise! Santa Ana's is the largest cabaret in the world, where the floor is lined off in half, and two bands play. Dancing partners are plentiful here. Dance tickets for a peso. Drinks are good, and not expensive. Then, after everything closes up, Tom Dixie's, in the heart of town, or the Great Eastern Hotel, will keep one busy till the sun

comes up. Everyone is allowed in the Silver Dollar, where you get that famous Gold Leaf Certificate if you can drink eight Singapore gin slings. The Silver Dollar and the Hub are spots that shouldn't be missed.

"Manila was a great liberty port," Ray Sparks recalled. "Joe Gans was our leader on liberty—one heck of a guy. Every payday we'd buy our cigarettes, our shaving cream, and stuff like that and have five dollars left over. The routine was a movie, chow, and the 'other thing'—and that only cost three pesos [about $1.50]."

Shanghai had been even more exciting, the oldtimers would boast. To missionaries it was the "sewer of the universe," but to sailors it was heaven. "This town would ruin anybody in no time," General "Vinegar Joe" Stilwell once said. "The babes that twitch around the hotels need attention so badly that it is hard not to give it to them." Whatever pleasure or vice one desired could be had in Shanghai, even on a seaman second's pay. At the French Concession, thousands of White Russians lived, and all seemed to have beautiful daughters. They claimed to be princesses and frequented the cabarets of notorious Blood Alley. On Friday nights at Short-Time Annie's the girls would dance in bras and panties, offering enchanting smiles and beguiling promises, which they would fulfill if the price was right.

The officers' diversions were more expensive. The Shanghai Club's 110-foot bar, reputedly the longest in the world, served delightful pink gins and gimlets. Farther down Nanking Road was the popular French club Le Cercle Sportif Français, the only club in town to admit Orientals. Some of the tables were set with foot-high tripods that looked like tiny water towers. A Chinese boy would pour a measure of absinthe into the top and it would trickle down through a lump of sugar, drop by drop, into the waiting glasses.

Some of the men who had been out in the Far East too long were said to have "gone Asiatic." In the words of a popular saying, they'd been up the river too long. They'd sit by the hour staring out to sea with a faraway look in their eyes. Some sported a gold earring in their left ear. But whether a sailor had been there too long or not, the liberties were something to remember, at least for those who were able to remember them the next day. Otto Schwarz said, "You just went along with all the other guys and had a good time. Or thought you had a good time. If you came back all drunk and dirty, you'd say, 'Boy, what a great time I must have had.' And if you looked down at your feet and saw tattoos, you'd say, 'Oh, my God, what did I do?'" According to an old Portuguese seamen's superstition, if you had a pig and a rooster tattooed on your feet, you would never drown. "A lot of guys in my division were having pigs and roosters put on their feet . . . you do a lot of stupid things that at the time you think are great fun."

Fights, too, came easily to a number of sailors on liberty. "You get wild when you're out to sea for a long time," said Joe Gans. "You get in a bar and you fight with anybody who wants to fight."

"The Navy was filled with characters in those days," Schwarz added. "That's why we were there in the first place. There were guys who could never go on a liberty without getting into a big fight. You'd always see them coming back to the ship all beat up with their uniforms dirty and torn."

Sometimes getting back aboard ship wasn't easy. After one memorable night in Manila, Ray Sparks and Raymond L. "Highpockets" Shireman were walking up the gangplank loaded down with bananas and other souvenirs, including a pint bottle of whiskey that Highpockets had stuffed in his sock. The OOD was a new ensign, J. B. Nelson, whom the men inevitably had nicknamed "Lord Nelson." A cigarette dangled from Shireman's mouth as he approached Ensign Nelson, an offense almost as grave as bringing booze aboard ship.

"Okay, Highpockets," Nelson said. "Throw it away."

"Yes, sir."

Shireman reached into his sock, plucked out the whiskey, and tossed it into the water. As Nelson looked on dumbfounded, Highpockets walked on by, still puffing on his cigarette.

Howard Brooks remembers the warning issued by his division officer before the first liberty in Manila. The men were lectured about venereal disease and urged to take all necessary precautions. "One thing that's going to happen," the officer told them, "as soon as you get any disease, your name's going to be put up there on that bulletin board." The VD list, the Monday-morning red badge of courage, was duly published. "Who was the first one on our list? The division officer!"

The morning after brought horrendous hangovers, a line of sailors and marines heading for the captain's mast, and the usual question, "What did I do last night?" Joe Gans, an old China hand, knew to take the first watch in the engine room. He'd send up a note to an old friend, a pharmacist's mate, requesting a little alcohol for medicinal purposes, and then he'd sweat it out in the engine room. Before long he was "raring to go" on the next liberty.

Admiral Hart was kept informed of the activities of his men on liberty—the arrests and fights, the damage done—and though he was a stickler on matters of military courtesy and discipline, he believed that after a long time at sea his men had a right to what he called a "rough liberty." He liked to say that there were never more than a hundred or so who would go on report, and that was really no worse than college boys after a football weekend back in the States.

The officers were expected to be more discreet. A favorite haunt was the beautiful Army-Navy Club, with its wide expanse of lawn sweeping down to Manila Bay. The management thoughtfully made provisions for those who had overindulged; the second-floor veranda contained a row of cots known as "drunkard's row," for those in no condition to return to the ship.

The exploits of three of the *Houston*'s pilots—Tommy Payne, Jack Lamade, and Windy Winslow—are still talked about today. When they came ashore at the Legaspi landing they liked to hail a cab, say "Follow that taxi," and take off wherever another cab happened to be going. When they finally wound up at the Army-Navy Club, Payne remembers, he would saunter up to the bar, hold out his cupped hands, and say, "Fill it up."

After one formal cocktail party, Lamade spied the remains of a turkey on one of the tables. He picked it up and wandered through the room. Whenever he approached anyone he would quip, "I have a bone to pick with you." Payne followed with the drumsticks, adding, "He doesn't have a leg to stand on!"

One afternoon the pilots stopped at the club intending to

have a drink before returning to the ship. Since they were not planning on dinner, they did not wear neckties. They were about an hour behind schedule because their launch had broken down and it was getting close to the time when ties were required.

"We had about eight old-fashioneds for our drink before dinner," Lamade explained, "and then the civilian in charge of the club came around and told us we had to leave since we didn't have on ties and it was after seven o'clock. We took off our shoelaces and put them around our necks as shoestring ties, but I guess they didn't like that either so they threw us out.

"We went from there down to the Manila Hotel, where on the way Windy threatened the taxi driver with extreme violence if he didn't give Windy his tie, so Windy ended up with a tie. Tommy, Windy, and I went in the hotel, where we went down to the haberdashery place in the lobby and started to help this good-looking girl at the necktie counter to sell ties. Tommy was in the process of rounding people up to buy ties when Captain Purnell [from Admiral Hart's staff] came through and said, 'Tommy, you know, I think maybe you all better go back to the ship.'

"We went down to the bar of the hotel and had another drink. We then went over to jai alai and went up to the top floor, where they had dancing, and Windy and I went up and down the line of tables where people were eating and took whatever food looked good to us. Tommy was helping pick out what looked good and about that time two big bruisers came over and took hold of Tommy and me and started escorting us out of the place.

"Windy grabbed a catsup bottle with one hand and the manager of the place with the other and told the manager he had better call his bouncers off or he would let him have it. About that time we disappeared in the elevator and Windy dropped the manager and ran over to help us. We went below before Windy could get in the elevator and then somehow or other Tommy put me in a taxi and went back to get Windy. He found Windy and they came down and Windy asked Tommy where I was. Tommy said, 'Oh, he'll be around,' and in a very short time they saw a taxi draw up with two feet sticking out of it and that was me. Well, we finally got back to the ship about nine-thirty. I will never forget that night as long as I live."

On one of their last liberties in Manila, Payne decided that they might run into trouble on the launch back to the *Houston* and so they needed some protection. He manhandled an ancient Spanish-American War cannon that was decorating the lawn of the Army-Navy Club into the bow of the launch. Upon reaching the *Houston*, he had second thoughts and instructed the coxswain to "do something about that thing." About three o'clock in the morning, the captain nudged him awake. "You wouldn't know anything about a cannon that's disappeared from the lawn of the club, would you, Tommy?" "What cannon, sir?" he asked groggily, wondering why the captain had come directly to him.

The wild times were coming to an end. There would soon be no more peacetime liberties, no more carefree nights where your only concerns were whether you had enough money for one more drink or if you would make it back to the ship on time and in good enough condition so that you would not be put on report.

Partly because of the shared experience of these liberties, of the persistent routine of work and training aboard ship, and of the length of time most men had served on the *Houston*, the crew had become a closely knit community. "I can't say they were like a family," Bill Weissinger said, "more like a lot of damn good neighbors." Ray Sparks looked upon the closeness of the crew from another point of view. "We were the best, and if we had nothing to do ashore, we'd fight amongst ourselves. But don't let anybody else mix it up with us—no outsiders."

They had been together long enough to form the bonds of trust, to have confidence in the next man in the turret, on the gun, and in the engine room. Each was sure the other knew his job and wouldn't let him or the ship down when trouble came. This was a comforting feeling, one that contributed to the cockiness they felt as the war approached.

But one man aboard was still an unknown quantity, one man whose full measure had not yet been taken—the captain. A battleship sailor in the prewar Navy described the role of the skipper this way: "Very few men in civilian life were ever exposed to such a close searching scrutiny as the crew of a Navy combat ship gives its new CO. For it is he who determined whether it would be a happy ship or an unhappy one; a taut ship or a slack one; a ship with esprit de corps or one morose and dispirited. He alone determined whether the food would be palatable, the quarters livable, the discipline harsh or tempered with mercy. Finally, the captain might well determine, by his competence or incompetence, whether any or all of us . . . lived or died."

For the men of the *Houston*, there was nothing in the background and training of Albert H. Rooks, Captain, USN, to raise any doubt about his competence. The 49-year-old career man had graduated from the Naval Academy at Annapolis in the class of 1910 and had served in a variety of duties, from submarines to battleships. Rooks had been gunnery officer aboard the *Northampton*, sister ship to the *Houston;* skipper of the USS *Phelps;* instructor in ordnance and gunnery at the Naval Academy, and later secretary of its Academic Board; and both student and instructor at the Naval War College. He was also qualified for command of submarines. He had handled this excellent progression of assignments in exemplary fashion. He was regarded favorably by his superiors, and it was assumed that he would make admiral before retirement. Rooks had been on the staff at Annapolis when Admiral Hart was superintendent. Hart had called him one of his best assistants, "a splendid officer of the intellectual type."

Rooks's background and qualifications for command of the *Houston* were excellent. What concerned the men was simply that he had been aboard only three months. In addition, the skipper he replaced—Jesse B. Oldendorf—had been worshipped by the crew. "It was obvious," said Lieutenant Bob Fulton, the assistant engineering officer, "that Captain Rooks was stepping into an awful big pair of shoes. Everybody knew they were in a tight situation there and that their future depended pretty heavily on the way the captain handled things, so they kept a sharp eye on how the situation was going. It was with a great deal of regret that they saw Captain Oldendorf leave the ship." "Well," added Lieutenant Commander Jack Galbraith, the air defense officer, "when you have a boss that you like very much, you're very worried about what the new recruit will be like."

The personal styles of these two captains differed greatly. Oldendorf was a "slap-'em-on-the-back" type, whereas Rooks was not so outgoing. To the crew, Rooks's ways took some getting used to. When the war started, Bill Weissinger said, "We still weren't in love with Captain Rooks. . . . He'd come aboard in

August and he was still the new kid on the block as far as we were concerned."

"Rooks was very stern and proper," Ray Sparks said. "Old Jesse B. had more humor about him." John Bartz, a 20-year-old gunner's mate on the 1.1s, also ran the captain's gig. He recalled that at first "the crew was concerned about the change of command, because Oldendorf was so nice, very congenial, very sociable, more so than Rooks." Marine Jim Gee also hated to see Oldendorf leave. "He was a man who was very close to the men. He had a lot of heart. My first impression of Rooks was that he didn't have that same type of heart. He wasn't down to earth. He was more standoffish. He depended on his officers to do what Oldendorf liked to do on his own. Oldendorf would walk around the ship and talk to you, but everybody respected him, because when he needed to get rough, he'd get rough."

In time, the crew would come to look upon Captain Rooks as the greatest skipper they could possibly have, but now, on the verge of war, they were uncertain about how he would react.

War came to the *Houston* quietly. There was no sudden roar of enemy planes overhead, no shattering explosions from falling bombs, no strafing Zeros tearing up the once-beautiful teak decks. No sudden death or screams of wounded men. War came at 3:45 A.M. on December 8 (December 7, Hawaii time), while the ship was anchored at Iloilo in 15½ fathoms of water with 90 fathoms of chain to the starboard anchor. Boiler number five was in use for auxiliary purposes. The antiaircraft batteries were set at Condition Three; one-third of them were manned.

Most of the crew, including the captain, were asleep. Some of the officers had been on liberty and had returned to the ship less than an hour earlier. Bob Fulton had spent the previous afternoon playing golf, his last game for five years. Jack Lamade was sitting in the wardroom drinking coffee, waiting to take over the morning watch on the bridge. Aft, at five-inch gun number eight, Sergeant Charley Pryor was on watch with a crew of five men, half the normal strength, standard for Condition Three.

In the after radio room, J. J. Bunch was on duty, waiting for his relief to take over so he could get some sleep. On the bridge, marine Pfc Jim Gee was on duty as orderly. One of the *Houston*'s launches bobbed up and down halfway between the ship and the entrance to the harbor. Bill Weissinger and others were waiting. They were on their way to relieve the 12-to-4 watch on antisubmarine patrol, and they were late. The officer in charge, Ensign Nelson, hadn't arrived.

"We were kind of teed off," Weissinger said, "because we were proud in the old Navy of relieving a watch on time. And we managed to do it, but just barely. We didn't like that just barely. Nelson told us the reason he was late was because just as he was finishing his coffee, a message came over the radio that a Jap convoy had been sighted off the Gulf of Siam. It was the one the British had been following since the first of December. So we talked about it for a while, but then we thought, Hell, that's Siam's problem. We're worried about the Philippines."

Aboard ship, J. J. Bunch's radio crackled to life. He hastily wrote down the message and called for the orderly. Jim Gee hurried to the radio shack and then raced for the captain's quarters. He knocked on the door. Rooks was in his bathrobe.

The message from Admiral Hart was simple and to the point: "Japan has started hostilities. Govern yourselves accordingly."

"I'll dress," Rooks said quietly to Gee.

Jack Lamade was draining the last of his coffee when the communications officer entered the wardroom. "You going to have the deck, Mr. Lamade?" he asked.

"Yes."

"Here," he said, "take a look at this," and he handed Lamade a copy of the message that had just been delivered to the captain.

Lamade hurried up to the bridge and took up his watch station just as Captain Rooks appeared.

"Do you have the deck, Mr. Lamade?" Rooks said.

"Yes, sir."

"Prepare the ship for war."

4

It's for Keeps Now

The first morning of war was not glamorous or romantic. In the last hour or so before dawn, most of the crew of the *Houston* were not yet aware of what had occurred. They did not know that the lives of all Americans would be irrevocably changed. The deck log recorded the momentous events in its usual sparse, unemotional style.

0345. At this time a message was received that Japan had commenced hostilities against the United States.
0350. Darkened ship.
0443. Lighted fires under boiler no. 6.
0505. Lighted fires under boilers no. 7 and 8.
0525. Sounded General Quarters.
0535. Secured no. 6 boiler.
0545. Hoisted out plane no. 4. Pilot Ensign J. B. Stivers. Hoisted out plane no. 3. Pilot Lt. T. B. Payne. Both planes conducting antisubmarine patrol.
0605. Set Preparedness Condition 3 on antiaircraft battery.
0617. Lighted ship.

0622. Tested main engines. Satisfactory. Placed engineering department on 30 minutes notice.

There was no inspiring call to arms, no rousing speech from
the captain, no cheers from the assembled crew. The captain
woke Al Maher, the gunnery officer, and informed him that war
had begun. Maher woke Jack Galbraith and told him to have the
antiaircraft guns fully manned as quickly as possible. Lee Rogers
was nudged awake by one of the Chinese stewards, who
shouted, "Hey, war Japan! War Japan!"

One by one the department heads assembled before the captain. By this time the messages from Admiral Hart were arriving
frequently, bringing more information on the attack on Pearl Harbor and announcing additional Japanese naval movements southwest of the *Houston*'s position, in the vicinity of Malaya. Captain
Rooks told his staff to make the ship ready to get under way.
They would go to general quarters at daybreak and he would
make the formal announcement to the crew.

Sergeant Pryor, on watch on the number-eight five-inch gun,
received a call from Galbraith to report the strength of his gun
crew. Over the phone he heard the same question being asked of
the other guns. All reported five or six men on duty, about half of
full strength.

"Go get all of them," Galbraith ordered. "Get your full crew
up and make ready your boxes." Then he added, "The Japanese
have hit Pearl Harbor. We are virtually at war with the Japs."

"That's how war came to us," Charley Pryor remembered.
"We didn't worry about it a whole lot. I guess we were cocky,
certainly ignorant of what war could be."

Pryor removed the waterproof door from the ready box and
opened its cover so the shells would be ready to ram into the
gun.

Merritt "Chips" Eddy, carpenter's mate second class, along
with some other sailors, was asleep in the carpenter's shop below
decks because it was too hot in his own quarters. At least the
shop had portholes that let in a breeze. At 4:30 in the morning,
the chief carpenter's mate, Maurice "Dutch" Weller, woke him
up. It was time to put the battle plates on over the portholes.

"Why?" Eddy asked.

"'Cause the Japs have bombed Pearl Harbor," Weller answered.

"We thought he was spoofing," Eddy said. "Four-thirty in the morning! Why is he pulling this stuff?"

Weller quickly convinced them that he was serious. Eddy took the keys to the storeroom and led the crew down to the deck below to get the battle plates. A few minutes later they were forced to wake Jack Burge, whose bunk covered the storeroom door.

"What are you doing down here in the middle of the night?" Burge demanded.

"Pearl Harbor's been bombed. We've got to black out the ship."

"So that was the way I found out," Burge recalled, "when they came down after those plates."

Slowly the word spread throughout the ship and the men roused themselves and prepared for war. As Al Maher rushed past the crew getting ready to relieve the antisubmarine patrol, he heard one sailor complain, "Now I'll never get that laundry I left at Cavite."

Windy Winslow was approached by E. A. "Joe" Bush, the aviation ordnanceman who served as gunner and radioman in Winslow's SOC. Bush had just heard the news.

"You know, Mr. Winslow, I understand the Japs bombed the New Senator Hotel [a well-known house of ill repute] in Honolulu."

"You don't say," Winslow said.

"Yes, sir." Bush grinned. "They killed two hundred white hats and one whore."

In his stateroom on the port side, senior pilot Tommy Payne had been asleep for less than an hour after some late-night partying in Iloilo.

The captain woke him up. "It's happened," Rooks said. "You'd better get up and send out a scouting party."

Jack Lamade saw Payne a few minutes later. "I will never forget Tommy as long as I live when he came down that ladder leading to the quarterdeck, weaving slightly on the deck, clapping his hands together and saying, 'Well, for chrissake, Jack, let's go get 'em. What are we waiting for? Let's go shoot 'em up.'"

Payne glanced up at the catapult, apparently forgetting for the moment that the SOCs couldn't be catapulted off while the ship was at anchor. The crane would have to hoist his plane overboard so that he could take off from the water. His spirit was willing, however, and he said, "Go ahead. Turn 'em over and we'll go fight 'em!" Years later, Payne put it more simply. "I just strapped on the airplane and went up."

At 5:25 the call to battle stations blared through every corner of the ship. No one ever slept through the nerve-shattering general alarm. First came the piercing shrill of the bosun's pipe, a seesaw sound of urgency, then the scream of the klaxon, followed by the bugle call. From every speaker boomed *"Now hear this! Now hear this! Man your battle stations!"*

Shortly thereafter came a voice that was unfamiliar to most of the crew. "This is the captain speaking. For the information of all hands, a state of war exists between the United States and Japan. Japan has bombed Pearl Harbor, inflicting some damage."

As Q. C. Madson recalled, "Everything was quiet for a few minutes, then everyone started talking at once. Things returned almost to normal, although there was an undercurrent of excitement."

No more than that, just an undercurrent of excitement. They had been expecting war and here it was. Now they had work to do. "We were finally going to get to put into practice what we had been working to perfect for this year and a half we'd spent on this ship," said marine Jim Gee. "We were ready to go," Otto Schwarz said. "We were jubilant and we wanted to get at them."

A few *Houston* sailors still did not know what had happened. Out in their launch at the mouth of the harbor, Ensign Nelson, Bill Weissinger, and the rest of the 4-to-8 antisubmarine patrol had not yet been relieved. Because they had no radio contact with the ship, there was no other way to inform them.

By 7:30, when a state of war had existed for some hours, they were concerned about food. Weissinger said, "We had some ham sandwiches and cheese sandwiches and a pot of coffee that would get cold in thirty minutes. We'd been gnawing on that stuff for four hours and we were all getting pretty hungry."

It was time for their relief to start heading out, but they didn't see any signs of a boat being made ready at the *Houston*'s gangway. Nelson peered through his binoculars but had nothing to report. The men were growing impatient. The signalman fired his signal gun several times. It drew no answer.

"Damn," he said. "Those people up there must be reading girlie magazines. I'll have to go semaphores."

He got out the flags and crawled up on the taprail to signal while Weissinger and the others held his legs. No response from the *Houston*, not even an answering recognition signal.

"What the hell's going on?" Weissinger wanted to know. "At eight we saw the band come out, saw the quartermaster raise the colors. It looked like everything was going normally."

Nelson continued to observe through the binoculars, and finally he turned and spoke to the men. "There's something funny going on. They've got shipfitters over the side putting those battle plates on over the portholes."

"They're not supposed to be on there!" Weissinger said. "That captain's crazy. It's all this heat. It's gotten to him. The ship wasn't built for tropical duty in the first place and now he's sealing the holes up. Those damn battle plates are not supposed to be on there until we go into action. That old boy's blown his stack. He's going to smother us."

About 8:30, a boat left the gangway. When it got within hailing distance, Nelson and his men knew that something was wrong. "They were waving their arms and hollering. We couldn't hear them because the wind had picked up and the water was rustling. They came alongside and we lashed the boats together and then they told us that Pearl Harbor had been bombed. I will never forget it. A guy by the name of Jim Ballew jumped over in our boat and beat me around the shoulders and yelled, 'The Japs have bombed Pearl Harbor! The Japs have bombed Pearl Harbor. We're gonna sink the sons of bitches.' He was just beside himself."

As Weissinger and his boat crew headed back to the ship, the *Houston*'s officers were addressing their men. On the fantail,

Lieutenant Commander Shorty Gingras, the senior engineering officer, called the men of the engine rooms together. He repeated the news about the attack on Pearl Harbor. They were now at war and everything they did counted.

"Just be sure and don't throw anything over the side," Gingras said, "because that would be a dead giveaway of our position."

Fireman First Class George E. Detre remembered that Gingras looked around slowly at all the men he had commanded for so long and then made one last remark. "It's for keeps now," Gingras said.

By this time there was not a man aboard who did not know they were at war. Most had no doubts about the outcome and some were anxious to strike back at the enemy, but Dutch Kooper was just plain angry at the Japanese and had a personal score to settle. He had bet a petty officer ten dollars that Pearl Harbor would never be bombed. Kooper paid up, but "ten dollars was a lot of money. I could make a couple of good liberties with that!"

Periodically throughout the day at Iloilo, Captain Rooks kept the men informed as much as possible about the developments in the war. Sometimes he spoke on the PA system himself, announcing another Japanese attack. At other times he plugged the radio directly into the loudspeakers.

Sitting in the wardroom, Lieutenant (jg) Harold S. Hamlin, Jr., officer in charge of number-one turret (the forward eight-inch turret), listened to the reports of civilian casualties in Honolulu with growing alarm. He had suggested to his wife that she stay in Hawaii once the dependents were ordered out of the Philippines. He had thought it would be safe, but now he was not so certain. As the radio reported the mounting Japanese aggression, the officers around him began to speculate on their chances for survival. Hamlin abruptly got up and left. He went to his cabin, determined to open the Christmas present he had received from his wife. The holiday was three weeks away, but who could predict what might happen in the meantime? If Pearl Harbor wasn't safe, then no place in the Pacific was.

In the early afternoon came the shocking news of another disaster. Clark Field, north of Manila, the largest American air base in the Philippines, had been bombed. Although the initial reports were vague, it sounded like the military had been caught napping, just like the fleet at Pearl. Those new B-17s at Clark were supposed to win the war against Japan. They had the range and the bomb loads to hit the Japanese bases on Formosa and destroy the Japanese invasion fleet. Now they had been destroyed—on the ground in broad daylight.

Crews manned the AA guns throughout the day, and lookouts scanned the skies all around, but the only planes to appear were the *Houston*'s own SOCs returning from patrol. On an early afternoon patrol, pilot Windy Winslow and his gunner Joe Bush sighted a large warship. It had to be a cruiser, they thought, perhaps even a battleship. They knew there were no U.S. or Allied ships in the area, so that left Japanese. They estimated its speed at 25 knots. Its present course would take it directly to Iloilo and the *Houston*, only 60 miles away.

They radioed the *Houston* to alert them that an unidentified cruiser or battleship was approaching. Then Winslow flew closer to see if he could make a better identification. Suddenly bright flashes of light erupted on board the ship. At first Winslow thought they were antiaircraft fire, but then he realized they were from a signal light challenging the SOC. Bush returned the proper recognition signals and the ship identified itself. She was the American light cruiser *Boise*, which had been at anchor in the port of Cebu. A modern radar-equipped ship, the *Boise* was part of the Pacific Fleet based at Pearl Harbor and had just escorted a troop transport to Manila. As long as the *Boise* was in his area, Admiral Hart had effectively commandeered her to reinforce his small fleet.

As more frequent reports were received of the Japanese attacks in the Philippines, as well as in Malaya and other points, Captain Rooks became increasingly anxious to put out to sea. He could not get under way yet, however. He had been ordered to await the arrival of Rear Admiral William A. Glassford, Jr., former commander of the Yangtze River Patrol in China. Glassford had been tapped to head Task Force Five, which Admiral Hart had designated as the fighting unit of the Asiatic Fleet. Glassford would command the task force from the flagship, the *Houston*.

Glassford had not been Admiral Hart's choice to command his only fighting unit. A few months earlier, when the Navy Department had asked Hart if he would recommend Glassford to succeed him when he retired in 1942, Hart had said no. Glassford had spent many years in China operating a small fleet of gunboats and engaging in delicate political maneuverings with the increasingly truculent Japanese. In Hart's judgment, Glassford had performed this job well, but Hart had reservations about Glassford's lack of experience in large-scale fleet operations.

In terms of seniority, however, Glassford was in line to replace Hart upon Hart's scheduled retirement, and now that war had come, Glassford was in line to command Task Force Five, even though Hart considered him unqualified to do so. Hart's objections to Washington had been overruled, and on the afternoon of December 8, 1941, Admiral Glassford boarded a PBY Catalina belonging to Patrol Wing Ten in Manila Bay for the long flight to the *Houston* at Iloilo.

Hart was not the only person dissatisfied with Glassford's appointment to Task Force Five. Officers aboard the *Houston* who had been in the Far East for some time shared Hart's opinion. "We just didn't have the same confidence in Admiral Glassford as we did in Admiral Hart," Lieutenant Payne said. "He hadn't had any fleet experience. That wasn't his fault, but that was the situation." But the decision had been made and Glassford was on his way.

About 6:30 that evening, Glassford's plane appeared over the bay and landed close to the *Houston*. The whaleboat was already under way by the time the PBY came to a stop. The water was choppy and the admiral was not a young man, but this was no time for ceremony or consideration for age. "Glassford had to make a white hat jump into the boat. There was no courtly way of doing it. He had to jump like everybody else."

There was also no time to wait. Rooks wanted to get the *Houston* out of the trap the Iloilo harbor placed them in. As soon as Glassford jumped in the boat, the *Houston* had the anchor up and got under way. The admiral's whaleboat had to "run like hell to catch us."

As soon as the *Houston* cleared the channel, Captain Rooks

ordered full speed, and to everyone's relief they were soon in
deep water again. They were only eight miles out of their Iloilo
anchorage when spotters in the foretop reported antiaircraft
bursts over the town. Japanese planes were on the attack. A few
minutes later a freighter that had been anchored near the *Houston*
went up in flames. On the radio that evening, the Japanese announced that they had sunk the *Houston*. Word spread around
the ship, and everyone felt pretty good about it. Better yet, they
were now steaming out to sea to do battle with the enemy.

That same day back in the States, a mother wrote to her son
aboard the *Houston*. Her thoughts echoed those of worried parents, wives, and sweethearts throughout the country:

> *Our hearts are sad and heavy, knowing you are sur-*
> *rounded by war, but we are trusting and hoping that you*
> *will come through all right victoriously. I hope this war*
> *will be a short one and hope you can soon come home. Put*
> *your trust in God for He will take care of you.*

The next morning at dawn, the *Houston* joined forces with
part of Task Force Five—the *Boise* and two World War I vintage
destroyers, the *Paul Jones* and the *Barker*. The force sailed south-
ward without meeting another ship, friend or foe, as they headed
toward a planned rendezvous the next day with a small convoy
that had fled Manila harbor.

Radio reports from around the Pacific area were gloomier
than they had been the previous day. Wake Island, Guam, Hong
Kong, and Malaya all seemed to be in danger. The news from
Hawaii indicated that the damage to the Pacific Fleet was greater
than anyone had imagined. It would be a long time before Admiral Hart could expect any reinforcements.

Sailors and marines remained on the *Houston*'s guns, and the
spotters were constantly alert. When they met up with the other
ships, many of the men remarked on the strange contraption on
the *Boise*'s foremast; it looked like a twirling bedspring. This was
the first time they had seen radar. Once they learned that it could
detect ships and planes that the human eye could not see, they
were grateful to have the *Boise* along.

December 9 had been a long, dull day. The officers and men continued to drill and maintain a condition of preparedness, not unlike all the days of the past several months. The excitement the crew expected to feel at the onset of the war had dissipated, and that was a harbinger of things to come.

The following day they picked up the rest of the convoy, five more ships, including two more four-stack destroyers—the *Stewart* and the *Edwards*—the old carrier (now seaplane tender) *Langley*, and the fleet oilers *Pecos* and *Trinity*. Shepherding them along at 10 knots, the oilers' top speed, the *Houston* continued south toward Borneo, and there was still no sign of the Japanese.

They heard a great deal about the enemy, however, because December 10, 1941, was a bleak day for the Allied naval forces. Two of the mightiest and proudest ships of the Royal Navy, the *Repulse* and the *Prince of Wales*, went down off the coast of Malaya. What made it worse was that both were sunk by Japanese air power alone. This tremendous loss inflicted a severe psychological blow to the Allies. The American battleships lost at Pearl Harbor had been sunk by enemy planes, but those ships had been at anchor, their crews under peacetime conditions. The *Repulse* and the *Prince of Wales* had been maneuvering in the open sea with their men at battle stations. In one strike, the Japanese had eliminated the most powerful ships in the Pacific west of Hawaii, causing the Allied naval forces to question their own abilities.

In Manila, Admiral Hart recognized the magnitude of the disaster. "It meant," he wrote, "that we entered the war in the Far East under a very grave handicap. We knew from the beginning that we might have to make a fighting retreat, but now the odds against us would be bigger as we tried to hamper and delay the enemy. To oppose a large and well-balanced Japanese fleet, we now had a small handful of vessels whose numbers did not include a single capital ship."

Hart witnessed another catastrophe that day from the roof of the Marsman Building. For more than two hours he watched in helpless rage as 54 Japanese planes crisscrossed the skies over Cavite unchallenged, destroying the Asiatic Fleet's only naval base. The Navy's obsolete three-inch antiaircraft guns could not reach the enemy bombers, and the remnants of the Army Air Corps offered no interference. Hart knew as he watched the pillars of smoke reach skyward that Manila was finished as a base for his fleet. Without air cover, he could not continue to defend the Philippines. He also realized that the islands were doomed as well.

Sounds of war reached the *Houston* that afternoon. The alarm rang out, sending men rushing to their battle stations. Off to port, the seaplane tender *Langley* was blazing away with all four of her three-inch guns. Men with binoculars strained at the cloudless sky, seeking the planes at which the *Langley* was firing, but no one could distinguish them. On the *Langley*'s flight deck, near the sandbagged fire-control center, Gunner H. E. Anderson heard a sailor say that the target's angle of elevation was not changing. Anderson squinted up into the bright sky at the little silver dot the guns were trying to reach, and he immediately realized their mistake.

A few hundred yards away on the *Pecos*, others had come to the same conclusion. The skipper, Commander E. Paul Abernathy, had just been brought a sandwich by his Filipino mess steward. The steward looked up in the sky for a moment and said, "Captain, why for *Langley* shoot at Venus?" The enemy plane in the *Langley*'s gunsights was actually the planet.

Aboard the *Houston*, Lieutenant Lee Rogers commented, "They're really protecting us."

Later that afternoon the spotters sighted a ship on the horizon. Admiral Glassford sent the destroyer *Stewart* ahead to identify her, and Captain Rooks ordered a boarding party to assemble. The 19-man party, under the command of Sergeant Charley Pryor, included both marines and sailors. The mission of the marines was to provide cover for the sailors who would actually take over the ship. The marines were well armed. Pryor himself carried a Thompson submachine gun, a pistol, and hand grenades. Two others were equipped with Browning automatic rifles. They had obtained their weapons from the armory and assembled on the fantail, eager to take to the water and do battle with the Japanese. By now the *Houston* was near enough to the other ship to make out a huge red ball on the side. "By thunder, this is it," Pryor said. "This is the real thing."

But it was not to be. The *Stewart* sent word that the ship had been identified as an American freighter. Her crew had scraped off the American flag when the war started and the rust had made it look like the Japanese rising sun insignia.

"We were kind of let down," Pryor said.

The next night the men of the *Houston* were thwarted again. Around dusk, the lookouts sighted two enemy ships, a cruiser and a destroyer, silhouetted against the setting sun. Perfect targets, and clearly outnumbered by the *Houston,* the *Boise,* and the four U.S. destroyers.

Admiral Glassford ordered the *Boise* and the *Edwards* to the convoy's perimeter nearest the enemy. General quarters sounded on every ship. Up in the *Houston's* foretop, gunnery officer Al Maher took his sightings and gave his three eight-inch turrets the range and bearing. The five-inch guns lowered their muzzles and took aim. Bill Weissinger, trainer on a five-inch gun, waited next to his sight setter and began to talk about what they would do when they opened fire.

The sight setter looked at him and started laughing. "What are you scared of?" he said.

"Nothing," Weissinger replied. "I looked down and my knees were shaking. It was nervous energy is what it was."

Up on the bridge, Admiral Glassford kept changing his mind and contradicting his own orders to the fleet. First he slowed to 10 knots, then sped up to 20. A few minutes later he slowed again. The gunners kept their sights trained on the Japanese, wondering why they had not been given orders to fire. Glassford was ambivalent about his primary duty. Should he attack enemy vessels when he had the opportunity or concentrate on getting his convoy through safely? Finally he decided that the latter was more important and, to the dismay of nearly everyone on board, he ultimately ordered a course change that turned them away from the Japanese ships.

"Oh, hell," Bill Weissinger said. "We were ready to go. We thought it was such a good opportunity. For a day or so, there were a lot of bad comments about Glassford. I mean, we signed up to fight. We were confident we could blow them out of the water. No doubt of that. We just wanted a chance to do it."

Many of the officers and men complained about the missed

chance and about Glassford's command. "We missed a great opportunity to strike the first blow against the Japanese navy," said Al Maher. "It was very frustrating, especially after I had given the order to load all turret guns and then had to unload them by hand as we avoided combat. It was hard to avoid criticism of the command, although Glassford had a difficult choice. Glassford knew China, but not what he was supposed to be doing with the task force."

On the afternoon of December 15, the *Houston's* convoy arrived at the port of Balikpapan on the east coast of Dutch Borneo, more than 800 miles to the south of Iloilo. The *Houston* moored at Pier Five to take on fuel. The crew on deck sweltered, looking longingly at the clean, attractive town. Although they would have liked to go ashore for a few beers, no liberty was granted. Their orders were to load up and get out as fast as possible. No one wanted to be caught in port by a flight of Japanese bombers.

Bob Fulton, the assistant engineering officer, went ashore to supervise the refueling from the huge storage tanks on the edge of town. As he stood for a moment atop one of the tanks, he wondered if the Japanese would move in before the ships could depart with their load of fuel.

Before dawn the next morning the convoy slipped out of the harbor and continued south, farther and farther from the war. The day after that, the *Houston's* crew received some good news. They had been ordered to leave the convoy and head for Surabaja on the Dutch island of Java. At last, a decent liberty port!

Otto Schwarz was in the foretop as the ship approached the harbor. His watch station on that highest point of the ship was sometimes a little precarious, particularly when entering a harbor known for its huge ground swells. The *Houston* rolled dizzily, and Schwarz was certain that the yardarms would touch the water each time the ship heeled over. All he could do was hang on tightly.

When the *Houston* docked at the navy yard she created quite a stir. She was the first American warship to call since the war began, and most of the townspeople came out to have a look. Both the VIPs and the ordinary citizens seemed reassured by her presence.

Surabaja showed few signs of war, and everyday life for the prosperous Dutch was little changed. The city bustled with vitality in big modern department stores, restaurants, nightclubs, and hotels. Lieutenant Winslow was impressed with the "beauty and cleanliness, especially the neatly landscaped white stucco houses with their red tiled roofs. The tidy Dutch had put their stamp on Surabaja and, in contrast to the filth and stench found in the cities throughout the Philippine Islands, this was refreshingly different."

The men were delighted to go ashore in a real city and anxious to relieve the tension and frustration of the previous ten days of waiting to get into action. Some of the officers headed for the Simpang Club, "a delightful place, spacious, with verandas and snow-white tables and cool wicker chairs where the maître d'hotel spoke English and where, besides marvelous Heineken's beer, there was the *rijsttafel*." Lieutenant Payne expressed amazement that the Dutch could eat such great quantities of food. "To watch them eat a *rijsttafel!*" he said. "It took twenty-one boys to serve all the courses. They'd eat for three hours. No wonder a lot of them weighed two hundred and fifty pounds or so."

Lieutenant Rogers was sitting in a restaurant with Lieutenant Harlan G. Kirkpatrick watching a youngster's birthday party at a nearby table. The sight of those beautiful blond children with their parents, all nicely dressed and so happy, saddened him.

"Jeez, Kirk," he said, "what a shame if the Japs ever took this place over with all those little kids there. Look how great they look."

"Ah," Kirkpatrick said, "they'll never take this place."

"And they didn't," Rogers recalled. "Not for about a month or so."

The sailors went to the Oranje Hotel and the Hollendorn Restaurant to feast on fresh tomatoes, tenderloin steak, and good Dutch beer, all for a very cheap price. More serious drinkers found what they wanted in Bols gin, still served in its original stoneware bottles. Inevitably for some, too much booze led to fistfights. Seamen Dutch Kooper and E. C. "Chuck" Isaacs were in a bar with some local girls. As Kooper's girl came out of the ladies' room, a Dutch sailor grabbed her. Kooper shouted, "Hey,

Mac," and let him have it. Instantly a brawl erupted and the *Houston* men grabbed their women and shoved off. "It was better for our health to leave," Kooper explained.

A lot of the men believed that they would soon be going into battle and might not make it back. What's the sense of money? they thought. Why not blow it and have ourselves a ball? They did, and the line at captain's mast the next morning was a long one. The deck log for December 18 lists a variety of offenses, including absent over leave (for anywhere from 20 minutes to five hours), drunk and disorderly, resisting arrest, profanity, smoking during general quarters, unauthorized absence from battle station during general quarters, and scandalous conduct attending to the destruction of good morals.

The punishments ranged from warnings, lost liberty cards, and a fine of 20 days' pay, to court-martial and confinement to the brig. Seaman Schwarz was amazed to find this happening in wartime. "Life went on," he said, "as if it were a normal peacetime situation. Some of the discipline was greater than if you got caught for armed robbery today, like bread and water in the brig for five days for fighting.

"Every time we came to a port where we got liberty, the deck logs would record all the deck courts-martial. . . . The deck logs record the action as almost incidental to the general running of the ship. That's the one thing about the Navy. In between those little interruptions—the battles—life went on and we were expected to shape up."

Navy life did go on during the first liberty in Surabaja. The ship remained at some condition of readiness, the AA guns were manned, and the alarm periodically sounded general quarters. At 11:00 on the morning of December 19, there was an air-raid alert. The guns, then in Condition Three, were fully manned in record time. One of the spotters found four planes winging in from the northwest, and the gunners began to track them. The men felt themselves growing more tense as the planes came closer, until someone recognized them as American B-17s. Before long, however, the only aircraft the *Houston* men would see would be Japanese.

The stop at Surabaja also meant routine work for the crew.

Fuel tanks were topped off and fresh provisions were brought aboard. The supply officer arranged for a huge lot of potatoes. Seaman Howard Brooks remembered the crew's surprise at seeing "these little thin short natives running up the gangplank with these big sacks." Most of the potatoes turned out to be rotten, and after a few days at sea the sacks had to be weighted and thrown overboard because the stench was so terrible.

The ship's supply of coffee was getting low. American sailors lived on coffee; to run out was unthinkable. Here they were in Java, the coffee capital of the world, the place from which coffee got its nickname, and there was no American-style coffee to be had. Green coffee beans were purchased and roasted in the ship's ovens. The mess attendants ground the beans and mixed that powder with cocoa beans to produce a kind of mocha. Most of the men didn't like it.

"Whatever it was," Lee Rogers said, "it was lousy. I swore at the time that I would never call a good cup of coffee a cup of Java anymore." It tasted so bad that the sailors, used to drinking their coffee black, resorted to adding powdered milk to make it palatable.

Most of the men agreed that one thing did change for the better in Surabaja. Admiral Glassford and his staff went ashore to work with the Dutch in facilitating cooperation between the two naval forces. Now if the *Houston* met an enemy ship, Captain Rooks would be in command and free to open fire. Ironically, the *Houston* would not meet a Japanese ship for quite some time. She was bound for Darwin, on the northwest coast of Australia. Her mission was more convoy duty.

Christmas Day of 1941 was not a time for celebration. The *Houston* had been at sea four days since leaving Surabaja and had seen no sign of the enemy. Indeed, for three days they had not seen another ship. On Christmas they made contact with the small convoy of merchant ships they were to escort to Darwin, then three days' sailing time away.

The men were annoyed with the inactivity, with their lack of participation in the war. They had trained and drilled to perfection and had had no opportunity to use their skills. In the Philippines, Japanese troops were swarming ashore. Enemy ships littered Lingayen Gulf, offloading supplies. That's where the *Houston* should be, the men thought, helping to defend the islands instead of steaming south.

All across the Far East, the U.S. and her allies were fighting, but nowhere was it going well. The news reports that Christmas Day were depressing. Manila had been declared an open city. Japanese troops marched across Luzon. Americans and Filipinos fought a series of delayed-action withdrawals designed to consolidate their position in the peninsula of Bataan, which was soon to become a death trap.

Farther to the east, tiny Wake Island, now a symbol of American courage, had been overrun by the numerically superior enemy force. The men on the *Houston* shared the country's pride in the valiant stand of the small band of marines on Wake, but that day it was another defeat to be entered in the history books.

To the north, the British were having an equally difficult time. Hong Kong fell on Christmas Day. In Malaya, the Japanese army raced from one victory to another, bringing them closer to the great British base at Singapore. Nothing, it seemed, could stop them.

In the doomed city of Manila, Admiral Hart was having similar thoughts as he prepared to vacate his headquarters. His small fleet was scattered throughout the Southwest Pacific. Under orders from Washington, his priority mission was to protect the convoys coming from the States to Australia, and to escort some of those ships northward from Australia to the Dutch East Indies.

On the day after Christmas, Hart found himself in the hot, cramped quarters of the USS *Shark*, a submarine. At two in the morning, as the sub slipped out of Manila Bay, he confided his despair to his diary. "I guess the jig is up," he wrote. "So 'Eighteen Days of Manila Bay' and T. Hart is running, yes it can be made out in that light, driven off by the Japs! It is not a nice thing to look back to."

Hart had planned to leave by PBY, but the Japanese wouldn't allow him that luxury. The day before, his plane had struck a native boat on takeoff and later was destroyed by Japanese bombs while undergoing repairs.

*   *   *

Two days later, after a week of the heat and humidity of the Indian Ocean, the *Houston* and her convoy approached the port of Darwin. The crew was eager for shore leave. If they couldn't fight the Japanese, at least they could have another good liberty, but they quickly learned that as a liberty town Darwin was a bust.

Bleak, barren, and only three blocks long and two wide, Darwin looked like a frontier town in the American West of a hundred years ago. The one-story wooden buildings had corrugated iron roofs, and all the windows were boarded up. Not a pane of glass was intact. A week before, the Australian soldiers stationed in Darwin had run out of beer and gone on a rampage.

This time of year Darwin was miserably hot and in the middle of the rainy season. Thick red mud clung to the men's shoes and soiled their white uniforms. Only narrow wooden sidewalks offered protection. The Aussies called Darwin the "asshole of the world," and it didn't take the men of the *Houston* long to figure out why.

"Of all the places I've been," Jim Gee said, "that's the one I'd like to stay in the least." "Darwin?" said Jack Lamade with a smile. "We used to say that's where we went to pick up our load of flies. Honestly, you'd take a bite of food and you'd just have to brush the flies off before you could get it in your mouth."

Nevertheless, it was a chance to get off the ship, away from the regimentation and the routine for a few hours, and to get something to drink. Some said that there were only two women in Darwin and they were otherwise engaged, so there wasn't anything else to do but drink—if you could find something, that is. But the men of the *Houston* were resourceful.

"Yeah, I had a famous liberty in Darwin," Jack Smith said. "The bars opened at two, and you could get one shot of rum and two warm beers. We met some Australian airmen, and they took us out to their air base and we went to their tea, and when their bar opened, I got me a couple of beers, and that's all I remembered. When I woke up I was minus one shoe and I understand they had to dig out a vehicle from all that red mud to bring me back to the ship. I made that one famous liberty. The funny thing was that they didn't have any more shoes aboard ship that fit me—I was size eleven and a half—and I was barefoot the rest of the time the ship was afloat."

"We just got paid and I went ashore looking over the sights," said Dutch Kooper. "Well, I couldn't get any beer anywhere because it was all warm. So Chuck Isaacs and me teamed up with some Australian soldiers—diggers, they called them—and we marched a couple of miles up the track where the army barracks were. Of course, those diggers didn't have any money, and between Isaacs and myself we bought some beer and, man, they just about carried us back to the ship. We blew all our money."

Tommy Payne, the senior pilot, became something of a hero to the Australians. When they ran out of beer again because the "bloody Yanks" had drunk it all, Payne went aboard an American supply ship that had put into port and requisitioned some beer for the locals. "I tell you," he said, "that's the closest I've ever been to becoming the president of Australia. They really did appreciate that. They were so glad to get that beer you'd think they never had any before."

In addition to depleting the local beer supply, the *Houston* sailors bought out the town's stores of canned food. They snapped up everything from peaches to hams, as much as they could carry. They ingeniously stowed their provisions near their battle stations and all around the ship so that they'd always have something extra to eat, even when at general quarters. By the *Houston*'s second day in port, Darwin's mayor formally complained to Captain Rooks that the shops were being emptied of food.

The ship acquired more food through normal channels, from a U.S. supply ship loaded with fruits, vegetables, and canned goods. It had been destined for the naval forces in Manila but had no hope of getting there now. American warships passing through were able to tap this valuable resource.

Bill Weissinger and other seamen spent all day transporting canned goods from the supply ship. "Each trip we'd break the cases open and by the time we got through, all the life jacket lockers were full of canned hams, peaches, fruit cocktail, and gallon cans of ripe olives. We managed to get us about a week's supply of food for each gun crew while we were transporting that stuff."

The *Houston* also took aboard a large supply of ice cream, and some of the crew invited Australian sailors to sample this treat. One Aussie seaman came away from the geedunk stand—the ship's soda fountain—marveling at his good fortune. He muttered to George Detre, "She's a bloody palace, mate! She's a bloody palace!"

The *Houston* held open ship for the Australians, and when the word got back from the first visitors about this bloody palace and the great chow, the locals arrived by the hundreds. Reluctantly, Captain Rooks had to close the ship because the Australians were eating too much.

On the morning of December 30, the *Houston*'s last full day in Darwin, Captain Rooks held mast for those who had managed to have too good a time on liberty. He issued the usual warnings and withheld future liberty cards, and one sailor was placed on bread and water for five days. A marine was awarded 20 days' bread and water in solitary confinement.

Before dawn on the last day of 1941, the *Houston* got under way. Most of the men did not know where they were headed, but they were aware that it was not into combat. They had another convoy to protect. More of the same. They looked ahead to 1942 and hoped it would be a better year.

On Java, Admiral Glassford was holding a press conference with reporters from CBS radio. Off the record, he offered his candid opinion about the situation.

"This is the blackest hour in United States history," he told them. The war was likely to last five to ten years. But as the reporters left, the admiral advised them to be optimistic in their stories.

On the bridge of the *Houston*, Lieutenant Hal Hamlin had the midnight watch. In keeping with Navy tradition, he wrote the first entry of the New Year into the deck log in rhyme.

> 00 to 04   1 January 1942
> Steaming on true course one zero eight,
> Enroute Port Darwin to Torres Strait.
> The standard compass reads one, two, three

(the degaussing increases the error, you see).
Alden, Whipple, and *Edsall,* destroyers lean,
About us form an inner sound screen.
Seven, six, three, and two are the boilers we need
For fifteen knots, which is standard speed.
To keep from sinking (and that's no joke)
Material is in condition "Yoke."
The guns in condition of readiness TWO,
Are waiting to sink any ship named *Maru.*
While all is dark as the ace of spades,
As a means of protection from enemy raids.

5

A Strange Way to Fight a War

"I can't tell you where I am, where I am going, or where I have been, but you can believe me when I say we are getting around." So wrote pilot Windy Winslow to his father, a New York physician, on the first day of January 1942. The elder Winslow did not receive the letter until the last day of January, and no one aboard the *Houston* would have believed that Winslow's words would be just as appropriate then as they were the day they were written.

Most of the crew shared the feeling of not knowing where they were or what was happening while the scope of the war continued to widen north of their position. They were not alone in that feeling; it was shared throughout the Asiatic Fleet, from Admiral Hart on down. While the *Houston* was heading east from Darwin, paralleling Australia's rugged north coast, Hart was completing his arduous submarine journey from Manila to Surabaja. He arrived in the Dutch port on the afternoon of January 2, after a passage of 1,000 miles.

For five days—most of the time submerged—Hart and 65 other passengers had been cramped inside the sub's pressure hull, enduring temperatures in excess of 100 degrees. It was difficult for a man of his age, but what was worse was being out of touch with the fleet and the war. Had he known of a decision reached in Washington during that time, he would have been even more concerned.

As soon as the submarine docked, Admiral Hart was rushed by car to his new headquarters, which had been established in Surabaja by Rear Admiral Glassford and Rear Admiral William R. Purnell, Hart's chief of staff. A great many official dispatches had accumulated during Hart's absence. Foremost among them was a message from Admiral Harold Stark, chief of naval operations, informing Hart of potentially damaging complaints filed by General Douglas MacArthur on Corregidor.

MacArthur had been openly critical of Hart's handling of the Asiatic Fleet, implying that the Navy had abandoned the Army by taking the fleet south so soon after the war started. MacArthur felt that his troops in the Philippines had been left defenseless.

Hart was furious. He replied to Stark that the fate of the Philippines had been decided at two in the afternoon of the first day of the war, when the planes at Clark Field were destroyed. Without air cover, Hart explained, his ships would have been at the mercy of the Japanese air force and would in all probability have been sunk by now.

Another dispatch waiting for Hart notified him that a supreme command for the Southwest Pacific would shortly be established, a unified naval force of American, British, Dutch, and Australian vessels. It would be commanded by an American admiral, "probably yourself," the message said.

Although Hart was the obvious choice, based on rank, he did not want the command. He cabled Stark, suggesting that someone else be selected. Hart believed that a combined naval force could not function effectively in wartime unless all participants agreed on a unified strategy. So far, such agreement had proved impossible.

Glassford and Purnell had already been in consultation with the Dutch naval leadership about Allied strategy, and these conferences had been marked by "bickering and recriminations." Hart foresaw no way of ironing out the differences, particularly with the Dutch, and he did not want to deal with a hodgepodge naval force that did not even speak a common language, much less share the same approach to the conduct of the war. The difficulties of a combined command nagged at him; the Allies should not be fighting each other when the common enemy was Japan. Hart slept poorly that night.

The next day he traveled by train to Batavia, the capital of Java, to meet with the Dutch naval commander, Vice Admiral Conrad E. L. Helfrich, and the governor-general of the Dutch East Indies, A. W. L. Tjarda Van Starkenburge. As soon as Hart had been ushered into the governor-general's office, he realized he was in trouble.

After curt formalities, the governor-general read aloud a press release announcing the formation of an Allied command known as ABDA (for American, British, Dutch, and Australian forces). Hart heard with dismay that he had been chosen to head the force. Further, it quickly became apparent that the Dutch resented the fact that an American was to lead them in the defense of their own territory. Helfrich believed that since the Allied navies would do battle in the waters of the Dutch East Indies, someone familiar with the area should command the fleet.

Hart understood the Dutch resentment, but he became angry when Helfrich demanded a detailed plan of attack. Hart was flabbergasted. How could he be expected to have developed operational plans when he had just learned of his unwelcome assignment? He replied that he had not wanted the command and had asked Washington to give it to someone else. He realized, he said, that the Dutch knew the area much better than he did. He also informed Helfrich that planning should be deferred until Field Marshal Sir Archibald Wavell, the newly appointed supreme commander in the Southwest Pacific, had arrived.

In Helfrich's view, Hart was much too cautious for the job. Helfrich believed that the American fleet should have been pursuing the Japanese for the last three weeks instead of wandering the Indian Ocean escorting small convoys. Thus Hart and Helfrich were off to a bad start, and their relationship was destined to get worse.

After the war, Admiral Helfrich wrote in his memoirs that Hart "was not optimistic and seemed somewhat downcast by Pearl Harbor and his rapid departure from the Philippines. . . .What disturbed me more was his opinion that the defense of the Dutch East Indies was a lost cause and that retreat to Australia was the next step to be taken." Helfrich wanted to hold the line; retreat was out of the question for him. After all, he was defending his homeland, territory possessed by the Dutch for 300 years.

Helfrich was correct about Hart's lack of optimism. The day after their meeting, Hart wrote in his diary, "I wish I could see some hope in it for [the Dutch]—but I can't see much. . . .[They] have utterly lost confidence in us. I can't blame them for that."

The new ABDA command began with pessimism, distrust, and a gloomy assessment of the future. Its failure to improve in the coming weeks would prove fatal for the men and the ships of all the navies involved. The fact that few of them would survive the next two months can be largely attributed to the ineptitude of the leadership and the awkwardness of the combined command structure.

Aboard the *Houston*, it was more of the same tedium, boredom, and frustration at failing to encounter the enemy. While Admirals Hart and Helfrich were meeting in Batavia, the *Houston* was anchored off tiny Thursday Island on the northeast tip of Australia, between the continent and the island of New Guinea. It was hot and it was dull. They stayed there until the next day when the light cruiser USS *Pensacola* arrived, escorting two American troop transports and a Dutch freighter. This convoy had been steaming toward Manila when Pearl Harbor was attacked, had been ordered back to Hawaii, and then diverted to Australia.

The cargo was an important one, consisting of 4,600 troops, 52 A-24 dive bombers, 18 P-40 fighters, 340 trucks and jeeps, 48 75-mm guns, 600 tons of bombs, three and a half million rounds of machine-gun ammunition, and 9,000 drums of aviation fuel. The American and Filipino troops on Bataan sorely needed these reinforcements and supplies, but there was no way to get the ships to Manila Bay. The Japanese now completely controlled the waters around the Philippines. The convoy's latest destination was Darwin.

The *Pensacola* turned over her charges to the *Houston*, which brought the ships to Darwin two days later. The town was even less inviting than it had been in December. The rainy season was continuing, and the men complained that they were constantly wet, if not from sweat then from the drenching downpour.

The war continued to pass them by. The *Houston* sat in Darwin for five days. The only real excitement was the arrival on January 9 of 61 new hands. The tiny town was overcrowded with American military personnel who had been slated for duty in the Philippines and were now stranded. There was no assignment for the Army units at present, but the surplus sailors were being distributed among the ships that called at Darwin.

Among the men reporting aboard the *Houston* was Private Lloyd V. Willey, from Iowa, a recent graduate of the Marine Corps radio school. No more radiomen were needed, so he was assigned to the five-inch gun commanded by Sergeant Charley Pryor. Willey and several other marines had been in Darwin for nearly two weeks. Eight of the men went to the *Houston*, seven to the *Boise*. Willey would be the only one of the eight *Houston* marines to survive.

Another new crewman was Pharmacist's Mate Griff L. Douglas, a 19-year-old from Waco, Texas, who had joined the Navy because he didn't like working in the cotton mill back home. Douglas was one of ten medical corpsmen to join the *Houston* that day, though the ship already had a full complement of sick-bay personnel. "There wasn't much need for us," Douglas said, "until we got hit, and then you could see the need. The rest of the guys kind of looked down on us because we weren't pulling watches like they were. After we got hit, they treated us a little bit different."

The following day the *Houston* got under way, but there was no word for the crew about their destination. With an escort of two destroyers, she headed north toward the Flores Sea around Timor Island, approximately 800 miles from Darwin. Rumors raced through the ship that something big was up, but it wasn't. For five days the *Houston* steamed in lazy circles. The men remained at their guns, and spotters continually watched the horizon, but no orders came from the bridge and no one saw the enemy.

Lieutenant Jack Lamade remembered how he, Tommy Payne, and a few others would break the monotony. "At night after chow we would all go up on the forecastle and sit for about three hours before going below. Tommy would break out his harmonica and we would sing just about every old song which was ever written. Coming out of harbors, we knew that Jap subs were laying for us and were all around us, but we would just lay up on the forecastle and sing with Tommy and his harmonica and know that if we were going to get it, then there was nothing we could do about it. We might just as well think about home as long as we could before they finally did catch up with us."

The only break in the routine came from the occasional sighting of a freighter. On January 13, Sergeant Pryor formed up his boarding party, but the unidentified ship turned out to be a Philippine cargo ship. The next day when the boarding party launched their whaleboat, they found the suspicious freighter they boarded to be Russian—and it even had women aboard. "We had a look at some of the women they had on there," said Boatswain's Mate Q. C. Madson, "and they looked like coal heavers. What a size!"

The following day Madson wrote in his diary, "Cruising slowly along the coast of Timor. We don't know what we are looking for." And the next: "Appear to be cruising aimlessly."

During these days of watching and waiting Captain Rooks took the opportunity to get to know his men, and to give them a chance to meet him. He visited every deck and battle station to talk with his crew. "Rooks would come around and make encouraging remarks," Howard Brooks recalled. "Just his presence was encouraging enough. He didn't have to say anything. His presence was a great comfort." The men still wondered how he—and all of them—would do in combat, but now at least the captain was no longer a remote figure on the bridge whom they knew only through stories and rumors. Rooks was taking on the dimensions of a human being and giving a great boost to the crew's morale.

Another officer who is fondly remembered from this time is the chaplain, Commander George Snavely Rentz. A graduate of Gettysburg College and Princeton Theological Seminary, Rentz joined the Chaplain Corps during World War I. Dedicated to the welfare of the crew, Rentz was tireless in his efforts to uphold morale. Bob Fulton, the assistant engineering officer, lived next door to the chaplain and recalls that there were always two or three sailors waiting outside Rentz's door to talk with him.

"The most wonderful thing I remember," Seaman First Class John Bartz said, "was that the chaplain came around all the time to the guns. He'd even offer you a little nip, which he was not supposed to do, but he would do that." A man of energy and endurance far beyond his years, Chaplain Rentz would become an indispensable member of the *Houston*'s crew in the trying days ahead, and a symbol of courage that remains vivid to this day.

The *Houston*'s engineers used the days of waiting to anticipate problems and develop contingency plans. Ensign A. F. Nethken developed a device to provide communications throughout the ship in case the normal communications system—the sound-powered or electrically powered phones—was damaged. Nethken built phones that would couple magnetically to the ship's pipes.

Bob Fulton in the engine room had encountered a problem with the fuel oil. Although the Asiatic theater was a major oil-producing center of the world, the *Houston* could not obtain the right grade of oil. The oil that was available was too thin to flow through the fuel pumps at a rate sufficient to provide full power to the engines.

The *Houston*'s pumps were designed for Stateside oil, which had to be heated to get a viscosity adequate to flow through the pumps. But the oil from Borneo was too thin and had to be thickened somehow. To accomplish this, Fulton designed and built seawater coolers made out of evaporator tubing and sheet metal. The coolers worked so effectively that they became the standard for the American navy. Without Fulton's engineering expertise and ability to improvise, the *Houston* would not have been able to make full speed.

At last, after five days of steaming in mile-wide circles, the *Houston* received new orders: Return to Darwin. "This was a strange way to fight a war," said Windy Winslow. The next day it got even stranger. As they were nearing the Australian coast, they were ordered back to the point they had just left. "This convinced me," Winslow added, that "we were operating under the control of a bunch of idiots."

In Java, the fledgling ABDA command was having difficulty getting organized. One Dutch officer confided in Jack Galbraith that "nobody knew what anybody else was doing. You've never seen such a mixed-up thing as that headquarters," he said. The turmoil was so widespread that "even the admirals hardly knew what their status really was." Lieutenant General Lewis Brereton of the U.S. Army Air Corps commented that "Sometimes we didn't know where we stood from one hour to the next."

The confusion pervaded even Admiral Hart's headquarters, and it was sometimes hard to say who was in charge of what. Because Hart now commanded the multinational naval force, he had delegated much of the operation of the Asiatic Fleet to his chief of staff, Rear Admiral Purnell. This meant that Purnell, whose headquarters was located on the Surabaja waterfront, was the acting commander of the American fleet. Admiral Glassford was retained as commander of Task Force Five and would be based on the *Houston* whenever the force went into combat.

A few days later, the Navy Department in Washington altered the American command structure. Glassford was promoted to vice admiral and put in charge of "United States Naval Forces in the Southwest Pacific." With that, the Asiatic Fleet effectively ceased to exist, although it was never formally abolished.

To make matters worse, Glassford was headquartered in Surabaja, while Hart, in the interest of working closely with Wavell and the other Allied leaders, established himself with them in Lembang, a resort town ten miles inland in western Java, at the opposite end of the island from Surabaja. His communications facilities there were primitive; the U.S. Navy's primary radio and coding facility remained at Surabaja.

In addition, the codes and ciphers used by the new command were the ones standard for the Royal Navy, but Dutch equipment and radio frequencies were used to transmit them. The best charts of the area were all in the Dutch language, unfamiliar to the other forces.

Further, Washington insisted that the Americans keep their supply and logistics base at Darwin, 1,200 miles to the southeast. Not only was this too far from headquarters, but as a port it was wholly inadequate to the task of servicing ships. It was vulnerable to air attack because there was virtually no fighter protection. But the chief of naval operations wanted to retain the Darwin base; Washington was not convinced that the Dutch East Indies could be held.

The supreme commander, General Wavell, arrived in Java on

January 10 and, five days later, took formal command of what he chose to call ABDACOM (American-British-Dutch-Australian Command). He selected as his deputy Lieutenant General George H. Brett of the U.S. Army Air Corps and as his chief of staff Major General Sir Henry R. Pownall. Hart was placed in command of all naval forces (ABDAFLOAT). His deputy would be Rear Admiral Arthur F. R. Palliser of the Royal Navy.

ABDACOM's complicated structure included four army, four navy, and six air force organizations (the latter included bomber, fighter, and reconnaissance groups). Molding all these components into an efficient military force would require considerable time, a commodity of which the Allies were short. Problems were compounded when it became clear that Wavell himself was far more interested in the fate of Singapore than in the Dutch East Indies. He was often absent from Java, and Hart was rarely informed about his departures.

Troubling personality problems began to emerge. Neither Wavell nor Pownall held a high opinion of Americans in general or of Admiral Hart in particular. To Pownall, Americans were "difficult and had to be put in their place." Hart was thought to be too old and tired. His known respect for Japanese efficiency was considered "bad form."

Relations between Hart and the Dutch Admiral Helfrich were deteriorating. Although Helfrich was commander in chief of the Dutch East Indies Navy, his ships were formally under Hart's control. Helfrich himself had no formal assignment in the new command. He resented his exclusion from the strategy sessions that were considering the fate of his homeland. He became increasingly critical of Hart and constantly needled him about the poor performance of American submarines, whose torpedoes usually failed to explode. Helfrich also harangued Hart about the amount of time U.S. ships spent in southern ports. Hart, on the other hand, was convinced that Helfrich often withheld important information from him and even deliberately misled him.

The Japanese were drawing closer to the Dutch East Indies every day. At the moment, their navy was concentrating on Singapore, but they had ships to spare, and some of these were probing for the best routes through the straits around Borneo, north of the Indies. One of these passages was the Makasar Strait, separating the islands of Borneo and Celebes, 800 miles northeast of Surabaja. Here was a chance for the Allies to strike at the enemy. The *Houston* missed the battle. She was too far to the south, convoying merchant ships between Darwin and Thursday Island. Task Force Five headed north from Timor with Admiral Glassford on the *Boise* in command. The five other ships in the force were the *Marblehead* and four old destroyers—*John D. Ford, Pope, Parrott,* and *Paul Jones.* None of the skippers could read the Dutch charts, and Admiral Helfrich had refused to supply the Americans with Dutch ship pilots, contending that he could not spare any.

Suddenly the *Boise* bucked and shuddered, ripping out her bottom on a coral reef. Glassford transferred his flag to the *Marblehead* and the damaged *Boise* made its way to Tjilatjap on Java's south coast, and from there to India for repairs. The only American ship in the Dutch East Indies equipped with radar was now out of action.

A short while later, the *Marblehead* burned out one of her turbines, reducing maximum speed to only 15 knots. Thus, before encountering any enemy action, the American cruiser strength had been drastically diminished. Now the *Houston* was the one remaining American ship of any size capable of confronting the Japanese.

The destroyers in Task Force Five made a determined attack in the Makasar Strait. They scattered the Japanese ships, but the delay was only temporary and the damage slight. This was, however, the first major surface battle for American naval forces since the battle of Santiago in 1898, in which a young Tommy Hart had participated.

The men of the *Houston* were eagerly anticipating liberty in Surabaja. They were exhausted from the weeks of tension and frustration and from maintaining a constant state of readiness. There had been no opportunity for shore leave in three weeks, since the heat and rain and emptiness of Darwin. On January 26, the *Houston* tied up at the Rotterdamkade Pier in Surabaja to take on fuel oil and as much in the way of provisions as could be obtained. This time they got 10 tons of canned ham.

Surabaja had not been attacked by the Japanese, and the civilians seemed unconcerned about the war. One change was evident to the sailors of the *Houston,* however. The schoolchildren were now carrying gas masks slung over their shoulders.

Lloyd Willey, the marine who had joined the *Houston* at Darwin, went ashore with four of his shipmates. "The main thing was to get away from the chow on the ship," he said. "The first thing we did was to pile into one of those two-wheel horse-drawn buggies. The five of us jumped on the back of this thing and the horse and driver went up in the air like they were on the other end of a seesaw. The driver was screaming bloody murder. I mean, those ponies are so small and [Sergeant Joe] Lusk alone weighed two-thirty at least. We finally got the horse and driver back down to earth and got into town. We just kind of walked around and drank this Heineken beer. You could get a big quart bottle of it for about thirteen cents American."

Some of the men had quite a bit more of Heineken beer, and Bols gin as well, judging by the length of the line at captain's mast the next day. This time the offenses included being out of uniform, returning to the ship unfit, direct disobedience of orders, being disrespectful to a petty officer, breaking windows, unauthorized possession of intoxicating liquor, and having clothing adrift in the starboard hangar. All hands agreed it had been a great liberty.

To judge by the news the men were hearing on the radio, it was "only a matter of time" before the Japanese would be spotted in the Java Sea. Unless the *Houston* retreated all the way to Australia, which no one aboard wanted to do, she would likely be in combat very soon.

Japanese troops had gone ashore in Borneo and were converging on the town of Balikpapan, where the *Houston* had refueled only a month before. The scuttlebutt was that they had also landed on New Guinea. If this were true, then they could effectively isolate Australia from the United States, because Allied convoys sailed within easy air range of New Guinea. The British were continuing to retreat down the Malay peninsula toward their fortress at Singapore. On Bataan, the Americans and Filipinos were holding on, but the men of the *Houston* knew that, without reinforcements, they could not survive much longer.

Admiral Hart, headquartered at Lembang, 400 miles west of

Surabaja, faced problems on two fronts: the conduct of the war and political problems in Washington. He could not do anything about the latter, but he was trying to do what he could about the war. He decided that despite Washington's ideas, the supply base at Darwin was too far away to service the fleet, and he ordered the auxiliary vessels there to sail to Java.

He was frustrated that he had been able to muster only a small force for the Makasar operation. "We are unready," he had written in his diary, "because of the ships having been at sea so long. They are run to death and simply must have some time in port to get tuned up. . . . We had made the mistake in all three Navies of convoying and escorting interminably . . . . There would have been no losses [in the convoys] if we had done none of that whatever." Convoying had robbed the Allies of the opportunity to take the offensive. This may have been the right conclusion, but it was reached too late; the Navy Department had insisted that warships escort all convoys.

Hart was unaware of much of the political maneuvering going on at the time. He found this out too late also. British and Dutch officials had complained to Washington that Hart was excessively pessimistic, and they demanded that he be replaced by Admiral Helfrich. The deputy governor-general of the Dutch East Indies arrived in Washington late in January and made no secret of his opinion that Hart was inadequate as a commander.

Wavell, too, was dissatisfied with Hart, primarily because of the opinion of his deputy, Pownall. Pownall had told him that Hart was "a nice man but with very little guts who always finds a good reason for not doing things." Wavell had had little opportunity to work with Hart, because he was spending so much time in Singapore, so he relied on Pownall's assessment. On January 29, Wavell wired Prime Minister Churchill with his views, suggesting that Helfrich take command. Churchill sent Wavell's "private and most confidential" telegram directly to Roosevelt, who agreed that Helfrich would be an ideal replacement.

The *Houston* was finally going to war. No official announcement had been made and none of the crew knew anything definite, but the rumors were strong and clear. On January 28, the men were told that all liberties would expire at midnight. Their planned layover in Surabaja for another two days had been cancelled. Lieutenant Payne confided to Winslow that he thought they would meet the Japanese sometime in the next few days.

The following afternoon, the *Houston* slipped out of Surabaja in the company of two destroyers, the *Paul Jones* and the *Whipple*. Shortly after they cleared the minefields, Commander Al Maher told the officers of his gunnery department that they were going to serve as a supporting force for the *Marblehead* and four destroyers in another assault on the Japanese forces at Makasar Strait. Some of the officers expressed disappointment that the *Houston* would not be in the attack itself and would be only a backup force, but this was at least an improvement over convoy duty.

On February 2, as they neared the strait, Captain Rooks received a message from headquarters calling off the attack. The moonlight was too bright and the attacking force would lose the critical element of surprise.

The *Houston* rendezvoused with the *Marblehead*, and the force turned back toward Surabaja. But Admiral Hart was not ready to give up. He organized a new attack on Makasar Strait, this time with a force so large that it offered the hope of a decisive victory.

Hart assembled every ship that was available. The British said they could not supply any, but the Dutch offered cruisers and destroyers. Hart decided, diplomatically, to put a Dutch naval officer in command. He tapped Rear Admiral Karel W. F. M. Doorman, the second-highest ranking officer in the Dutch East Indies Navy. Doorman, a 53-year-old pilot, had led the Royal Netherlands Naval Air Service in the Indies and had, more recently, been in command of the Netherlands Squadron, the navy's fighting unit.

He was a determined man (some called him stubborn) and had a reputation for being difficult to get along with, but no one questioned his eagerness to fight. Unfortunately, he suffered from a long-standing tropical illness that sometimes sapped his energy. He had never led a sizable naval force in battle.

The *Houston* dropped anchor at Bunda Roads at Madura Island, about 50 miles east of Surabaja, at 8:00 P.M. on the night of February 3. Throughout the night, the ships of the strike force congregated, and at dawn the crew of the *Houston* saw anchored around them in the bay more ships than anyone had seen since they had last been in Pearl Harbor. There was the *Marblehead* and four American destroyers along with the Dutch cruisers *Tromp* and *De Ruyter*, and four Dutch destroyers.

Admiral Doorman summoned the skippers to the *De Ruyter*, his flagship, for a conference on strategy and tactics. He outlined his intelligence on the enemy. Three Japanese cruisers, escorted by several destroyers, were shepherding 20 troop transports at the southern end of the strait. Obviously they were preparing for an invasion somewhere to the south and could be expected to leave the area at any moment. For maximum effect, the Allies would have to strike while the enemy was still confined in the strait. If the American and Dutch warships could get in among the transports, they could cripple the Japanese invasion force and disrupt their island-hopping campaign.

The only problem was the lack of air cover. Neither the Americans nor the Dutch could send any planes up, and Doorman, above all, knew the value of air cover for a fleet. But there was nothing he could do about it. They would have to take their chances.

While the officers conferred on the morning of February 4, the sailors were summoned to general quarters. Following the alarm, the shrill and unforgettable notes of air defense were sounded by the bugler. The *Houston's* men raced to their battle stations. Antiaircraft crews uncovered the ready boxes and rammed shells into the five-inch guns.

The pilots rushed to the quarterdeck to get to their planes, pulling on their flying clothes as they ran. Whenever air defense sounded, it was standard practice to get the SOCs airborne. They could inflict no damage on an attacking force. The little biplanes were incapable of doing more than 100 knots on a good day and were no match for Japanese fighters, or even bombers; but if left on board during an air raid they were a danger to the ship. Their gas tanks were always kept full.

The planes got off just in time. Above them the pilots saw the massed formations of some 50 Japanese bombers. "Hmm," said Tommy Payne. "Geese, no doubt. Headed south."

Fingers tightened on triggers. Spotters watched the planes drone steadily on. Each gun barrel tracked their leisurely progress. Everyone knew that the entire force was trapped. No one could get under way in time.

The Japanese planes continued on course. Not one altered its flight path to attack the helpless ships. They had another target that day—their first attack on the city of Surabaja. The Japanese had not known about the fleet assembling in Bunda Roads, though they surely knew now and would be back.

That afternoon, Commander Maher summoned his officers to his stateroom and revealed the new plan of attack. Other department heads were doing the same and in turn passed the word to their men. The strike force would depart at night to avoid the air attack they all expected to take place at dawn. The following night they would attack the Japanese convoy at the south end of Makasar Strait.

At midnight, Admiral Doorman on the *De Ruyter* led his ships out into open water. They assumed a cruising formation, with the four cruisers in line, each about 800 yards astern of the other. The four U.S. destroyers guarded the flanks while the four Dutch destroyers brought up the rear.

"How formidable we appeared," Lieutenant Winslow wrote. "Never before had I seen four cruisers steaming in column." The long gray column of armed might appeared invincible.

At 9:35 A.M. the force reached latitude 7°28' south, longitude 115°37' east, placing them about 45 miles north of Bali. The crew of the *Houston* could see the mountain peaks of Bali and its neighboring island of Lombok to the south. To the north were the lush green mountains of Kangean Island, 35 miles away. The sky was clear and the sun already hot, with only a few cumulus clouds to promise any relief.

Admiral Doorman signaled his ships that enemy bombers were on their way to Surabaja. He was wrong. This time the ships were the target.

6

Man Your
Battle Stations

The klaxon screamed into every corner of the ship. There was no escape from its raucous, insistent call, nor from the urgent voice that followed it:

"Now hear this! Now hear this! All hands man your battle stations!"

The bugle call for air defense blared over the PA system. "That bugle call sent chills down your back," Bill Weissinger said. He was scrubbing on the boat deck when the alarm sounded, and he dashed for his battle station on the number-one five-inch gun on the starboard side.

It didn't take any of the crew long to reach their battle stations, no matter what they had been doing when they were jolted into alertness. The hundreds of hours spent drilling before the war and the scores of calls to general quarters since Pearl Harbor were preparation for this moment. "We did it so often we could do it in our sleep," Al Maher said. This time there was a greater urgency. This was not a drill. The men of the *Houston* knew that their lives and those of their shipmates depended on manning the battle stations fast.

Some men had been asleep between watches. When the alarm sounded they were on their feet before they realized what was happening. Before the klaxon and the shouts and the notes of the bugle registered in their brain, they were running up ladders, down ladders, through passageways and compartments, across open decks, down through hatches that were quickly sealed behind them, into hot little closed steel rooms that might become their tombs. They raced into cavernous, noisy engine rooms protected from the sea and from torpedoes by only three inches of steel, wrapped by miles of pipes that carried scalding steam. They rushed up to the bridge with its glass and only one inch of plating, and into the eight-inch gun turrets protected by a mere three-fourths of an inch of steel on sides and rear. They packed themselves below decks in repair parties and waited, ready to stop the sea from pouring in or to fight a roaring fire in the bowels of the ship where a spark in the powder magazines could blow them all to dust. They sat behind the skimpy splinter shields of the five-inch guns and the 1.1s and in the open to man the .50-caliber machine guns.

They reacted instantly, without conscious thought. As their footsteps resounded on steel decks, as watertight doors and hatches slammed above them, as men below gripped powder bags and live shells and men topside strapped on helmets and clenched their weapons, there was no thought of home and family, of past or future. For the seasoned professional and for the 17-year-old kid, there was only the moment and the fading notes of the bugle call, the steel hot to the touch from the sun, the gun sight and the shell and the valve, the pumping heart and the throbbing tension that seized them like a drug. There was also fear, and some felt it more than others, but there was no hesitation, no delay, no holding back.

Within minutes each man had settled into his own personal place of war, a seat, a piece of deck space, a bulkhead that for now was his reason for being. From stations all over the ship, the talkers, poised to receive and transmit messages, waited for the reports that the various stations were manned and ready. They stood rigid, with the hot and heavy bakelite earphones clamped over their ears, with the breastplate pressing on their chests and the microphone a few inches from their mouths, listening for word that their little part of the war was ready for action.

In the foretop, 140 dizzying feet above the waterline, Commander Maher waited for his talker to get word from all the ship's gun crews, the battle stations under Maher's command. "Yes, I was in a vulnerable position up there," he said, "but I could see everything that was going on."

The foretop consisted of a circular steel structure balanced atop the tripod foremast. An area approximately eight by ten feet and crowded with a half dozen people, it was crammed with equipment—lights to show the condition of readiness; instruments giving the range of targets; telephones to the plotting room far below, to the bridge, to the conning tower, to the air-defense directors. Maher paced back and forth in the cramped space, scanning the sky and waiting. He had trained for this moment through 19 years of service to his country.

Some 300 feet aft of the foretop, behind the second smoke-stack, Lieutenant Commander Jack Galbraith also waited. Part of his job was to report to the gun boss that all the antiaircraft guns were manned and ready. His position was out in the open, and he alternated between two swivel seats he had had welded to the deck, one on the port side and the other starboard. Under his control were the eight five-inch guns, four on each side of the ship (two forward of him and two aft), the four 1.1 pom-poms (two near his station and two forward by the bridge), and the dozen or so .50-caliber machine guns. Two talkers stalked Galbraith's every move, ready to pass on his orders.

Just forward of Galbraith's station was a six-by-six-foot steel cubicle; its twin was located atop the bridge. These were the five-inch antiaircraft directors. Lieutenant Leon Rogers in sky forward joked that he had "a grandstand seat." The director was another cramped little place. Rogers and his pointer and trainer all stood with their heads poking out of the top. Rogers raised his binoculars to spot for enemy planes, and the pointer and trainer held their scopes ready, poised to fix the crosswires on the target. Behind them a seaman worked the range finder, a bulky apparatus with two protruding ears; and the cross-level operator, with his telescope set at 90° to the line of the bearing, kept his horizontal crosswires level with the horizon, compensating for the roll of the ship. Two talkers completed the crew, alert and waiting for orders.

Back in sky aft, commanded by Lieutenant Joe Dalton, Ray Sparks took up position as talker and Q. C. Madson reported as trainer. In both directors, the officers were waiting for their individual gun crews to report in.

Up forward on the starboard side, Gunner's Mate John Bartz, age 20, was at his battle station. He was a pointer on the starboard 1.1-inch gun, and his job was to elevate the weapon. The trainer next to him would bring it left or right. When it was pointed properly, Bartz would fire it. "I'd get it on the plane and if I could see the bomb, then I'd close my eyes and I'd start firing. I was a young kid and I was petrified." Now Bartz reported his gun manned and ready.

When Sergeant Charley Pryor reached his five-inch gun, number eight, the last one on the port side, it was already fully manned by the crew that had been on duty when the alarm sounded. Pryor took his men below to the magazine to take ammunition from the racks and place the shells on a hoist to send up to the gun.

Topside, Lloyd Willey waited in his bucket seat by gun number eight. He was a fuse setter. "You've got a dial in front of you with a handle on it that goes from one to one hundred twenty. As you get a call down from the gun director, they give you the timing on how many seconds they want from the time the shell leaves the gun until it explodes. Those shells weigh seventy-three pounds, and on the tip were these two little notches, and the nose cone turned. They'd call down that they wanted ninety seconds, and then I would put the shell in and turn the handle to ninety seconds. When you got down to about ten seconds, then you knew the bombers were right overhead and it was time to take whatever cover you could."

Bill Weissinger was the trainer on gun number one on the starboard side. Opposite him, at gun number two to port, Dutch Kooper was standing by as first loader. The job required considerable strength, and Kooper was built for it. He had to take the 73-pound shell out of the fuse pot after the timing had been set and throw it in the gun.

The five-inch guns were manned and ready. One at a time, the gun captains reported in to Galbraith.

Although the attack was expected to come from the air and no enemy ships had been reported in the vicinity, Commander Maher had ordered the massive eight-inch guns to be loaded and ready. They could not be raised high enough to fire at aircraft overhead, but Maher had to be prepared for the possibility that the Japanese would use torpedo planes that would come in low over the water. The Fleet Gunnery School had suggested that the eight-inch guns would be effective against such a low-level attack, aimed so that their shells would explode in front of the torpedo planes. The theory was that the explosions would create huge geysers of water that would swamp the planes. The idea had been borrowed from the British, though no U.S. ship had ever tested it. Today it would turn out to be a fatal mistake for the *Houston*, but five months later this method of defense against torpedo planes would be practiced by American cruisers at Midway with great success.

The *Houston* had three eight-inch turrets, each housing three guns; number one and two forward, and number three aft. The topside of each turret was a large square metal structure that was capable of training 180° from one side of the ship to the other. A deep well within the turret accommodated the gun breeches when they were elevated. Instruments, levers, and dials covered every available bulkhead space, and the entire enclosure was kept highly polished and greased. On the starboard side was a small compartment for the powder handler. The powder came up from below on an electric hoist, and the handler transferred it into the turret chamber.

A small booth with thick armored-glass windows served as the turret officer's battle station. There was barely room for one person inside. Lieutenant (jg) George E. Davis, Jr., was the turret officer on number three. Ensign Nelson was his assistant.

Below turret number one, Otto Schwarz had reached his battle station, the shell deck, a cramped compartment filled with the imposing three-foot-tall shells for the eight-inch guns. The shells weighed 150 pounds apiece and they were covered with grease. The ammunition was stored completely around the bulkhead, with more on a shelf about five feet above the deck. The bottom of each projectile had a lug on it, which was put in a hoist. The shell handler pulled on a chain to bring the shell to the hoist, which lifted it into the turret chamber.

The eight-inch ammunition was the semi-fixed type; the projectile and the powder that fired it were separate. The powder was stored deep in the powder magazine in 55-pound bags; two bags were needed to fire each shell. The bags were sent up on another hoist to the handling room in the turret. In turret number three, Jack Smith was at his station in the handling room. Like most of the enclosed battle stations, it was hot, cramped, and crowded. Smith's job was to manhandle the 55-pound bags and feed them onto the hoist. The drill called for 12 bags of powder in the hoist at any one time, with three more bags lying out on the flameproof door, ready to be placed on the hoist.

Smith was a conscientious young man and curious about the operation of his battle station. Behind him were two valves, and he wondered what they were for. He asked Gunner's Mate Second Class C. J. Kunke about them.

"What do we do about those two valves if we have something happen in here?"

"Don't you worry yourself about those valves," Kunke always said.

Smith did worry about them, and he questioned Kunke so often that the mate finally told him. The function of one of the valves was to sprinkle the hoist with water. The other was to submerge the three powder bags on the flameproof door to keep them from catching fire and exploding.

"I used to sit there," Smith said, "and kind of imagine, 'Well, if anything happens, it'll be dark in here,' and I'd turn around and try to hit that valve, practicing it in my mind."

"Turret one manned and ready."

"Turret two manned and ready."

"Turret three manned and ready."

Commander Maher called the bridge: "Gunnery department manned and ready."

Meanwhile, the *Houston*'s pilots were racing toward the quarterdeck, hoping to get their planes aloft before Japanese aircraft appeared. Lieutenants Payne and Lamade were scheduled to go off first and their SOCs had already been loaded on the catapults.

The other two planes were being rolled out of the hangar, ready to be hoisted up.

An aviation machinist's mate was turning over the engine in Payne's airplane when he climbed into the cockpit, but Lamade's engine was slow to catch. The starboard catapult was cranked out to about a 45° angle from the ship, and Payne ran a practiced eye over his instruments. He motioned to the catapult officer that he was ready to run up the engine. The little SOC vibrated madly.

Payne clenched the throttle with his left hand to make sure it stayed all the way forward. He gave the thumbs-up signal to the catapult officer and instantly lowered his right hand to the control stick, bracing it against his right knee. The catapult officer checked to make sure the locking pins on the plane cradle had been pulled and waited for the next up-roll of the ship. He sighted down the catapult until it hit the horizon, slapped the gunner's mate on the back, and the man pulled the trigger. Payne was off!

The launch sounded like gunfire. The catapult operated not unlike a cannon, firing a powder charge that resembled the cartridge of a five-inch shell. It shot the plane forward instantly. The little aircraft reached a speed of 80 miles per hour in a distance of only 30 feet. As soon as it cleared the end of the catapult, the g-forces that had held the pilot motionless in his seat dissipated, and he eased back on the stick to begin a long slow climb. Of the four planes in the *Houston*'s small complement, Tommy Payne's was the only one to get airborne that day.

While the other planes were being rolled out of the hangar, Pharmacist's Mate Griff Douglas was taking up his battle station there. He stood by a huge first-aid box that was clamped to the bulkhead on the hangar's port side. At his feet was a first-aid satchel light enough to carry easily to any wounded man in his vicinity. It contained the essentials of his trade: bandages, splints, scissors, and the all-important morphine.

Other corpsmen stood by stations around the ship, above and below decks, ready to respond to the first call for a medic. They reported in to Commander William A. Epstein, the chief surgeon, that their stations were manned and ready.

Forward, and two decks below, Commander Epstein and his

assistant, Lieutenant (jg) Clement D. Burroughs, USMC, were preparing their instruments and equipment and waiting for the inevitable aftermath of armed combat. Epstein informed the bridge: "Medical department manned and ready."

Far below the waterline, sealed in with one inch of steel overhead and a meager three inches to protect the hull against torpedoes, were the officers and men of the black gang, the engineering department. The noise and heat were worse in the forward and after engine rooms than in any other part of the ship. Sweat poured off the men even when they were resting. The metal around them, particularly in the firerooms, was too hot to touch without getting burned. Communications were carried out by hand signal. Men standing beside each other could shout and still not be heard over the din of the turbines and the whine of the forced-air blowers.

Each engine room had two firerooms and two giant steam turbine engines. The four engines together produced in excess of 100,000 horsepower, which drove the *Houston* at a maximum speed of 32½ knots. Lieutenant Commander Gingras, the senior engineering officer, was in charge of the after engine room controlling the two inboard propellers. Bob Fulton had the forward room controlling the two outboard propellers.

The men did their jobs efficiently and rapidly. They knew that no matter how good the officers, the gunners, and all the other mates topside might be, the *Houston* was a dead hunk of metal without the throbbing engines to drive her. When general quarters sounded, the black gang instantly went to work. They put all the boilers on the line and then isolated the plant. This was fundamental to damage-control work, to compartmentalize every system.

The *Houston* used a split-plant operation; the two engine rooms could operate independently. If one was knocked out, the other could continue to function. The same caution applied to the turbines and their boilers.

The engineering personnel changed all the valve settings to allow for maximum maneuverability, so that the captain could achieve rapid shifts in speed. All the auxiliary operating equipment necessary for battle was brought up on the line—the pumps, blowers, and generators needed to keep vital equipment working. The auxiliaries that would not be required—the water evaporators, the anchor engine room, and the machine shop—were shut down.

Fulton was on station at the forward end of his engine room. In front of him stood a gauge board approximately eight feet square. Almost two dozen gauges dotted its surface, indicating steam pressure in the main and auxiliary steam lines. Two talkers were with him at all times.

In the firerooms forward of the engine rooms, the men worked on two levels. On the lower level, four firemen under the supervision of a watertender cut burners in and out as needed to maintain the desired steam pressure. On the upper level, another watertender perched on the open metal grating, ready to perform one of the more crucial jobs on board. He watched a column of water in a glass tube, the indicator for the water level in the steam drum. The level in the glass had to be maintained within a couple of inches of the halfway point. If the level dropped, the boiler would burn out in seconds. If the level rose too high, water could overflow into the pipe leading to the turbines and knock the blades out of the turbine casing.

"Forward engine room manned and ready." Fulton reported to Shorty Gingras that all his men were at their stations, all systems were on line. Gingras was waiting to hear from the rest of his personnel. Some were stationed at key auxiliary equipment, such as the steering engine. Others were at electrical distribution points throughout the ship. Still others were assigned to damage-control parties. Joe Gans and Howard Brooks joined their repair parties, waiting with a dozen others one deck down. Brooks's group was the farthest one aft, next to the mount of the number three turret. All parties reported in and Gingras notified the bridge: "Engineering department manned and ready."

It all went smoothly, just like a peacetime drill.

The planes appeared off the *Houston*'s port beam at 9:49. They came from the north at an altitude of 9,000 feet—nine twin-engine bombers flying in a large and perfect V formation.

A marine gun captain at a 1.1 leaned against the rail near

Lloyd Willey's battle station. He chewed on a big wad of tobacco and watched the planes for a moment. "Well," he said, "I know those are not our planes. I think we're gonna have a little bit of trouble pretty soon."

In sky forward, Lieutenant Rogers told his crew, "The bridge reports some Japanese planes in the area, up north of here."

"I see em! I see em!" shouted one of his spotters.

"Stand by for attack to port," warned the PA system.

In the gun directors, the pointers and trainers quickly took the range and bearings of the planes and transmitted the information to the antiaircraft guns. The crews on the port side made ready to fire the instant the flight came within range.

In the foretop, Commander Maher watched the progress of the planes with a feeling of confidence. "We weren't worried," he said. "We thought the Jap planes were sitting ducks. We thought we'd shoot the whole outfit down."

Lieutenant Commander Galbraith followed the progress of the planes through his binoculars. Soon he'd learn the truth about his five-inch ammunition. Was the Fleet Gunnery School report correct about the batch of shells the *Houston* carried?

Lieutenant Lamade's plane was still on the catapult. He thought the enemy planes were heading directly for him. If his engine didn't catch in the next few seconds, he would not be able to take off before the Japanese were overhead.

Galbraith gave the order to fire. The four five-inch guns on the port side sent a salvo of shells into the middle of the enemy formation. Perfect shooting! But only one shell exploded. They fired a second salvo with the same results. Galbraith knew then that his ammunition was defective. Still, he thought, there was always a chance that something else was responsible. Maybe the fuse settings were wrong. Seaman Ray Sparks in sky aft heard Galbraith yell, "Goddamn it! How come they aren't going off? Check your fuse settings!" The crews checked. There was nothing wrong with the settings. The shells themselves were at fault.

All those drills, all that practice, all the training . . . The crews could hit their targets, but what good was that when the shells didn't explode? "That was a big disappointment," Ray Sparks said. "It was a morale thing. Here you put up all those shells just where they're supposed to go, and nothing falls down."

Down in the engine rooms, despite the noise and commotion, the men could feel the impact each time the five-inchers were fired. That was the only way they knew what was happening topside. "We knew we were heading into trouble when we heard those guns fire," Fulton recalled, "but that was about all we really knew."

Jack Lamade knew he was in trouble also. No amount of flight training or prewar drills had prepared him for this moment. His plane was still sitting on the catapult when the five-inch guns boomed. "My engine was running," Lamade said, "but the fabric was all blasted off." He was left in the cockpit of a plane that was nothing more than a skeleton. And when he looked up, he saw a string of nine bombs falling toward the *Houston*.

"Take cover! Take cover!"

Captain Rooks immediately ordered flank speed and a sharp turn to port. In the forward and after engine rooms the bells rang on the telegraphs, the large round dials by which the bridge transmitted speed orders. When the handle on the bridge annunciator was moved, the movement was duplicated in the engine rooms. Now the handles swung all the way forward.

The throttlemen responded at once, turning the 2½-foot wheels as fast as they could to their full open position. As the men strained against the 20-pound force required to tug the wheels, all four engines revved to their maximum capacity and the *Houston* sped forward.

"That first string of bombs!" said Seaman Kooper. "I had never heard a bomb before, and suddenly I look up and I could see something flickering in the light, and boom! A great big geyser of water splashed up, and it seemed like the waters parted like the Red Sea when Moses went through and we were steaming right through the center of that opening where the water parted. All of a sudden the water seemed to close in on us and all I could see was the stack. And here we come like a submarine breaking the surface steaming along."

A sailor on the *Marblehead* later said that from a distance "it looked like the *Houston* was a goner. There was just a wall of water and [the *Houston*] completely disappeared. All this water just sort of hung in the air. Then it started to fall back, and out from underneath all this stuff comes the *Houston* going thirty knots."

Aloft, Tommy Payne also saw the first bombs hit close to the ship. "It looked like it lifted the ship right out of the water," he said.

"Those bombs sounded like sand running down a tin roof," remembered Bill Weissinger. "They just kept getting louder and louder and all of a sudden here goes some brown streaks right by us. They just missed the ship. And old [Seaman Second Class Richard L.] Adams from Kentucky beat me on both shoulders and said if you look real close you can see the shadows of those bombs."

None of the bombs hit the ship directly, but they exploded near enough to do some damage. "The bombs were high-explosive and armor-piercing," wrote gun boss Maher in his official report of the fighting of February 4, 1942. "They exploded well under the surface, throwing great masses of water as high as the forward machine-gun nest. The ship, as she drove into these columns of water, caught tons of it forward and as far aft as the flight deck. The water, which was about a foot deep in the flight deck, became so deep as the ship listed in her turns that the loading crews were swept from their feet and washed about the deck with shells still in their arms. The ship was given such a violent thrust to the side that the forward AA director was jammed in train." Something had gotten stuck in the groove and it could not be moved.

The men below decks felt the effects too. Seaman Second Class Donald C. Brain, stationed in one of the five-inch magazines, remembered the shock waves. "It popped loose some rivets down below the waterline, and you could hear them let loose."

"Oh, yeah, we could hear those near misses all right," added Joe Gans. "They can kill you. Oh, God, it was just like someone banging on the side of the ship, but big bangs. You could hear them just as plain as day. They'd scare the hell out of you."

One of the bombs struck about 10 feet outboard of the

number one engine, close to where Bob Fulton was standing in the forward engine room. Lights and gauge lines snapped instantly, and the numercators—four-foot high glass tubes that measure the oil level in the various tanks—shattered.

The enemy planes passed over and the noise and cascading water, the popping rivets and the shattering glass, ceased. For a moment all was peaceful. In place of the turmoil came fear, anger, and frustration. The *Houston* had had a close call—any closer and some of them would have died—but they had been unable to strike back. The planes were now beyond reach, their perfect formation undisturbed.

"I don't think any man can go through a bombing raid like that without saying that he's frightened," Jim Gee said. "But I just say that we were frightened in such a way that we were hoping to God that we could just get our hands on that shell, on that gun, that would bring down a Jap plane. We just wanted to kill the Japs. That's all we could think about. And even in all of the fear and all of the frustration that you have when you see those bombs falling—and you see them splash right over at the side of that ship, and you see maybe a plate buckle, or you might even see the shrapnel or the results of shrapnel that hits pretty close to home—you still are just so fighting mad that it really doesn't bother you all that much. It's a tremendous feeling to think that you have the power to shoot down this enemy that you've waited for for a long time, that you've prepared for a long time."

But three out of every four of the *Houston*'s shells were duds. "If you can't reach them, you don't knock them out. And we were dedicated to knocking them out."

During the lull after the first wave, Lieutenant Lamade quickly climbed out of his wrecked airplane and watched silently as the catapult officer gave the necessary order. It was fired over the side, to sink into the sea. The other two planes were rolled back into their hangars. There was no point in trying to launch them now.

All around the ship, men were working to fix the damage. The broken telephone connections were repaired, the moisture was wiped from the telescopes and range-finder lenses that had become fogged, and the water was swept off the decks. An attempt was made to get sky forward, the AA director, moving freely on its track again, but the *Houston* didn't have the equipment on board to fix it. It was jammed and would remain so for two days. The air defense would now have to be conducted solely by the after director. Men rushed to load the guns and to hoist more shells up from the magazines.

The planes came over a second time. The spotters counted 54, in six formations of nine planes each. One group was heading for the *Houston*. Obviously the Japanese were concentrating on the *Houston* and the *Marblehead*, the two American cruisers, the biggest ships in the task force. The fleet had scattered; prewar planning dictated that ships should not stay together in a bombing raid. No one had yet learned that keeping the ships in formation would increase and concentrate the amount of antiaircraft fire they could deliver. In those early days of the war, it was every ship for herself, and the men braced themselves for the next attack.

The planes came off the port beam at about 10,000 feet. All guns would be controlled from the after director. The air-defense officers visited each five-inch gun to make sure the shells were being seated properly in the fuse pots. They were still hopeful that something could be done to improve the percentage of shells that exploded.

The gunners manning the 1.1s and the .50-caliber machine guns pleaded with Lieutenant Commander Galbraith to let them open fire. "My people want to shoot, sir," said the sergeant in charge of the machine guns. Although the planes were well beyond range of those guns, Galbraith let them open up. He knew how frustrating it was for the gunners to do nothing.

What was good for the morale of the gunners, however, turned out to be bad for the men below decks, who could only know about the action by the sound of the guns. When the engine-room crews sensed the machine guns going off, they assumed that the planes were so low that they would soon "knock down the masts."

In the forward five-inch powder magazine, Seaman Brain knew that something terrible was going on. "The five-inchers were being fired, then all of a sudden, you could hear the pom-poms—the 1.1s—and then you heard the fifty-calibers going off. When I heard the chatter of those machine guns, I thought, My God, they can't be that close!"

The AA crews worked furiously, sending shells up as fast as the hoists would move. The fuse setters took extra care placing the shells in the fuse pots. Dutch Kooper and the other loaders hefted the shells one after another and rammed them into the guns, but the ammunition was no more effective than before. Three of every four shells failed to explode. One salvo did jar two Japanese bombers slightly out of their perfect formation, but only for a moment. They quickly slid back into place and flew on with all the precision of a training exercise.

When the planes were directly overhead with their bomb bay doors open, the order came from the bridge to take cover. Bill Weissinger and his number-one gun crew scrambled for shelter. "I looked back at my gun," Weissinger said, "and here was an ol' boy laying back there flat on his back, ol' [John M.] Warhead Williams. He was the fuse setter, and when they said take cover that second time, he had a pair of headphones on and he just jumped out of his seat and took out across the deck. The cord was about ten feet long, and when he hit the end of it, it just jerked him flat on his back. And there he lay with these planes coming over. Of course that was a big laugh. Tense as the situation was, people couldn't help but laugh. He managed to scramble in and—here they come!—and they drop their load again and these brown streaks go right by and Adams hits me on the back and yells, 'That's the goddamn bombs!'"

Once again the bombs came uncomfortably close, popping rivets below decks and sending tons of water cascading over the ship. The *Marblehead* seemed to be in greater difficulty. For a moment, the old light cruiser disappeared, obscured by the fountains of water, but when she reappeared, she was still moving. No bombs had struck her either.

The attack continued for two hours. Every 15 to 20 minutes, another formation of planes appeared. The *Houston*'s antiaircraft crews did their best, despite the jammed forward director, which could not get the range of the enemy planes. The after director was located directly behind the after smokestack, and gases from the stack were interfering with the delicate range-finding equipment. Air-defense officers knew this would happen when maneuvering at high speeds—and they had been reporting it since 1939—but no action had been taken by the Navy Department to correct it. As a result, the director could not supply range information to the gun crews, forcing them to go to local control.

Despite the faulty ammunition and the problems with the directors, the well-trained gun crews kept up their fire. Once they saw a plane drop out of formation. Observers in the foretop watched it go into a spin and plunge into the sea with a satisfying splash. Two other Japanese planes fell out of formation, but the gunners could see that they remained aloft. The next day they learned from the Dutch ship *De Ruyter* that the damaged aircraft had also crashed at sea. Three hits for the *Houston!* The gun boss reported that the *Houston* had the best air-defense capability of any ship in the task force.

Three planes out of 54, however, was not many, and the rest of the Japanese attack force returned to bomb the ships again and again. Captain Rooks maneuvered the *Houston* as though she were a destroyer, some said like a yacht. He slowed to 15 knots between attacks. As soon as he saw the enemy bomb bay doors open, he would order flank speed, and the instant he saw the bombs leave the planes, he would call for a hard turn to port or starboard. Sometimes he called for a crashback situation, the sudden lurch from full speed ahead to full speed astern. At least once, to make a sharper turn than anyone thought possible, he ordered two engines ahead and the other two astern.

"I never in my life expected to see the engine annunciators go in opposite directions," said Fireman George Detre of the black gang, "but by golly he did it. He put one side emergency astern, which was everything you could give it astern, and the other side flank ahead, which is the same for ahead. That ship just quivered, but it went."

The engine-room crew had never worked at such a pace. Although they were close to collapse from heat and exhaustion, they answered every call from the bridge instantly. Captain Rooks was truly testing their training and skill that day, particularly with his crashback orders. That demanding maneuver required a complex and precise series of actions that, if not properly coordinated, could permanently damage the engines. The black gang responded like the pros they were.

Upon receiving that signal from the bridge, the throttleman would instantly tug his big wheel shut, crank open the astern throttle, and feed it just enough steam to bring the shaft's rotation to a stop. Then he rapidly spun it open all the way. Within seconds, the circulating pump was started to pump seawater through the condenser.

Forward in the firerooms, the burner operators started cutting out half the burners right away, but only for a few seconds, then they quickly resupplied oil to the burners. High up on the gratings, the watertender watched the water level drop, but he knew why it was occurring and realized he'd have to do just the opposite of what was normally called for. He quickly shut down the fuel supply, and soon the water level rose as the engines sped up to move the ship astern. All this was performed in a matter of seconds without additional communication; the engine-room personnel knew what they had to do. The entire ship was gripped by intense vibrations as the limits of men and machines were tested.

Up on deck, these violent maneuvers flung the men around. They grabbed on to whatever handhold they could find, and the loaders scrabbled to keep from dropping their shells. The men in the magazines had the same problem. "We had a bunch of water on the deck, and it got pretty slippery," said Donald Brain. "One of the fellows slipped and lost control of the brass charge that he had, and it rolled across the deck. When he went to get it, it rolled back the other way. So we were having a little problem down there trying to keep good footing."

Captain Rooks continued to take evasive action and to stop and start the ship as each wave of planes came over. "He would lay that ship over so far in the water to turn it that the water would be scooped up by the hangars and it would go right back out through the ship and out over the fantail." Most of the crew had never seen a ship handled that way before.

Through it all, the gun crews kept firing, the men below decks kept sending up shells, and the black gang kept meeting every demand. Chaplain Rentz made the rounds of the guns, hanging on gamely and never taking cover, "always there with his thermos jug of cold water and pockets full of candy."

"Everybody adored that man," Ray Sparks said. "There he was going from gun to gun. 'Need any help?' he'd ask. 'Get in there, son. We'll get 'em. Don't you worry about it.' He didn't just stay at one station. He was all over." "He was right up there with us on the guns," Dutch Kooper said. "And if he could help out in any way, he did."

Time lost all meaning as the enemy bombers crisscrossed the task force to drop their loads. They focused on the *Houston* and the *Marblehead*. The *Marblehead* had obsolete three-inch guns and could not fire high enough to inflict any damage. The men of the *Houston* watched wave after wave of bombs descend on the *Marblehead* and saw the ship engulfed by looming geysers of water. But she always came through, charging out of the deluge as fast as her antiquated engines would take her.

Finally her luck ran out. Two bombs hit, one forward and the other on the fantail. The fires were brought under control, but the greater damage was in the steering room, deep in the bowels astern. One bomb exploded there and destroyed all the gear. The rudder would not answer to the helm, and the *Marblehead* was out of control. She was listing 10 degrees to starboard and steaming to port in endless circles.

Captain Rooks turned the *Houston* toward the stricken ship to see if he could assist, but another formation of Japanese planes headed for the *Houston*. It would be the last wave. The bombers bore in from the port side. Once again, gases from the *Houston*'s after stack covered the after director so that no range figures could be obtained. The gun crews had to estimate altitude and speed on their own. The formation flew in an almost perfect V, but one plane lagged slightly behind the others.

The crews resumed their routine automatically. Aim, load, fire. Aim, load, fire. Hold tight when the ship lurches forward. Aim, load, fire. Hang on while she heels over. Run like hell when the PA system warns *Take cover!*

The bombs were all released at the same instant and fell in the usual pattern, except for the one from the straggling plane.

They hit the water to starboard, drenching the gun crews but doing no damage. The last bomb was still falling. Al Maher watched it from the foretop, but he didn't think it would hit. John Bartz at his 1.1 watched it and he heard it as well. "You could hear this last bomb coming, the whistling of it, and hear the crunch when it went through the machine-gun deck."

The bomb sliced through a stay at the top of the mainmast. It did not explode but cut through the thin metal of the searchlight and machine-gun platform. It didn't explode then either, but the impact triggered its delayed-action fuse.

The bomb was deflected slightly from its vertical course and battered its way through the thick leg of the tripod mast, leaving a 10-foot hole. Still it didn't explode.

Next it rammed diagonally through the roof of the after radio shack and headed for the main deck at a point midway between the crew's head and turret number three, which was trained to port. It hung no more than three feet above the deck. Then it exploded.

The launching of the USS *Houston* (CA-30) at Newport News, Virginia, September 7, 1929. (*Courtesy Cruiser* Houston *Memorial Exhibit, M.D. Anderson Library, University of Houston*)

The USS *Houston*, flagship of the Asiatic Fleet. *(Official U.S. Navy photograph)*

The USS *Houston* passes beneath New York City's Brooklyn Bridge. *(Courtesy Cruiser* Houston *Memorial Exhibit, M. D. Anderson Library, University of Houston)*

President Franklin D. Roosevelt aboard the USS *Houston* in the 1930s. *(Courtesy Cruiser* Houston *Memorial Exhibit, M. D. Anderson Library, University of Houston)*

The ship's band in action. (*Guthrie Layne album, Cruiser* Houston *Memorial Exhibit, M. D. Anderson Library, University of Houston*)

The crew's Gulbransen upright piano, a gift from the people of Houston, Texas. (*Courtesy Otto Schwarz*)

The USS *Houston* at Shanghai. (*Courtesy Cruiser* Houston *Memorial Exhibit, M. D. Anderson Library, University of Houston*)

Two of the USS *Houston*'s SOC scout planes. (*Courtesy Otto Schwarz*)

Recreation party going ashore at Tawi-Tawi in the Philippines en route to Darwin, Australia, late 1941. *(Guthrie Layne album, Cruiser Houston Memorial Exhibit, M. D. Anderson Library, University of Houston)*

Seaman Jack D. Smith (lower left), a powder handler in turret three, with some of his buddies on liberty in the Philippines. *(Courtesy Jack D. Smith)*

Seaman Otto Schwarz, taken in Manila just prior to the beginning of the war. *(Courtesy Otto Schwarz)*

Volume 3, No. 6   Pearl Harbor, T. H.   May 30, 1940

GOING ASIATIC! . . . CHINA BOUND!!

Masthead of the ship's newspaper, the *Blue Bonnet*. *(Courtesy Cruiser Houston Memorial Exhibit, M. D. Anderson Library, University of Houston)*

Captain Albert H. Rooks, U.S.N.A. 1914, on his first inspection party aboard the USS *Houston*, August 30, 1941. *(Courtesy Cruiser Houston Memorial Exhibit, M. D. Anderson Library, University of Houston)*

Captain Jesse B. Oldendorf (left), skipper of the USS *Houston* from October 1939 through August 1941, with Admiral Thomas C. Hart, Commander in Chief of the Asiatic Fleet. *(Courtesy Roy Coats)*

The USS *Houston* going through the Panama Canal. *(Official U. S. Navy photograph)*

The USS *Houston* showing turret three, which was later damaged by an errant Japanese bomb causing a heavy loss of life. *(Official U. S. Navy photograph)*

Arthur L. "Al" Maher, U.S.N.A. 1923, the "Gun Boss." Maher later commanded a minesweeper in Korea. *(Courtesy Arthur L. Maher)*

W. Jackson Galbraith, U.S.N.A. 1929, the air defense officer, taken after the war when he was serving as naval attache to the government of Norway. *(Courtesy W. Jackson Galbraith)*

7

Fire in Turret Three

Pers-8249-maj   15 November 1945
CONFIDENTIAL

From: Senior Survivor (Former Gunnery Officer) USS
Houston
To: Chief of Naval Operations
Subj: Action Report—USS *Houston* on 4 February
1942 against enemy aircraft.
The one direct hit caused the following damage:

1. Forty-eight men were killed and twenty
   wounded.
2. The powder charges in turret III were ignited by bomb fragments which pierced the
   side plating. The fire and the fragments
   which struck the roller path placed the turret out of commission.
3. A hole about twelve feet in diameter was
   blown in the main deck.
4. The crew's head was demolished.
5. Three searchlights were badly damaged.
6. The radio transmitter room was badly damaged.

7. The lockers in the D-202-L and the clothing in these were ruined.
8. Fragments entered the cold storage at frame 118, and the meat in the storage room spoiled.
9. Two motor launches on the main deck were demolished.

Forty-eight dead and twenty more wounded, maimed, and horribly burned by the raging fires, a casualty rate of almost seven percent, all caused by a single 500-pound bomb in a fraction of a second. In less time than it takes for a man to scream a warning, huge jagged pieces of shrapnel tore through the ¾-inch steel on the side of the turret as though it were paper. Once inside, the shrapnel ripped through bodies and ignited all the powder bags in the hoist. Most of the men in the turret and the handling room below were killed instantly.

Below the main deck, where a 12-foot hole now stood open to the sky, the after repair party had been waiting quietly before the fire and shrapnel burst overhead. The group of a dozen sailors was completely wiped out with the exception of two. Howard Brooks was one of them.

Inside the turret, Gunner's Mate First Class Roger P. Poirier had barely survived the fire and the ripping shrapnel. Badly burned and seriously wounded by the fragments, he tried to activate the turret's sprinkler system, but it had been damaged. He crawled out from the turret and despite his pain was able to keep several men from abandoning ship before he passed out.

Seaman Second Class Samuel J. Marsh escaped unharmed from the flaming shell deck, but he quickly noticed that no one else had followed him out. He hurried back to the inferno, grabbed a wounded seaman, and dragged the man clear of the flames. The man died four hours later.

Down in the powder magazine, Smith and Kunke were knocked flat by the explosion, which also cut the lights. Kunke switched on the emergency battle light while Smith kicked the flash door shut. Then, remembering what he had learned about the valves, Smith reached around and turned on the sprinkler system, flooding the hoist. Kunke flooded the magazine. "We didn't have any orders to do any of that," Jack Smith said, "but it seemed like the thing to do." Their quick action saved the ship by preventing the fires from spreading to the magazine.

Then they tried to save themselves. They undogged the hatch and came out below the main deck, only to confront the grisly remains of the after repair party. There was "a guy leaning over with his head gone. It was just blown right off," Smith said. "We started going into the debris trying to find someone who was alive. The people left were all dead. One guy was laying over on his side and he looked like he was in pretty good shape, but little red specks were all over his body. I went over and checked him but he was gone."

Moments earlier, Carpenter's Mate Chips Eddy and two others had been sitting nearby. The blast knocked Eddy unconscious, but he remembered that one of the other men had been hit pretty bad. The third man didn't even have a scratch.

Forward of that point, in the after five-inch magazine, Charley Pryor was getting back on his feet after the explosion. He had been talking to a chief just before the bomb hit. Now two corpsmen were carrying the man out. "His right leg was blown completely off. He told the corpsmen to leave him be, that he was going to die in a few minutes, and to go try to help some of the other people."

A few feet away, Howard Brooks came upon Boatswain Joseph B. Bienert "sitting there with his whole insides out and he said to take care of someone else. 'I'm too far gone,' he said."

Topside, the bomb claimed its victims just as quickly and randomly. Bill Weissinger was one of the lucky ones. "All of a sudden, there was just a big puff of white smoke and wood and splinters and everything flying by and the first thing I thought was, Boy, they just knocked the whole aft end off this ship, because you couldn't see anything at all. Just this white smoke with a sort of brown tinge in it just boiling."

John Bartz at his 1.1-inch gun was also fortunate, sustaining only a shrapnel wound in his leg. "I felt a burning sensation when it hit. I never thought much of it. A corpsman came along and took it out and bandaged me up. I was the only one in my gun crew hit, and we were all standing around close together."

Lloyd Willey thought it was all over for him. The bomb

passed through the edge of the radio shack and missed him by about four feet. "All this shrapnel blew everything out from underneath me and all the paint and stuff right off the stanchions around me. I looked down and I was covered with blood. I was shaking my head from the concussion and there was a great big dent in my steel hat. It turned out that all this blood on me was just paint chips. I wasn't hurt at all. I dug paint out of my knees and chest for weeks afterward. Things were spinning for a while though, and for a time I didn't know whether I was alive or dead. But then it cleared up and I went back to my battle station."

On the hangar deck, Pharmacist's Mate Griff Douglas had a close call. The concussion threw him flat on the deck. "The shrapnel ate the deck up right in front of me and hit right over my head and went into a box right next to my shoulder and didn't come through. I didn't get a scratch." But others around him were wounded. "There was a boy no farther than six feet away who got hit bad. I took my bandage scissors and finished cutting his leg off. It was blown off—just a piece of skin holding it on. I threw it over the side. He was laying there conscious and he was hit all over. I stopped the bleeding and put tourniquets on and gave him a shot of morphine. He said, 'Doc, that hurts!' Here he's got holes all over him and he's saying the needle hurts. He died."

Some men on the ship still did not know what had happened. Those down in the magazines and the shell decks far forward felt and heard nothing when the bomb exploded. Amidships, in the forward engine room, Fulton and his crew felt little more than a mild vibration. But then over the PA system they heard the terrible words: *"Fire in turret number three."*

They realized the danger instantly. The turret was loaded and ready to fire. Shells and powder bags were in the three eight-inch guns, and more were in the turret waiting to be loaded. If they exploded, the *Houston* would be lost. The aft end of the ship would disintegrate and she would go down in seconds. The fire had to be put out.

Commander Maher phoned the bridge to tell Captain Rooks that he would go aft and assess the situation. As gunnery officer, Maher was well aware of what a fire in a loaded turret could mean, and he was sure it was going to explode. He assumed that the after damage-repair party would be on the job trying to extinguish the blaze. He did not know that these men had been killed.

After the first moments of shock, men started running for the turret to help the wounded. They too expected the repair party to be on the job, dousing the flames. Not many men were available topside who could assist. Most of those on deck were gun crews, and they could not abandon their battle stations. But the aviation machinist's mates and ordnancemen, the pilots and radio operators, raced aft.

Windy Winslow and Joe Bush reached the port hangar and met the wounded who were streaming back from the turret area. "We took blankets, canvas, and anything else we could use to carry the wounded down to sick bay. Many men were badly burned. I reached in my first-aid kit for burn lotion to apply to a man whose skin was scorched to a dirty brown. His skin came off in my hands. He moaned in pain. I gave him a morphine shot and had him carried to sick bay. Some men had deep wounds in arms and legs. One lad told me he thought he had been hit in the back. There was a hole in his back as big as my fist. I told him he'd been hit, but I thought he'd be okay. He gave me a big smile of appreciation and died seconds later."

Jack Lamade helped carry Boatswain Bienert. He looked like he didn't have a chance. Bienert noticed Lamade's .45. "He was conscious," Lamade said, "and I gave him three shots of morphine, but it didn't affect him a bit." Bienert looked up at Lamade and pleaded with him. "Shoot me. Shoot me, please, please shoot me." He died within the hour.

Chaplain Rentz did what the corpsmen and the surgeons could not. He administered last rites to the dying and gave consolation and support to those who would live.

When Al Maher reached the burning turret three, he found to his dismay that nothing was being done about the fire. A few men stood around dazed, and Maher immediately got them organized. He spotted Winslow and shouted, "For chrissake, get hoses up here, Windy. If this fire hits the magazines, we'll be blown to hell."

"This man was absolutely fearless," Winslow said later about Maher. "He was standing beside a blazing gun turret, knowing full well the ship could blow sky high at any moment, and he was yelling orders as though it was some kind of fire drill."

Maher was awarded the Navy Cross for his actions that day. "By his inspiring valor, gallant leadership, and selfless devotion to duty at a time of grave peril, Captain Maher undoubtedly prevented *Houston* from being destroyed," read the citation. This was one of five decorations he would receive for his conduct aboard ship and later as a prisoner of war.

While Winslow was running forward to get fire hoses, Lieutenant Lamade and Aviation Machinist's Mate First Class John W. Ranger, from Gillespie, Illinois, leaped into action. Ranger had glanced upward and noticed that the American flag had been torn away from the mainmast. He raced aft, grabbed a flag from a motor launch (ordinarily used when the launch carried liberty parties ashore), and lashed it to the *Houston*'s stern stanchion, a symbol for friend and foe alike that the ship was still in the fight.

Ranger returned to turret three and entered it through the door, which had been open when the bomb hit. The compartment was strewn with bodies and the piles of shells were so hot that the grease was sizzling. Tongues of flame lapped at the shells, and others sprung out from the powder bags. Lamade passed him carbon dioxide bottles that were designed to suffocate fires. Ranger broke the bottles directly on the flames. He had no asbestos suit or any other protection against the fire and the intense heat. As soon as he broke the bottles, he stepped halfway out of the turret, gasping for air. Lamade was about to hand him more carbon dioxide containers when the fire hose was brought up.

"Get out of there," he yelled to Ranger.

"I'm all right," Ranger said.

He grasped the bulky nozzle and dragged the hose inside the turret. The grease on the shells was bubbling and hissing and the powder was aflame. In only a few seconds' time the fierce heat would penetrate the steel shells and set off the detonator caps. Every shell in the turret would explode, along with all those stored below.

The pump was activated and water gushed through the hose. Ranger sprayed it all around the turret. Lamade climbed in after him, helping him control the high-pressure stream of water. As the water hit an electrical short it set off one of the big eight-inch guns, and it fired with a deafening roar. The crew thought that the end had come, that the turret had blown, but it hadn't, and in a matter of minutes the fires were put out.

As Lamade and Ranger stepped back outside the turret, they spotted a grim sight, the remains of the turret officer, Lieutenant George Davis. When the bomb fell, Davis had been sitting in the doorway with his feet hanging over the sill, close to where the bomb exploded. "I'll never forget Lieutenant Davis," Lamade said. "There was practically nothing left of him, just his white canvas shoes pitted with holes."

Ensign Nelson had been luckier. He had been called out of turret three just moments before the disaster; no one can seem to recall why. The summons saved his life. "You talk about a young fellow who was greatly relieved!" Jack Smith remarked.

The fires were out, the wounded were being treated, the sky was free of enemy planes. Admiral Doorman faced a difficult decision—whether to continue with the mission. He decided to scrub it. With two cruisers badly damaged, no air cover, and the likelihood of further air attacks, this was probably the wisest course of action, though Admiral Hart later disagreed. The *Houston* and the *Marblehead* were ordered south to Tjilatjap, the port on the south coast of Java, where they would be beyond the reach of Japanese planes, or so all hands hoped. Captain Rooks offered to stand by the crippled *Marblehead*, but her skipper, Captain Arthur G. Robinson, said she could make it on her own.

Captain Rooks set course for the Bali Strait, and the *Houston* left the scene of her long-awaited contact with the enemy. Now the men were dealing with the consequences. They needed to remove the dead and to determine the extent of the damage beneath the turret.

Merritt Eddy had regained consciousness, and he realized that as a member of a damage-control party he would be needed. He made his way aft toward turret three. "There were people running around everywhere. [Warrant Officer Louis E.] Biechlen looked at me and said, 'Do you think you can handle that breathing apparatus? We don't know what's happened down below the turret.'"

"Yeah," Eddy said. "If I can find it."

Eddy went below deck to the repair locker and found the breathing apparatus and a bottle of oxygen. He yelled up through the 12-foot hole in the deck to tell Biechlen that he'd gotten what he needed. He strapped on the bottle, clamped the mask over his face, opened the hatch, and walked into the shell-handling room. It was waist-deep in water from the sprinkling system, but he saw no casualties.

He came out into the passageway where the after repair party had been sitting when the bomb hit. "I thought there was a couple of them alive," Eddy said. "They were bubbling from the nose, like they were breathing. Two guys were sitting right there by the door. I reached down to pick one of them up and grabbed a whole handful of flesh. It just came right off. I kind of got a little sick."

He wasn't the only one. Marine Sergeant Pryor saw men trying to remove a dead sailor from his seat inside the turret. "I know a couple of sailors went to move him, and when they took him, the flesh stuck to their hands, and it made them sick—just as sick as all get-out." A voice behind the men said quietly, "I'll do it." Commander David W. Roberts, the soft-spoken, scholarly exec, cradled the sailor in his arms and placed him gently on the deck.

Bill Weissinger went aft to see what he could do. The first thing he saw was the remains of a good buddy. "They had him covered with canvas and the guy carrying him out of the hatch said, 'We almost didn't get him up here 'cause his skin's coming loose. The guy's been parboiled.' When he said that, I just turned around. That did it for me."

Donald Brain came aft from the forward five-inch magazine. "Some of those boys were pretty bad, and some of them were . . . Really, it was just horrible, and the odor of the burnt flesh there! I got to the point where I couldn't go down below deck to sleep. You just had that pungent odor of burnt flesh, and it lasted for weeks."

Brain examined the turret and wondered "how we still had it. It looked just like a piece of wood that termites had got into. There was a series of little burned holes in there, like somebody had taken a cutting torch and burned holes all the way through this thing. It was really shocking to me."

Otto Schwarz climbed out from the forward powder magazine and went back to turret three out of curiosity. "We were hearing all kinds of stories. They sent us around some apples, and somebody said the blood from the men in the turret had been dripping down on them. I went back to see what it was all about, because up to that time we were just as cocky as could be. We had never seen anybody hurt.

"I just couldn't believe what I saw. The blood and the bodies! It was terrible—and that was just outside the turret. Then somebody grabbed me and said, 'Come here, we can use you.' They needed someone to get out a couple of bodies from the tiny room in the turret where the shells and powder come up from below. They're passed out through a little window and that little window is the only entrance or exit.

"They were looking for someone small enough to go in there and get out two bodies that were welded together by the heat. Other people have told me I was mistaken, because there wasn't room for two people in there. But I swear, my memory tells me that there were two people in there. They gave me a piece of rope and I crawled through and I'll never forget when I put the rope around them and they started pulling the bodies out. One of them was a fellow I used to go on liberty with.

"That's when I found out that it was not going to be fun and games, that war was not all glory, and that maybe we wouldn't finish the Japanese off in five weeks. I wasn't so cocky after that. I grew up immediately."

A lot of the men of the *Houston* shared his feelings, and they came to look upon the war more soberly. Jack Smith was one of them. "For hours and hours that day we were bailing out bloody water from down in the ship below the turret while they hoisted bodies through the hole made by the bomb. And there we were taking buckets of bloody water out, and the cook finally sent us around some food. And you know what they were? Bloody-looking corned beef sandwiches!"

Far forward of the damaged area, the sick bay was full. The medical corpsmen had run out of room for all the wounded. Some were bedded in the wardroom and in the captain's and the admiral's cabins. The two surgeons, Epstein and Burroughs, did their best to save lives, but some men slipped away that after-

noon and evening before the *Houston* reached port. More would
be likely to die if they didn't reach a hospital soon.

Down in the engine rooms, the black gang kept the engines
turning over at maximum revolutions, 420 rpms. Captain Rooks
wanted every bit of speed the *Houston* could make. When Jack
Lamade took over as OOD at four o'clock that afternoon, the captain told him, "Don't stop for anything, Jack. Just keep going."

The master-at-arms made the rounds of all the battle stations
asking if the men had any messages for the skipper. Many of the
men did have something they wished to say. They wanted the
new captain to know that they thought he had done a great job in
their first encounter with the enemy.

Bill Weissinger, up on the boat deck, watched the master-at-
arms climb the ladder, cross the navigation bridge, and approach
Captain Rooks. "We saw the master-at-arms go up and salute and
tell the skipper what the crew thought of what he had done. The
skipper stood there and looked at him for a moment, then turned
away and started looking aft. And when the master-at-arms came
back, he told us the captain never did say anything but that the
tears started coming down his cheeks and he just stood there at
the rail and cried. That made quite a hero out of him to us. We
knew then he was a great man. He was some kind of skipper, I'll
tell you that."

There was hardly a man aboard who did not agree. "After
our first meeting with the Japanese," Otto Schwarz said, "the legends started to go through the ship about this great skipper."
George Detre added, "After that first bombing, there was nothing
we wouldn't do for that man—and nothing he wouldn't do for
us."

Among the senior officers, along with gratitude and admiration for Captain Rooks's expertise in maneuvering the ship, came
feelings of dissatisfaction with the official Navy procedure he had
had to follow. Lieutenant Tommy Payne, the senior aviator who
had been circling in his SOC during the bombing raid, huddled
with his fellow pilot Jack Lamade and the assistant engineering
officer Bob Fulton in the wardroom that afternoon to try to develop a different approach.

They agreed that quick changes in speed were not the best
way to fool a bombardier. In addition, these actions were hard on

the engines. "The only way to do it," Payne explained, "is to go full speed, as fast as you can go, and to detect the point at which the bomb is going to drop, which can be done with a sextant."

The men set to work compiling mathematical tables for various combinations of altitude and speed. From this information, the angle at the instant of bomb release could be determined. An officer on the bridge could read the position angles of the attacking planes with a sextant. When the planes reached a point five to ten degrees before the dropping point for that particular combination of altitude and speed, the ship should be ordered to turn.

They discussed the problem in detail, drew a diagram of how the system would work, and brought it to Commander Maher. He approved and sent it to Captain Rooks. The skipper liked the plan and agreed to implement it the next time they were under air attack, though everyone hoped they would not have to use it that day.

Fortunately, they were running into heavy weather. Quite a few rainstorms dotted their course, protecting them from enemy aircraft and greatly increasing their chances of making port.

As the sun set on Admiral Hart's headquarters at Lembang, he recorded his thoughts in his diary. "Was a bad day—the result seems to be that there are no cruisers left in the Asiatic Fleet that are capable of service. In fact, there is worry lest [*Houston* and *Marblehead*] not even *reach* port."

On his desk was the radiogram he had received from the *Houston* at five that afternoon: "Direct hit close to turret three. Turret is on fire. Numerous casualties." It was an indication of how poor communications were with his task force that he had received the message so late in the day. It had been sent many hours before.

Hart was disturbed not only by the crippling of his most powerful ships, but also by the failure of the strike force to engage the enemy. For a time that day, he had considered relieving Admiral Doorman of his command, believing that he was being too cautious. Finally he decided against it but ordered Doorman to meet with him in Tjilatjap on February 8, to discuss future strategy.

If February fourth seemed like a bad day to Hart, the fifth

would be catastrophic, for it would mark the end of his active naval career. The combined pressures from the British and Dutch to relieve him of his command had been successful. A telegram was on its way from Admiral Ernest King in Washington advising Hart that "an awkward situation has arisen." It would be best, King wrote, if Hart would request to be relieved for reasons of ill health. Admiral Helfrich would be named to replace him.

Hart had once said that he would like to end up catching "a fourteen-inch shell in the midsection" while on the bridge of a ship. Now he was being sent home under a shadow, relieved of command of a fleet that had been insured of failure from the beginning. He knew he would be blamed for that, but he was sure in his own mind that he had done his best. "It's all on the laps of the gods," he wrote in his diary, "and, whatever happens, I don't now see any forks over the long road back where I feel that I took the wrong turn."

Hart would be given 10 days to formalize the transfer of command and to conclude his own affairs. On February 15, he would depart, forced to leave the men and the ships of his fleet to almost certain defeat.

A somber event took place on the *Houston* that evening. Forty-eight bodies were laid out on the fantail, not far from the wreckage of turret three, where most of them had died. The sailors had not been issued identification tags, the dogtags that became commonplace later in the war. That, coupled with the deplorable condition of the bodies, made identification of the remains difficult. But it had to be done.

Because most of the dead were from the turret crew, Ensign Nelson, who had escaped death there by moments, was called upon to do the grim job. Slowly he made his way among the rows, trying to recognize the features, to match a corpse with a name. Tears streaked his face as he recorded their names. When he was finished, the bodies were covered with canvas to await burial at Tjilatjap.

John Bartz stood watch by turret three that night. "They had all the dead laying out there and they were under tarps. It was scary because rigor mortis was setting in and an arm or a leg would suddenly pop up. When midnight came and that guy came to relieve me, I was sure ready to get out of there."

To Jim Gee, it was sobering to see his buddies laid out on the deck. "This brings a lot of reality to you real fast." There was no escaping the presence of death. As Bill Weissinger recalled, "that odor that kept drifting forward . . . once in a while a breeze would come up and there would be a cloud of this odor coming over the boat deck. We were all topside because it was too hot to sleep below and this odor would come over and you couldn't help but think, There lay our shipmates. I had a lot of good friends back there."

The *Houston* arrived at Tjilatjap, an uninviting native village, late on the morning of February 5. At the best of times, maneuvering was difficult because the harbor had dangerous shoals and narrows. Today it was crowded with Allied ships, including some of the Asiatic Fleet's auxiliary vessels that Admiral Hart had ordered up from Darwin. The tiny port was also jammed with refugees who were abandoning cars, furniture, and clothing as they tried desperately to board any ship going south, to escape the menace of the Japanese.

As soon as the *Houston* tied up at the dock, Q. C. Madson rounded up a working party to go ashore and scour the town for wood. Sixty-one coffins needed to be built—48 for the *Houston* dead and 13 more for the *Marblehead*. The only lumber available was "that darned rough mahogany and it was harder than hell," Merritt Eddy said. "We worked all that day and most of the night, the whole carpenter gang."

"We built coffins for them," George Detre recalled. "I say 'we' because it was an all-hands evolution, and everybody was friends and they were friends going. One of the saddest things I remember was the carpenter. He was making coffins. He had a very good friend who was a commissary chief. He was watching these coffins go by his shop, and he was building them as fast as he could, pounding nails. He looks at one and says, 'Who's that?' And they said, 'This is old Cookie.' He took his hammer and belted the coffin shut and said, 'So long, Cookie,' and went right on with his work."

In the morning, a group of Dutch army trucks lined up be-

side the ship to transport the dead to the cemetery. The men of
the *Houston* donned their dress whites. The 48 coffins were
stacked in the starboard hangar. The entire crew stood at attention as one by one the coffins were carried off the ship. Lieutenant Lamade was the officer of the deck. "I was standing right
there when they lifted those coffins off. You could see the blood
running out of them."

The bandmaster, George L. "Bandy" Galyean, led his musi-
cians in Chopin's funeral dirge. As the last coffin left the ship the
marine bugler sounded the mournful notes of "Taps." The crew
saluted. "It is hard," wrote Q. C. Madson in his diary, "to describe the emotions which ran through us, and what we were
thinking of the Japs is not to be put on paper."

There were guns to be manned, supplies to be loaded, and
repairs to be done, but all the crew who could be spared marched
behind the trucks to the cemetery. The band continued to play
the funeral music and the men walked in a slow, measured cadence through the tropical heat and dust, past the little town, to
the burial ground overlooking the Indian Ocean. They marched
in a column of twos in reverse order of rank, in accordance with
Navy protocol. Behind engineer Fulton at the end of the column
came Captain Rooks. "It's striking, isn't it?" Rooks said. "These
boys are being buried in a town they'd never even heard the
name of before."

Immediately following the last truck in the convoy came the
honor guard in full dress uniforms, carrying their rifles. "God
almighty!" Jack Smith said. "It's a heck of a cadence and all those
bodies right in front of us stinking in the tropical sun. It was a
long way that we marched behind this truck. The cemetery was
down at the beach and the graves were very shallow, only about
four or five feet deep. The tide was coming in and the bottom of
the graves was full. We're standing out there at attention and we
present arms every time a casket comes by and the guys are passing out from the heat. I know I had two rifles leaning on me.

"I could have shot [the officer in charge of the funeral detail].
He's got his saber and all, and says, 'Boy, this is really going over
good.' I'm standing there smelling these bodies and he's putting
on a show! I thought we were out there honoring the dead."

Chaplain Rentz led a brief service, and the honor guard fired three volleys over the graves. The haunting notes of "Taps" were heard once more, and it was over. The men returned to the *Houston*, leaving behind at the gravesite two Dutch women. No one knew who they were. No one had invited them. They wept throughout the ceremonies and when last seen by the sailors were still weeping, all alone. "In their grief," thought Lieutenant Lamade, "was the grief of America's faraway womanhood."

At three in the afternoon the *Marblehead* arrived at Tjilatjap. She had sustained so much damage that those who watched her being towed in wondered how she had remained afloat. Tradition dictated that the men of the *Houston* come to attention and salute. Instead, they broke into wild cheering.

A Dutch hospital train backed slowly down the dock and stopped beside the two ships, now one behind the other. Waiting to receive the 50 wounded from the *Marblehead* and the 20 from the *Houston* was Corydon McAlmont Wassell, Lieutenant Commander, U.S. Navy Medical Corps Reserve. Wassell was a middle-aged, chain-smoking doctor from Arkansas who had spent most of his adult life as a medical missionary in China, until the war caught up with him. He was worn out and in poor health. Some called him "Shaky Jake" because of the recurring tremors he experienced from various tropical illnesses. Commander Wassell would soon receive the Navy Cross and become famous throughout the United States. The 1944 Hollywood motion picture *The Story of Dr. Wassell* would depict his heroic exploits in evacuating most of the *Houston* and *Marblehead* wounded from Java before the island was occupied by the Japanese. He would be played by Gary Cooper.

From the dock at Tjilatjap, Wassell supervised the transfer of the wounded to the train that took them to the Petronella Hospital in Djocja. There, a Dutch woman, Mrs. C. E. Reddingius-Soeters, whose husband was a local pastor, visited them.

"I shall never forget what I felt when I entered the room where they were laying on their beds, suffering enormously, burned all over the place, but still so brave in the way of suffering. I went from one bed to the other and talked to them. The only thing I could do was bring them ice cream and iced fruit. My husband put an article in the newspaper and so we gathered some money to give them their ice cream and their cigarettes [Lucky Strikes]."

Mrs. Reddingius-Soeters was later interned by the Japanese and, after the war, in 1946, wrote to the U.S. Navy Department to find out what had become of the men. "I can tell you better than any other person that they were heroes in the way of bearing their pain. God bless them for all they have suffered. For the relatives of the boys who died in Djocja, I can tell you that up till December 1945 flowers were brought by girls and ladies of our church to their graves. I went there myself and I was pleased to see the graves were well looked after. We have not forgotten them."

While the train bearing the wounded was pulling away from the dock, two men who were sitting together were silent. Captain Rooks of the *Houston* and Captain Robinson of the *Marblehead* were thinking of their men, "who were, through iron necessity, being abandoned in their hour of need."

The men of the *Houston* had considerable work to do to prepare the ship for sea duty again. Normal refueling and provisioning were always time-consuming, but now the *Houston* was taking on a different cargo. Before the *Boise* departed Tjilatjap for repairs after ripping her bottom on the coral reef, several hundred rounds of her five-inch ammunition were transferred to the *Houston* in exchange for the obsolete, corroded, and defective shells with which the *Houston* was fighting the war. As the only U.S. Navy ship in the area equipped with five-inch guns, the *Houston* got the ammo, and it was a welcome addition indeed. The next time the gun crews met enemy airplanes, they'd have a better chance of inflicting some damage.

Sky forward, the antiaircraft director that had become stuck in the bombing, was being repaired. The weatherstripping that was designed to protect the path on which the director turned had been bent by the concussions from the bombs. When the weatherstripping was removed, the director once again trained freely. To make sure the same problem would not occur with the after director, its weatherstripping was also taken off.

The biggest repair job involved turret three and the 12-foot hole in the deck just forward of it. The eight-inch guns could not be fired, nor could the turret train, without undergoing extensive work, repairs that could only be done in a well-equipped naval shipyard. What they could do at Tjilatjap was to make the turret look like it was operational. The force of the explosion had lifted the turret off the big ring of gears on which it turned. Slowly workmen were able to jack the turret around until its guns faced aft. Then they welded sections of railroad track to the deck, securing the turret in place.

Four-by-eight sheets of steel were affixed over the hole in the deck. To work through the night undetected by enemy planes, the crew built a canvas hood over the opening. Now they could use their lights. The only plating they were able to find was not very substantial, but at least it would keep out the water in rough seas. Below decks, the weakened area around the hole was shored up. From a distance, the ship would appear to be undamaged.

Captain Rooks was constantly concerned that the *Houston* would be caught in port by Japanese bombers. The harbor was so small and crowded that there would be no time to get up steam and get under way once planes were spotted. Further, he had no room to maneuver to avoid falling bombs. So far, Tjilatjap had not sustained any air raids, but Surabaja was now being hit regularly every morning at 11:00, and it was only 300 miles away.

One of the officers suggested that in the event of an air raid in port, all personnel not essential for defense, such as the engineering gang and the eight-inch turret crews, be allowed to go ashore. This might prevent unnecessary casualties. When the men were informed of the decision and told it would be voluntary, all hands agreed to stay on board. They knew they could always help out repairing damage, hauling ammunition, or tending to the wounded. The men of the *Houston* would stay with their ship.

Liberty was a different matter, even in a place like Tjilatjap. "They had a blackout," Seaman Weissinger said, "so you couldn't see much of the town. There was a little square in the center and all the bars and gin mills and such had candles and small lanterns in them. We made a couple of bars and they were jammed full, so we said, 'Hell, if we can't get something to drink, we'll just go back to the ship.' So we started back and were walking down this road and someone called out, 'Are you American sailor?'

"It was a Javanese, and we walked across a deep ditch on a log to get to his house. He invited us over and asked if we had had supper. We said no, so he invited us in for a meal. We'd been warned not to eat native food or drink water that hadn't been boiled but we thought, 'What the hell, we're gonna get a decent meal somewhere. We didn't recognize anything they had on the table.

"There were three teenage girls there and they got the biggest kick out of us. They'd pass us something and we'd look at it and say, 'What the hell is this? Do you really eat this stuff?' We had one heck of a good time. We were there a good hour and when we got ready to leave the father asked us if we would like the girls. Sure, who wouldn't? So he gave us the pleasure of his daughters." It was the kind of liberty sailors dream about.

Lloyd Willey had a different experience trying to find something to eat. He and another Marine Corps private, Jack Winters, went to a little restaurant. "We didn't know how to order anything, so we drew a picture of a chicken. And that's all we got—a chicken. They had taken the insides out and deep-fried it. Just a chicken on a plate. So then we drew a picture of a loaf of bread, and Jack wanted a bottle of beer, so he drew a bottle. They brought us a bottle of French champagne. It was only about fifty cents a bottle. Jack had never had any champagne and he said, 'Oh, boy, this is going to be great,' but he was so disappointed in the taste. We managed to tear the chicken apart in our hands. They didn't even bring us any knives or forks."

Jim Gee's liberty was also memorable, though today he thinks that Tjilatjap is a place he would like to forget. The 22-year-old Gee was not a drinking man, but he had promised his Marine Corps buddies that whenever they made liberty in Singapore, he would get drunk with them. Young H. R. Cray had made a similar promise. It looked as though the *Houston* would never get to Singapore, and after the close call they had just had, who knew how many chances there would be to fulfill the promise?

"After that bomb hit, I just told them the next port we go into, I'll just go ahead and get drunk with you. There were maybe fifty of us, all marines, who went ashore. We went into this bar and they pulled up all the tables and made a big T, and sat Cray on one end and me on the other. Each man would order a drink and we had to drink it. They had everything you could think of to drink—some I wish I'd never heard of.

"We just went along with it like we were having fun. I got to the point where I couldn't speak. I certainly couldn't move a muscle. They had to manhandle me to get me back to the ship, and there they fed me some hot pepper and some chocolate. Then we went up to the quarterdeck and they sneaked me by the officer of the deck and went up on the forecastle. I slept there, with a bunch of marines just ringing me so I wouldn't walk off the side.

"The next morning, they woke me up about eleven and I thought, My God, they'll throw me in the brig for this. They were all just standing around and somebody'd come by and check on me from time to time. They were all laughing, and not the captain or anybody ever said a word to me about the condition I was in. Everybody was kidding me about what a good time I had."

Jack Smith and his buddies also found something to drink on their liberty and they returned to the ship carrying souvenirs. "I had two bottles of South African brandy tied in my socks. And we were all loaded when we came aboard, and there was Lord Nelson as the officer of the deck, an officer who always went by the book. But you know, he didn't say anything that night. I know damn well he knew we had that booze with us, but he let us pass."

Admiral Hart arrived in Tjilatjap on February 7 to meet with Admiral Doorman and to inspect the damaged cruisers of his Asiatic Fleet. He was still troubled by Doorman's decision to abort the attack after the air raid. Admiral Helfrich agreed with Hart. "I am afraid," Helfrich wrote to Hart, "that the first air attack [Doorman] got during the *first* operation of the combined fleet has upset him a little, and I hope that he will recover soon, especially after you meeting him at Tjilatjap."

No record remains of Hart's conversation with Doorman, but Hart later recorded his own thoughts in his diary. "[Doorman] was found to be rather overapprehensive of enemy bombing attacks. [At this point in Hart's written narrative, someone has added the word "scared" in the margin.] Admiral Doorman was naturally a very cautious sea commander and not inclined to take commensurate risk."

They talked about the growing Japanese menace and what steps, if any, could be taken to slow their advance in the Pacific. No formal plan emerged. Doorman knew that Hart was a lame duck commander. It would be Helfrich's job to formulate strategy and Doorman's to carry it out. The only important role left for Admiral Hart was to decide the fate of his cruisers. Should he send them to safety and for their much-needed repairs and overhaul, or keep them in the war?

Hart also had to weigh the political considerations. How would it appear to the Dutch allies and to the rest of the world if the United States withdrew the major elements of the Asiatic Fleet? The U.S. Navy was already drawing criticism at home for the debacle at Pearl Harbor and for leaving the Philippines. Even Tokyo Rose was asking on the radio, "Where, oh where, is the United States Navy?" The only naval force near the fighting was the small Asiatic Fleet.

As he began his inspection tour, Hart had little doubt about the *Marblehead*. Her damage was so extensive that she was clearly in no condition to continue the fight. It was doubtful then that she could be patched up sufficiently to make it back to the United States. Temporary repairs effected at Tjilatjap did put her in seaworthy condition, just barely, and she embarked on the 9,000-mile voyage home, arriving at the Brooklyn Navy Yard 48 days later; for half the trip she had been without a rudder.

The decision to send the *Marblehead* home left Hart with one capital ship in the war, a ship that had lost one-third of her firepower. Most of the men of the *Houston* believed they would be getting out of the war for a while. "The biggest rumor at that time," Jim Gee said, "was that we were going to go back to the States. I mean, we were crippled. How can a crippled man fight? At least we thought we'd go to Australia and repair the ship and get more ammunition. We thought we would get out for a while and come back with reinforcements." Commander Maher thought they would be ordered to Pearl Harbor for repairs.

Hart and his staff were piped aboard the *Houston* with all due honors and ceremony. Bob Fulton remembers that the admiral moved rapidly about the ship to inspect the repairs, walking so fast that others had to run to keep up with him. This was certainly not the pace of a man returning home for reasons of poor health.

This was the first the men knew that Tough Tommy Hart was being relieved. "He told us he was leaving," Lieutenant Payne said, "and he told me good-bye and thanked us for all we had done. He was obviously very upset emotionally about having to leave and not being able to take us with him. He said, 'You're under a new command now,' and he hoped we would give them the same devotion we'd given him.

"There was a general feeling that we were losing an awfully good director, and we had no idea of what the new situation was going to be like. We did know that there was a difficulty as far as language and operational experience together. We knew that was going to be a problem."

"There was some reaction against the Dutch command," Commander Maher added. "We didn't figure the Dutch were qualified to take over command at sea."

Hart inspected the ruined turret three and talked alone with Captain Rooks on the quarterdeck. The two men walked down the gangway to the dock. Otto Schwarz was standing the gangway watch. He recalls that Hart and Rooks stood on the dock for a long time, talking and looking back at the ship. Schwarz wondered about the conversation. "It was quite evident from the events that followed that some kind of a decision had been made at that time."

Many years after the war, Schwarz wrote to Admiral Hart about his visit to the *Houston* that day. Schwarz had founded an association of *Houston* survivors, and he published Hart's reply in his newsletter, the *Blue Bonnet*, named for the *Houston*'s shipboard newspaper.

"Captain Rooks and I were on the wharf," Hart wrote. "He was just back from burying the men who had been killed by that bomb. I had to make up my mind on the *Houston*'s future. I said that I was thinking over whether or not I should send her out of the war zone because of what that bomb hit had done. Rooks thought for some time and said, '*Marblehead* has to go out and the [*Boise*] has already gone with a torn-out bottom. We are the only one left. *Houston* has one good strike on her [indicating the after turret], but she has two good strikes left there [indicating the forward ones], and we can shoot all the ammunition that is left from there. We don't think we should go out.'

"Of course I was the one who had to decide it. But it would have been very hard to send you home when the ship's people felt that way."

"There it was," Schwarz said. "Our future had been decided on that dock in Java."

In 1946, Admiral Hart wrote his official "Narrative of Events, Asiatic Fleet," recording a similar version of the meeting with Rooks. "I was thinking of sending her out of ABDA but decided that it would be wrong, with which [Rooks] agreed. After telling me he would take his ship out again in a few hours, Rooks pointed to the wreck of his after turret and said, 'A Jap cruiser will have one strike on us, but with the two remaining we will try to break up his game.' Such was the spirit."

When interviewed by the Oral History Research Office of Columbia University in 1962, Hart offered a personal insight about his decision. "I had to make a decision which I now wish that I had reversed. It was largely her captain's decision."

Captain Rooks came back aboard the *Houston* after Admiral Hart departed, and informed his senior officers of the decision. He told Commander Maher that they were not going to get repaired.

"We're a two-turret ship now," he said, "and we'll have to stay and do the best we can."

8

We're Going to Hell

On the morning of February 8, the *Houston* departed Tjilatjap, setting course for Darwin. Another convoy was assembling, waiting for the *Houston* to escort it northward so its troops could try to reinforce the crumbling defenses of the Southwest Pacific. The *Houston* was the only ship powerful enough to provide protection for the group. The journey to that isolated outpost on the northern tip of Australia took three days, and the *Houston* arrived at 11:00 on the night of February 11. She refueled immediately and tied up at the dock near four merchant ships. These vessels were in the process of embarking two U.S. National Guard outfits, the 147th and the 148th Field Artillery, plus a large number of Australian troops. Their destination was the island of Timor at the eastern end of the Dutch East Indies.

The *Houston* sailors felt an instant comradeship with these soldiers. The crew tossed cigarettes, candy, and other items from the PX over the rail to the soldiers and kidded them about the dangers they would be facing.

At sundown on the following day the convoy set sail. Along with the *Houston* and the troop transports were the old four-stack American destroyer USS *Peary* and two small Australian corvettes, HMAS *Swan* and HMAS *Warrego*. The convoy's top speed was only nine knots, the best the transports could do. Within an hour after they left port, the men were startled to hear Tokyo

121

Rose on the radio describe each ship in the convoy and give their heading! It was unnerving. Obviously the mission had not been kept secret. And if the Japanese already knew where they were, it was only a matter of time before they would attack.

The crewmen believed, however, that they were safe for a while because Japanese airplanes had never been seen so far to the south before. But at 8:00 the next morning, when they were 150 miles out of Darwin, spotters sighted a Japanese four-engine flying boat. It circled slowly, careful to stay beyond range of the *Houston*'s five-inch guns. Nevertheless, Captain Rooks radioed Darwin for air support. The troop transports were vulnerable, and if the enemy arrived in force, the *Houston* would have a difficult time protecting them all.

For two hours the flying boat shadowed the convoy as it moved slowly to the north, ever closer to Japanese-occupied territory. Finally, the air support Captain Rooks had requested arrived—a single P-40, all the Allied forces could provide for a convoy of several thousand men. It was the first American aircraft the *Houston* crew had seen since December, except for their own SOCs.

The P-40 was at least a fighter plane, capable of shooting down the enemy aircraft, but first the pilot had to find it. The cumulus cloud cover was increasing, and the P-40 pilot was unable to catch a glimpse of the Japanese flying boat. Rooks ordered the five-inch guns to fire a few rounds in the direction of the enemy, but the American pilot appeared to pay no attention. Air-sea communications at the time were primitive at best; the pilot and the *Houston* were using different radio frequencies.

Ensign C. D. Smith watched the U.S. fighter plane flit back and forth through the clouds. "The flying boat would disappear into a cloud going north, and the P-40 would be ducking into the clouds going south. This cat-and-mouse chase lasted for about fifteen to twenty minutes."

When the P-40 disappeared from view, the Japanese plane banked and made an approach to the *Houston*. The five-inch guns swung into action and the plane quickly veered away. Several minutes later the flying boat made a pass over the ship at 10,000 feet. The gunners, using the new ammunition taken from the *Boise*, pinpointed the plane, and the accuracy of their fire forced it to a higher altitude. It changed course so abruptly that when the pilot released the bomb, it fell at least 1,000 yards away from the *Houston.*

The enemy plane flew off to the north, into the cloud bank, and in a few moments the P-40 reappeared, apparently tracking it. Five minutes later the *Houston's* gunners saw a huge explosion on the horizon.

Neither plane ever returned to its base. On a subsequent trip to Darwin, the *Houston* crew members were questioned about the missing American fighter plane. Months later, in a Japanese prisoner-of-war camp, they were questioned by the Japanese about the missing flying boat.

The morning of February 16 brought perfect weather conditions for an air attack. The ceiling was unlimited, with extremely high and light cirrus clouds. The sea was calm and the wind zero. All of the *Houston's* antiaircraft guns were manned, and the spotters had been instructed to be especially alert. The *Peary* and the Australian corvettes led the convoy, acting as an anti-submarine screen. The *Houston* was next in line, followed by the column of transports. Not only were they vulnerable to air attack today, being nearer to Japanese territory, but they were also at the risk of submarine attack. None of the ships was equipped with sonar, the underwater listening device. The *Peary* and the corvettes had a few depth charges on board, but the *Houston* was not rigged to carry any. Traveling at nine knots, they certainly could not count on speed to offer them any advantage.

By 11:30 the waiting was over. The spotters reported a force of 45 aircraft off the starboard beam at 11,000 feet. The *Houston's* klaxons and the air-defense bugle call sent the men racing to battle stations. The planes were quickly identified as twin-engine Mitsubishi-97s, flying in four V formations of nine each. Behind them, in two groups, were nine four-engine flying boats, of the type that had harassed the *Houston* the day before.

Lieutenant Jack Lamade pulled on his flying suit and raced for his plane. Tommy Payne, the senior aviator, who had been the only one launched during the last air raid, had promised Lamade that the next turn would be his. But now the mission of the SOCs would be different. Captain Rooks had decided that if a plane were successfully launched, it was not to circle overhead but was to make for Broome, Australia, instead. There the pilot would await orders about when and where to rendezvous with the ship.

Lamade did not know the exact location of Broome so he grabbed the *National Geographic* map of the Southwest Pacific that was tacked to the bulkhead in the wardroom. To reduce the plane's weight, he and his radioman, Robert Lee Tubbs, jettisoned everything that wasn't absolutely necessary. When they were ready, Lieutenant Payne came over to say good-bye.

"Tommy came up to me," Lamade recalled, "and he said, 'Well, Jack, I don't know where you can land, but I hope we can meet some time again. Good luck to you.' There were tears in my eyes when I shook hands with him," Lamade added. "I told him we'd be together again someplace and be able to go out and scrag those Japs with some decent equipment."

Lamade gave the thumbs-up signal to the catapult officer, and the little plane shot forward. As it gained altitude, Lamade banked and turned south, looking back at his ship and the approaching enemy aircraft. It was the last time he ever saw the *Houston*.

Lieutenant Winslow and radioman Bush waited in the cockpit of the second SOC, ready to be launched, but the Japanese planes were already too close. The *Houston*'s five-inch guns opened fire and again the shock waves ripped the fabric from the plane. They clambered out and the SOC was lowered into the hangar. They had already lost one plane that way and Payne wanted to try to salvage this one.

The engineering gang had the *Houston* up to full speed and Captain Rooks was circling the convoy, hoping to draw enemy fire away from the troop transports. His strategy worked. For nearly an hour, the *Houston* was the sole target of the air raid. The Japanese planes made bombing runs overhead every four to five minutes. With the new ammunition, however, the *Houston*'s AA fire was much more effective. The planes were forced to change course and altitude so frequently to evade the exploding shells that sometimes they turned away without dropping their bombs.

The captain maneuvered the ship all around the convoy, anticipating that the Japanese might alter their plans and go for the transports. The five-inch guns were firing continuously and even the 1.1s got off some rounds. The *Peary* had nothing larger than .30-caliber machine guns and so could offer no assistance. Nor could the Australian corvettes. Everyone's fate depended on the *Houston*.

Again and again the Japanese bombers concentrated their attack on the cruiser. At one point they tried a well-coordinated run from three different directions. Nine bombers approached off the starboard bow, nine more from port, and nine astern. All dropped their bombs at the same time and it looked as though there was no chance for the *Houston* to evade a direct hit. Gunnery officer Al Maher reported that 27 bombs fell within an interval of no more than 15 seconds, but none of them struck the ship.

Captain Rooks issued rapid-fire orders from the bridge, weaving the ship around and through the convoy. "The skipper [nearly] turned the *Houston* over protecting those ships," Griff Douglas said. "In fact, he dipped the quarterdeck at one point; the water came up to my knees." Lloyd Willey guessed that Captain Rooks must have thought he was back on destroyers!

Charley Pryor, on gun number eight, said that the bombs dropped so close that "the shrapnel just pecked all along our splinter shields all around us. And when that last group dropped its bombs, the skipper gave the change. He ordered the port engines reversed and a hard right rudder and the water just washed right across the fantail. The deck was awash. Those guys up in the foremast, all they could see under them was green sea—no ship, just green sea.

"I know that there were old chiefs who came out of those boiler rooms and engine rooms down there who'd been in the Navy twenty-four years or so and had never seen anything like that. One of our marines [Pfc Howard C. Corsberg] was the orderly on the bridge that day and he heard Captain Rooks say, 'Well, I didn't know whether she'd do it or not, but that was the time to find out. They would have destroyed us otherwise, and we just had to know. But now we know what she'll do.'"

After the three-pronged raid on the *Houston* failed, the next wave of planes, five flying boats, made a run on the transports. Rooks deftly edged the *Houston* in among the helpless ships and the five-inch guns opened up at their maximum rate of fire. To a seaman on one of the transports, the *Houston* "looked just like a wall of flame when it went along the line of ships, from the flashes of the guns firing." The captain of the transport *Meigs* watched from his bridge in amazement. He kept repeating, "Look at that bastard go," as the *Houston* flashed by with all guns firing.

Aboard the *Houston*, Q. C. Madson said that the ship was "twisting in and out of that convoy like a mother hen protecting her chicks."

Down in the magazines for the five-inch guns, 120 men worked furiously in their hot cramped quarters, sending up shells as fast as the guns could fire them. Many of the men would require treatment for heat exhaustion before the battle was over. On the guns themselves, the first loaders were under such a strain that only one was able to continue loading throughout the entire attack. The others had to be relieved by members of the off-watch crews.

When the smoke cleared and the roar of the guns faded, when the skies were once again free of enemy planes, the men assessed their situation. It was found that the convoy had sustained only one casualty, a merchant seaman on the *Mauna Loa* who had been hit by shrapnel from a near miss. Pharmacist's Mate Griff Douglas went by whaleboat to the transport to bring the wounded man back to the *Houston*. "He had a hole as big as your fist in the small of his back. He died right on our operating table."

As the *Houston* passed down the line of merchant ships after the attack, the troops and merchant seamen lined the rails of all four vessels to cheer as she went by. To Al Maher, they looked and sounded like "a crowd at a football game."

"They cheered at the top of their voices," Otto Schwarz said. "I shall never forget that. It was one of the most exciting moments of my life, to have those people so thankful for actually having saved them."

On the bridge, Captain Rooks was pleased to receive a message from the commander of the troop convoy.

FROM: USAT *Meigs*
TO: USS *Houston*
EXCEEDINGLY WELL DONE

The convoy re-formed and resumed its course for the island of Timor. The men of the *Houston* remained at battle stations.

Each mile brought them closer to Japanese air bases and they would not have been surprised if the enemy had launched another raid sometime during the long afternoon. That same thought concerned Admiral Helfrich in Java, who was now in command of ABDAFLOAT. His intelligence reports indicated that an enemy carrier force was approaching Timor from the north. Early that afternoon he radioed the *Houston*, ordering the convoy to reverse course and return to Darwin. He no longer wanted to risk the ships and troops by attempting to reinforce Timor.

On the return voyage, Captain Rooks once again radioed Darwin, asking for air support. It arrived a few hours later and consisted of a twin-engine Hudson bomber, a type used as a trainer back in the States.

Lamade and Tubbs reached Broome after a six-and-a-half-hour flight. "I landed with a spoonful of gas left," Lamade said, and Broome was "an even worse place than Darwin." He telegraphed his location to the base at Darwin and settled down in Broome's lone pub to await orders to rejoin the ship.

The previous day, February 15, soon came to be known as Black Sunday to all the men of the Asiatic Fleet. Singapore, thought to be the invincible bastion of the Far East, had fallen to the Japanese. If Singapore, with its thousands of troops and massive fortifications, could not hold, what could? Certainly not the Dutch East Indies with only a fraction of the troops and almost no heavy fortifications. Now the entire Japanese armed force that had been committed to the capture of Singapore was free to roam farther south. The Dutch islands would be their next stop.

Jack Lamade heard the news about Singapore over the radio in the pub. With him was a "typical Englishman, a tall lanky fellow with khaki shorts and pith helmet. He was stunned. He walked up and down saying over and over again, 'It can't happen. It can't happen. England rules the waves.'"

Another piece of sad news that Sunday was the departure of Admiral Hart. Late that morning the admiral was riding in a battered sedan to the port at Batavia, accompanied only by the driver, a young lieutenant. From a makeshift mounting on the car's fender fluttered a small four-star flag. The driver stopped the car, opened the door, and surreptitiously slipped the pennant into Hart's raincoat pocket. Then he drove away, leaving Hart alone on the dock.

A short time later, D. A. Harris, skipper of the old destroyer USS *Bulmer*, arrived at the dock. "I noted, as the only other individual in sight, an elderly man in civilian clothes. He was tall, thin, erect, white-headed, and resembled Admiral Hart. But it could not be. You do not dump a four-star admiral, particularly one who within the past few days had been commander of ABDAFLOAT, on the dock in a strange country where little English is spoken and leave him to fend for himself like the newest recruit. A closer look proved that it was Admiral Hart, now reduced to the status of a seaman second—waiting on the dock."

Harris loaned the admiral his gig, which took him out to the HMS *Durban*, a damaged British cruiser that was on the way to Ceylon. Her captain had agreed to take Hart along as a passenger.

The evening before, Hart's staff officers had hosted a farewell dinner at the Savoy Hotel in Bandung, Java. When it came time for the admiral to bid his 16 officers good-bye, he stood awkwardly at the dining-room door, shaking hands formally. It was a difficult moment for them all.

The first few officers shook Hart's hand in silence, unable to speak, but then Lieutenant Commander Redfield Mason approached, took the old man's hand in both of his, and said, "Good-bye, sir. You are the finest man I've ever known."

Admiral Hart was overcome with emotion. Tears filled his eyes and he could not say a word to the rest of the men who filed past. That night in his room—the management had lodged him in the honeymoon suite—Hart wrote in his diary, "Oh, it was hard . . . leaving them out here in the face of a dangerous enemy and commanded by God knows whom or how."

Later, to close friends, he confided, "I did the best I could with what I had, and under the conditions present. I was defeated. That's all there was to it."

On February 18, the *Houston* and her convoy were 30 miles from Darwin when Captain Rooks received a new set of orders: return to Surabaja as quickly as possible to join Admiral Doorman's strike force. The *Peary* was detailed to escort the merchant ships in, and the *Houston* steamed full speed ahead to Darwin to refuel.

By five that afternoon the *Houston* was ready to get under way. Captain Rooks sent a message by telegraph to Broome, informing the pilot Jack Lamade of the coordinates for the ship's position the next morning. The *Houston* would wait for him off the coast. Lamade did not receive the message until two days later. By then, the *Houston* was well beyond the SOCs flying range and Lamade's career on the ship was over.

Lieutenant Lamade returned to the United States in July of 1942. He served as a flight instructor at the naval air station at Jacksonville, Florida, and later commanded Air Group Seven aboard the carrier USS *Hancock*. Under his aggressive leadership, Air Group Seven inflicted enormous damage on enemy sea- and land-based facilities in Japan. Lamade named his F6F Wildcat fighter plane *T. Benny*, in honor of the *Houston*'s senior aviator, his old friend Thomas Benjamin Payne.

Captain Rooks had gotten the *Houston* out of Darwin just in time. Had he adhered to the original plan, laying over until dawn, the ship would have been caught at the dock in one of the heaviest Japanese air raids of the war. Nearly 200 carrier-based fighters and dive bombers plus more than 50 land-based bombers devastated the little town and the ships in the harbor.

There was no warning. Darwin had no radar and too few planes for continuous air reconnaissance. When the raid was over, eight ships had been sunk, including the *Peary* and two of the four transports the *Houston* had saved just a few days before. Nine other ships were severely damaged. Eighteen planes had been destroyed and tons of supplies and equipment were lost. For a time, the base was abandoned, out of fear that the Japanese would return.

The *Houston* crew learned of the Darwin raid that night from Tokyo Rose, who announced once again that the *Houston* had been sunk.

Their voyage from Darwin to Surabaja was a long one. To make sure of having sufficient fuel aboard, Captain Rooks stopped at Tjilatjap for refueling at dusk on February 21. As they approached the harbor, a Royal Navy PBY flew right overhead and dropped a depth charge. Everyone thought the pilot had spotted a submarine. Rooks immediately reversed course and headed back out to the open sea. Later he learned that there had been no submarine. The PBY had been damaged by Dutch AA fire. Unable to land with its depth charges aboard, the pilot had recklessly dumped them, disregarding the harm he might have caused to the *Houston*.

Meanwhile, the Dutch harbor pilot went home for dinner. He assumed that the *Houston* was late and he was not inclined to wait for her. After two and a half hours, the ship managed to dock, only to find that the Dutch fueling crew had quit work for the day. The *Houston*'s ragged engineering force had to rig their own lines from the dock and take on fuel. Although the men were exhausted, they worked through the night, but by the first light of dawn the *Houston*'s tanks were still not full.

The captain, not wanting to be caught in a morning raid on Tjilatjap, ordered the fueling halted, and by 7:30 the *Houston* was once again at sea, heading west along the south coast of Java.

Only Rooks and a few of the senior officers knew that their destination was Surabaja, and most of the men were openly curious. Lieutenant Windy Winslow asked Commander John A. Hollowell, the ship's navigator. "In a concerned fatherly way [Hollowell] draped his arm around my shoulder and, as though talking to himself, gravely said, 'Son, we're going to hell—we're going to hell.'"

Hell turned out to be the familiar port of Surabaja on Java's northern coast. The *Houston* arrived at 3:30 on the afternoon of February 24, after an uneventful passage through the Sunda Strait that separates Java and Sumatra. An air raid was in progress, but the ship docked without being attacked. As she tied up to the Rotterdam Pier, the all-clear sounded.

All along the shoreline the huge warehouses spewed smoke and flame. The entire port area, once so attractive, was now a scene of desolation. The naval air base at nearby Morotrambangan had been leveled. The beautiful Dutch naval officers' club, the Modderlust, with its wide terraces and balconies, modern architecture, and leaded windows had been broken by bombs, disfigured by dull gray camouflage paint. The entire city looked drab and melancholy, as if all the vibrant colors had been bleached out by the war.

Wherever the men of the *Houston* looked they saw signs of a city under siege. In the harbor, the burning hulk of a large cargo ship lay aground on a rock. Thick smoke from her burning cargo of rubber rose high in the air. An American destroyer, the USS *Stewart*, lay over on her side amid the fragments of a drydock. A Dutch destroyer shored up nearby sported a gaping hole in her stern, and a Dutch hospital ship was laid up for repairs.

At 11:30 that night, the *Houston* shifted her berth to the navy yard dock to take on more fuel. The cargo ship was still burning fiercely, the flames serving as a beacon for the enemy. A Dutch minelayer fired more than 30 shells into the hull in an effort to sink her but it did not work. The flames rose higher and brighter. "There was little sleep for any of us that night," Lieutenant Winslow commented.

The next morning the *Houston* moved again, this time tying up to the *De Ruyter*, a Dutch cruiser that was moored to a dock. Shortly after 11:00 A.M. the air-defense bugle call blared over the PA system and the crew raced to battle stations. This was only the first of two raids the Japanese had planned for them. The next one occurred at 3:30 that afternoon. During both attacks, while the *Houston* crew manned their battle stations, the crew of the *De Ruyter* abandoned their ship and went ashore to the safety of the air-raid shelters, leaving all of their antiaircraft guns unmanned. The reaction aboard the *Houston* was surprise, then anger.

"By gosh," Charley Pryor said, "that was something we didn't understand. Why in the Sam Hill would they do that? They'd head for those air-raid shelters like a bunch of rats." Don Brain added, "The feeling aboard ship was, 'Well, you can't trust [the Dutch]. They aren't going to fight.'"

Although these feelings were understandable, they proved to be unfair to much of the Dutch navy. The *De Ruyter* crew left the ship during air raids because their AA guns were not capable of reaching aircraft at high altitudes; the gunners would not have been able to hit anything. The Dutch would soon demonstrate that they were willing and eager to fight.

Neither cruiser was damaged in these raids, though some bombs did land close by, setting new fires in the warehouses. The

Houston's five-inch gunners discovered a new danger, however. This was the first time they had fired while at anchorage, and they found their own shrapnel falling back on them.

"That was altogether a new experience," Pryor said, "having your own shrapnel coming back on the ship, tremendous jagged pieces. Some of them weighed three pounds. The first time it happened, we ceased firing and took cover and I stuck my head under the platform of the gun. Then I happened to think, Well, by thunder, I've only got my head covered. The rest of me is still out there. I don't know how I scrooched under there, but I got all the rest of me under that thing."

During the air raids, the guns of the *Houston* provided the only defense. Surabaja might otherwise have been a ghost town. There were no signs of life until the all-clear sounded.

The Japanese forces were closing in on Java, and the Allies had little with which to stop them. Indeed, nothing had even delayed their timetable of conquest except for the American and Filipino forces holding out on Bataan. Elsewhere in the Southwest Pacific one disaster followed another. The enemy now occupied, in addition to Singapore, the islands ringing Java—southern Sumatra to the west, Borneo to the north, and Celebes, Timor, and Bali to the east. Far to the south in Australia, Darwin had been crippled as a naval base, and the Indian Ocean was no longer safe from air attacks. It was obvious that Java was next in line.

Admiral Helfrich knew he could expect no troop reinforcements and no additional ships. Still, he and Admiral Doorman were defending their homeland and were determined to fight to the end. Three days earlier, Doorman had sent a signal to all the ships under his command:

". . . the situation is very serious. I wish to impress upon all of you the necessity for every effort against the enemy to prevent his landing on Java. Every opportunity for offensive action must be seized and sacrifices must be made to this end. . . . I fully trust that every man shall understand the earnestness of this message and will realize that we will have to do our duty until the last moment."

The last moment was rapidly approaching, but two of the

major partners in the ABDA command were less than enthusiastic about the possibility of holding Java. In Admiral Hart's final directive to Admiral Glassford, he noted that "The expenditure of all U.S. naval forces in the ABDA will be fully justified, providing such expenditure results in measurable contribution to the success of such defense." Privately, Hart had expressed the view that the situation was hopeless and that there was nothing he or Glassford could do about it. The U.S. was formally committed to helping its Dutch allies.

The British were even less optimistic. On February 21, Field Marshal Wavell, the supreme commander of the Southwest Pacific, cabled Prime Minister Winston Churchill: "I am afraid the defence of ABDA has been broken down and the defence of Java cannot now last long. Anything put into Java now can do little to prolong struggle: It is more question of what you will choose to save. . . . I see little further usefulness for this HQ. . . . I hate the idea of leaving these stout-hearted Dutchmen, and will remain here and fight it out with them as long as possible if you consider this would help at all."

Four days later, on February 25, Wavell and his air commander were driven in a Lincoln Zephyr to the nearest airfield. The car and its Dutch driver were the only hint of ceremony left in a command that had been announced with such enthusiasm only six weeks earlier. Wavell boarded an American B-24 bound for India and never returned to the Southwest Pacific command.

The day before, with the approval of Wavell and General Henry "Hap" Arnold in Washington, Lieutenant General Lewis Brereton, commander of the U.S. bomber group on Java, also left for India. He arranged for his planes and their crews to evacuate to Australia. ABDA was disintegrating.

The Dutch, now in sole command, had some 7,000 British and Australian troops, 541 American soldiers (mostly antiaircraft and artillery), plus their own 25,000-man army composed largely of Javanese units with Dutch officers. These native troops were poorly equipped and trained and their loyalty to the Dutch was questionable. In addition, they were scattered in small, isolated units over the islands of Java and Sumatra.

For air power, the Dutch could rely on 13 U.S. P-40 fighter planes, flown by American and Dutch pilots, 6 Australian Hurricane fighters, 3 U.S. twin-engine A-24 attack bombers, and 6 Brewster Buffaloes. These, plus the ships of ABDAFLOAT, did not add up to an impressive defensive force against the Imperial Japanese war machine.

Helfrich was in a desperate situation. A British historian later wrote that Helfrich "inherited the crumbling remains of a command which in its short existence never became unified, which rarely secured joint action between land, sea, and air forces of a single nation, let alone of differing nations; it was," he concluded, "a command doomed to defeat even before he could assert his influence—and the final defeat came just a few days later."

The men of the *Houston* were not unaware of this situation. The realities of the ABDA command could not be kept secret, even from the rawest seaman. Rumors, tales of inefficiency, and stories of disagreement on goals and tactics had spread throughout the Asiatic Fleet. "The stories always filtered down," one seaman said. "We knew that we were having problems in that the observers from the different countries were stationed aboard various ships, and they were having great difficulty in communicating. We also knew that we were part of a ragtag outfit. Here we had some Dutch ships and some British ships and Australian ships, and really, none of them was a top-notch modern vessel. Even the *Houston*—as beautiful as she was and as good a ship as she was—had not been refitted with any modern gear. So we knew we were members of a very hastily put together operation."

The officers felt much the same way. Lieutenant Bob Fulton, the assistant engineering officer, reported that they had very little confidence in the high command. "We could not understand what they were trying to do."

The radio broadcasts from home did not help. In a fireside chat, beamed to the Far East by station KGEI San Francisco, late on the night of February 22, 1942, President Franklin D. Roosevelt spoke of the global war facing the United States. He listed the impressive production goals set for 1943 and 1944, the thousands of planes and tanks and ships that would soon be rolling off the assembly lines and sliding down the ways. It sounded very grand, but the men of the *Houston* would have been grateful for the reassuring sight of a few airplanes overhead that day. And it was unsettling to hear the President talk about defeating Germany, making little mention of the Pacific war. Anyone who still harbored hopes of reinforcement could scarcely do so after that speech.

Secretary of the Navy Frank Knox made a similar broadcast, noting that America's primary effort would for some time have to be directed against Germany. The *Houston* sailors knew that meant precious little to spare for the war against Japan.

"We did not expect reinforcements," said Seaman Otto Schwarz, "especially after the *Boise* came out and ran aground. We figured that was our reinforcement. It was obvious every time we were under attack that the Allies didn't have anything to help us with, because only one time did we see even one P-40 . . . and he never did find the enemy. You didn't have to be a genius to know that you were pretty much alone."

Seaman John Bartz added, "Finally we got the feeling that you knew you were going to be left there, that there was nothing or nobody who was going to come out and help us. The word was going around that we were there more or less as a sacrifice."

So many things had gone wrong. There was too much dissension and confusion at the top, too many aborted missions, too many mistakes, too little modern equipment, too little opportunity to maintain the ships properly. The fleet was literally wearing out, and so were the men. After weeks of continuous duty at their battle stations, they were reaching the point of exhaustion. The weariness and strain were taking their toll and there was no hope of any relief.

"I know I stayed up every night," Sergeant Pryor said, "and then in the daytime when you might be permitted to get a little sleep, well, these [Japanese] planes were over you so many times during the day that you were at battle stations pretty much the whole day, and then again at night. At one stretch we were at battle stations about twenty-one hours without relief."

The men never could count on a full night's rest. Even an hour of uninterrupted sleep was a luxury. So was eating. The *Houston* was not in danger of running out of food; the soda fountain still offered ice cream until two days before the ship went down. The problem was simply having enough time to eat. "We just didn't have time to eat," said Seaman M. L. Forsman.

"They'd just grab a hunk of meat and a hunk of bread and bring it around to your battle stations."

"Toward the end," said Otto Schwarz, "we were at sea all the time and under air attack quite often, so there were many times we were lucky to get sandwiches. And if we were at general quarters and they decided to serve food, it didn't come down to us, because they couldn't break the watertight integrity. Those of us locked up down below heard them talking about passing the food around, but we didn't get any. When we did get food it was mostly ham sandwiches, apples, and coffee. And boy, it was great!"

In the engine rooms, the black gang concocted a mulligan stew of meat and vegetables and cooked it on the hot feed pumps or on any other hot, flat surface. The men could not be released to go to the galley, and when the ship was closed up at general quarters, no food could be brought down to them. Like sleeping, eating had become a haphazard occurrence.

Without adequate sleep and food, the men grew tense and jittery, particularly when the bugle sounded over the PA system. Chips Eddy said, "After a while, it got to the point where every time that bugle sounded, no matter what it was for, you ran for your battle station." The air-defense call, in particular, was screeching and horrible. "It just sent me almost in a state of panic momentarily, until I got my wits about me."

"Everybody was so jumpy," Lieutenant Leon Rogers said, "that at the first note of that bugle, everybody hit the deck running, even if it wasn't the air-defense call."

Finally, Captain Rooks restricted the use of the bugle to emergency calls for general quarters and air defense. He decided not to sound it for routine matters such as mess call.

Yet the men bore up under the lack of sleep, the ham sandwiches and coffee wolfed down whenever they could, the frequent summons to general quarters, the air attacks. Their spirits did not suffer. "Under those circumstances, morale was absolutely marvelous," Lieutenant Tommy Payne said. "It was that tremendous loyalty they had to the skipper that did it. They'd do anything for him. They didn't care what it was, as long as he made the decision. The men would do it, no matter what he said."

The long months of training and drilling before the war were paying off. The men of the *Houston* were professionals, and their attitude, their morale, their willingness to pull together to do the job never wavered. Nor did their confidence in themselves and in their ship ever slacken. "Up to the very night we went down, I don't think any of us for a moment didn't think we were going to succeed."

The ship lacked the latest technology of war, her machinery was wearing out, and her armament had been reduced to two turrets, but her crew remained proud of the *Houston*. The men were tense and tired and not as cocky as they once had been— certainly, they no longer expected the war to be easy and quick— but they believed they would come through it all right.

They were wrong. At that moment, most of the more than 1,000 men aboard the *Houston* had only three days to live.

Northwest of Surabaja, ships for the largest amphibious operation ever mounted were converging on Java. The Japanese had organized three forces. Their Western Attack Group, composed of 7 cruisers, 25 destroyers, and 56 transports and freighters, had sailed from Camranh Bay in Indochina, expecting to land troops on the western end of Java at the northern passage of Sunda Strait. Its anticipated arrival date was February 28. The Eastern Attack Group—one cruiser, 6 destroyers, and 41 transports—had come from Jolo in the Sulu Archipelago. Ahead of it steamed the Eastern Covering Group consisting of 3 cruisers and 7 destroyers. These forces were due to reach the waters north of Surabaja on the 28th.

Dutch naval intelligence had been following the movements of the Japanese ships. Admiral Helfrich directed Admiral Doorman to attack the Eastern Covering Group, because it seemed as though this group would arrive first. After that, Doorman was to shift his attention to Batavia to deal with the Western Attack Group. "Pursue attack," Helfrich ordered, "until you have demolished the Japanese force."

At dusk on February 25, a strike force composed of the *Houston*, the Dutch cruisers *De Ruyter* and *Java,* and seven Dutch and American destroyers steamed out of Surabaja to find the enemy. As usual for that time of day, there was a rain squall. The weather was gray and dismal. "The whole atmosphere was one of apprehension," recalled one *Houston* sailor. "All we knew was that the Japanese were coming and we were going out to meet them."

9

Follow Me

The *Houston* was finally steaming to war against an enemy fleet. This was the sort of combat the ship had been built for, the kind of battle the Navy traditionally fought. Ship against ship, aggressively trading shells over great distances, not defending against airplanes or maneuvering to avoid falling bombs. A cruiser was a platform for her big guns, and the bigger and more accurate they were, the more destruction she would leave in her wake.

Now, on a sultry tropical evening, February 25, 1942, one fleet was seeking out another. When they met at last, it would be the biggest sea battle, in terms of number of ships, fought since the battle of Jutland in the last great war. Its outcome, however, could be foretold before the first shot was fired. The Allies did not have a chance.

Numerically, the two fleets were almost equal, with the Japanese having only a slight edge. But on other measures it would be difficult to find more unequal combatants. The Japanese ships were new, of the latest design and firepower, with superior torpedoes and air reconnaissance. The fleet had trained and fought together, their crews were at the top of their form, well rested and fed, fresh from a string of easy victories.

The ABDA ships were old and undergunned. The *Houston* was the best of the lot, and she had only two turrets working.

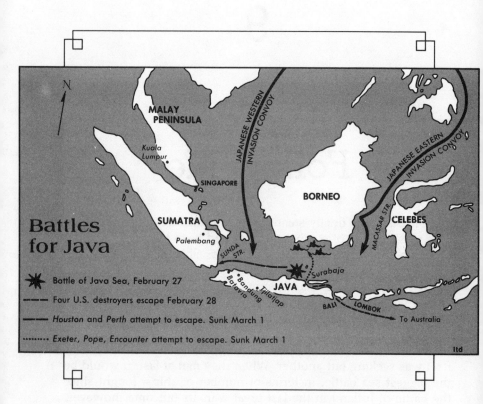

Battles for Java

✸ Battle of Java Sea, February 27

----- Four U.S. destroyers escape February 28

—— *Houston* and *Perth* attempt to escape. Sunk March 1

.... *Exeter, Pope, Encounter* attempt to escape. Sunk March 1

N

MALAY PENINSULA

Kuala Lumpur

SINGAPORE

SUMATRA

Palembang

BORNEO

CELEBES

JAPANESE WESTERN INVASION CONVOY

JAPANESE EASTERN INVASION CONVOY

MACASSAR STR.

SUNDA STR.

Batavia
Bandung
Tjilatjap
JAVA
Surabaja

BALI
LOMBOK

To Australia

ltd

The *Java*, the Dutch light cruiser, had been designed at the time of Jutland and was an excellent ship—by the standards of her day. Her biggest guns were 5.9s arranged in single turrets, giving her a broadside firing power of only five guns. The *De Ruyter*, while slightly more modern in design, was similarly lacking in long-range firepower. The American and Dutch destroyers were also products of World War I and, like the light cruisers, were in desperate need of maintenance. All the ships had been at sea almost constantly since the war began.

The officers and men of the American and Dutch navies had never worked together. There had been no time for combined exercises in fleet maneuvers, signals, or fire control, all so vital for the smooth coordination required by ships at sea. No joint doctrine had been developed, no agreement on tactics had been reached, and, what was worse, no effective communications system had been established. There was simply no efficient way of sending messages from one ship to another.

None of the ships had an English-Dutch signal book aboard and there was no code that both nationalities could understand. There was not even a common system for signaling with flags. In addition, the ultra-high-frequency radio transmitters and receivers did not stand up well under the shocks and vibrations that occurred when the ships fired their big guns. On the *De Ruyter*, Admiral Doorman's flagship, the searchlights, which could have been used for signaling purposes, would be destroyed by the firing of the ship's own guns!

The crews were weary from too many alarms, too many air raids, too many aborted missions, and too many sleepless nights. Indeed, Admiral Doorman had radioed Admiral Helfrich to report that the men had reached the limit of their endurance and would soon exceed it. Although their morale and their courage remained high, that would not be enough to win the battle.

The battle, however, did not take place that night. The Allied fleet sailed 100 miles across the Java Sea, as far north as Bawean Island, but saw no sign of the enemy. Doorman had arrived too early. He ordered the ships to return to Surabaja to refuel. The crews had been at battle stations throughout the night, and when they arrived in port at daybreak, they were greeted by a Japanese air raid.

There were more raids throughout the day, more calls to general quarters, more interrupted sleep. Captain Rooks received a strange request from the local government authorities. They ordered the *Houston* to cease firing on enemy aircraft for fear that the shells would fall on the city.

"What the hell!" said Q. C. Madson. "There's a war going on, so any time they come into range, we open up."

Japanese bombs were falling as close as 100 yards, but by now the men were so used to it that the distance wasn't close enough to worry about. "There were plenty of dead fish floating around when it was over, though. The concussion knocked them out and they floated belly-up on the surface until they came to and swam away."

Every time the all-clear sounded, the band assembled on the quarterdeck to entertain the men with swing tunes of the 1930s. As tired as they were, the men would gather around to listen, to tap their feet and clap in time with the music. But Lieutenant Payne could not hear them where he was. Before the first air raid of the day, his airplane had been hoisted over the side and he had taxied it to shore. He had been sitting in a bug-infested swamp, waiting for orders. Later, when it was decided that the big battle against the Japanese would be fought at night, he was instructed to remain ashore. His plane was the only one the *Houston* still had in flying condition and it would be a lot safer where it was.

Throughout the afternoon, Admiral Doorman and his staff planned their strategy. They had received new intelligence reports and orders from Admiral Helfrich, pinpointing the location of the approaching Japanese force. It had been spotted by reconnaissance planes and submarines and was believed to be between Borneo and Java, about 200 miles from Surabaja. The force of 2 cruisers, 4 destroyers, and 30 transports was heading southwest at a speed of 10 knots.

Doorman was ordered to "weigh anchor and attack at night," then to take his ships to Tanjong Priok, the port of Batavia, to be prepared to repel the Western Attack Group. Four hours later he received another directive from Helfrich: "Pursue attack until you have demolished the Japanese force."

At four that afternoon, the men received a welcome surprise.

Reinforcements arrived. Several ships sailed into Surabaja from Batavia, detached from the British force Doorman was keeping in reserve. Previously on convoy duty, they included three relatively modern British destroyers—HMS *Electra, Jupiter,* and *Encounter*— the Australian light cruiser HMAS *Perth,* and the British heavy cruiser HMS *Exeter.* All hands aboard knew of the *Exeter.* In December of 1939 she had taken part in the action that bottled up the German battleship *Graf Spee* in Montevideo harbor, where she was finally scuttled by her crew.

The ABDA force was larger now, but it was no more prepared to act as an effective fighting unit. The added presence of British and Australian naval vessels compounded the communications and logistics problems. The British semaphore system was different from those of the Americans and the Dutch. Further, like the Americans, the British and Australians had had no opportunity to hold maneuvers with the Dutch. The only apparent advantage seemed to be greater firepower. The *Perth* had six-inch guns and the *Exeter* boasted eight-inch guns in two turrets, one fore and one aft.

At sunset, the ships got under way with battle stations manned. On the *Houston,* Lieutenant Winslow remembers sailing past the "burned-out hulks of ships and ruined docks. Small groups of old men, women, and children, no doubt relatives of the Dutch navy men, assembled along the bomb-blasted docks to wave tearful good-byes to their men, most of whom would never return."

As the fleet left the harbor, the *Exeter* began to pass the *Houston* to take a position forward of the American ship. When the ships pulled even with each other, the *Houston* crew could hear music from the *Exeter*'s PA system. It was playing "A-hunting We Will Go." The sleek British cruiser was an impressive sight. "They had this huge battle ensign that must have been twelve feet by twelve feet," said Bill Weissinger. "I had never seen such a big flag in all my life. It was flying from the mainmast.

"It was sort of overcast and cloudy, but just about the time the *Exeter* got even with us, off our starboard beam, the sun broke through a little hole and this ray of bright light fell right on this bright white battle ensign. You talk about a beautiful sight! And she had the bone in her teeth, with the old bow wave coming up, and I saw the destroyers over here and the cruisers over there. That's the scene I'll always see—the *Exeter* coming up alongside us. It looked like the hull was about to go out from underneath the mast, she was going so fast. Just like everything was leaning back. Boy, it was a magnificent sight."

The whole fleet was magnificent. As the ships reached open water they formed up in column. First the flagship, *De Ruyter*, then the *Java*, followed by the *Exeter*, the *Houston*, and the *Perth*. The destroyers arrayed themselves alongside and behind—the British ships *Jupiter*, *Encounter*, and *Electra;* the Dutch *Kortenaer* and *Witte de With;* and the American *John D. Ford*, *Alden*, *Paul Jones*, and *John D. Edwards*. To the Dutch civilians waving from the bomb-scarred docks, they must have looked invincible.

Admiral Doorman led the ships due north to meet the enemy. The guns were manned and the ready boxes were filled with shells, with the hoists loaded with more. Down in the magazines, the handlers were prepared to send up ammunition as fast as the hoists would work. Spotters scanned the darkening sea, each man wanting to be the first to sight the enemy and give the warning. In the engine rooms, the throttlemen and burner operators stood ready to feed more oil to the burners. Throughout each ship, the damage-control parties and corpsmen waited, hoping their skills would not be needed that night.

Surely now, they thought, they would join the battle that had eluded them the previous night. The Java Sea was not endless; the intelligence reports had been specific about the location of the Japanese force. One hour passed, then another, and there was no sign of the enemy. Doorman turned his striking force to the east for an hour, then sailed west for another hour. On and on they steamed, every man at his battle station, alert and straining for some clue to the enemy's whereabouts.

The first pale light of dawn shone in the sky to the east. The morning clouds hung low, but they were not dense enough to keep the Japanese planes away. At 8:55 they came, not in their usual tight V formation but individually, making sporadic runs on the Allied fleet. Most of them concentrated on the British destroyer *Jupiter*, but none of the seven bombs dropped on her did any damage. The *Houston's* five-inch guns threw up a protective wall of fire, but they did not score any hits. Q. C. Madson observed tersely, "Bombs missed fleet, we missed planes, so no one is out anything."

Admiral Doorman felt angry and frustrated at having failed to find the Japanese ships for the second night in a row. Obviously the reconnaissance reports he had received were incorrect. He was also concerned about the lack of air cover for his ships, their dwindling fuel supply, and the fatigue of the crews after two nights and the intervening day at battle stations. The men needed rest and the ships, particularly the destroyers, would soon need to refuel. At 9:30 in the morning, he ordered the force south to return once again to Surabaja.

When Admiral Helfrich got the news a half hour later, he reacted with anger. He radioed Doorman at once. "Notwithstanding air attack, you are to proceed eastwards to search for and attack enemy. Air attacks had been expected and this attack should not have been a reason for withdrawing from the area of action."

Helfrich believed that Doorman was being excessively cautious, but Doorman was the commander on the scene and had the better grasp of the condition of his men and the limits of his fuel supply after a night of fruitless cruising. He chose to disregard Helfrich's order and continued on course for Surabaja.

The force entered the harbor at 3:15 that afternoon and was greeted by the shrill wails of the air-raid sirens. Surabaja was under Japanese air attack again. But before they could drop anchor, Doorman received another position report from naval intelligence. This time the sighting of the Japanese fleet seemed more definite.

Forty minutes earlier, reconnaissance planes had spotted four groups of enemy ships. One group, consisting of 2 cruisers, 6 destroyers, and 25 transports, was 20 miles west of Bawean Island, less than 100 miles from Surabaja. The second group, reported to be 65 miles northwest of Bawean, included more transports and destroyers. The third sighting was of a single cruiser 70 miles behind the second group. The strong covering force of two heavy cruisers and a large number of destroyers was about 35 miles southwest of Bawean, no more than 40 miles from Surabaja. This last group was out looking for Doorman's ships and the Dutch admiral had no choice but to meet it. If he remained in port, not only would he risk additional air attacks, but also the possibility of being bottled up in the harbor by the Japanese covering force.

Doorman turned his flagship in mid-channel and signaled his commanders. "Am proceeding to intercept enemy units. Details later. Follow me." An American liaison officer aboard the *De Ruyter* translated the message from Dutch into English and sent it to the *Houston*, which transmitted it to the other ships. Throughout the operation that was to come, some captains never received their instructions or received them in the wrong order. Others obtained messages only after they were relayed from headquarters on Java.

"We were hoping to get a bit of rest first," said one *Houston* seaman as the ship reversed course, "but here we go again. It looks like the circus is about to start."

The Allied fleet steamed northwest on a course of 310° at a speed of 25 knots. A 15-knot wind blew from the east, making the sea choppy. The sky was clear and visibility was excellent, which meant that the ships would be easy targets from the air.

The cruisers formed in column with the *De Ruyter* in the lead, followed by the *Exeter, Houston, Perth,* and *Java.* The three British destroyers were sent ahead as scouts. The four American destroyers were in column astern, and the two Dutch destroyers were about 4,000 yards aport. The Dutch destroyers were trying to make their way ahead, where Doorman wanted to position them, but the *Kortenaer* was having boiler trouble and her best speed was 24 knots. The American destroyers were also having difficulty keeping up. Their machinery was wearing out, their bottoms were fouled, and their condensers were leaking.

Doorman had had no opportunity to formulate a new battle plan. His earlier strategy had been based on a night battle, which was why the *Houston*'s airplane had been left behind, but now the striking force would encounter the enemy in daylight. The skipper of each ship had no idea then of the best tactics to employ when they all finally met the Japanese. There had been no formal agreement. The only orders were Doorman's cryptic signal, "Follow me."

The officers of the *Houston* noted the disposition of the ships and thought it to be an unorthodox arrangement at best. It suggested to one that "Admiral Doorman knew little about proven naval tactics or chose to ignore them completely." Another would say, "We should have done a lot better in that battle." After the war, several *Houston* officers endorsed a report that was highly critical of Doorman and his handling of the Java Sea battle.

An Australian historian was charitable. "The Dutch admiral," he wrote, "was as gallant as any in Netherlands naval history, but his battle experience was limited, and he should never have been in command. His was a political and rank appointment made in haste at a time of chaos and collapse."

Specifically, the *Houston* officers disagreed with the placement of the ships. Instead of having the destroyers in the rear, they should have been ahead, where their torpedoes could be used. The heavy cruisers should have been behind the light cruisers, instead of being intermixed, where their big eight-inch guns could rake the enemy forces and remain safe from the return fire of all enemy ships except other heavy cruisers.

The American officers also criticized Doorman for failing to exercise the fleet in maneuvers and signals, something he could easily have done that morning and early afternoon while they were at sea. In addition, Doorman had not worked out any fire plan for the ships. As a result, each captain was forced to select his own targets. Thus, some targets were fired upon by more than one ship, while others were not fired upon at all. Finally, they felt that Doorman was wrong to send the *Houston*'s spotting plane ashore, to have no contingency plan for a daylight battle, and to choose to engage the escort vessels instead of attacking the transports.

But there was no time to correct these problems. No sooner were they out in deep water than enemy planes were spotted. The antiaircraft gunners tracked them, but they stayed out of range. They were there to spy on the fleet, not to attack it. Doorman radioed headquarters with a final request for air cover, but was informed that no planes could be spared.

A few minutes later, three Japanese float planes—cruiser-based spotting planes similar to the American SOCs—were seen to the north. Doorman's fleet was now 30 miles out of Surabaja.

At 4:15, the British destroyers screening the column reported the sighting of Japanese ships. At first, they reported two battleships. That announcement was unexpected and caused a great deal of consternation. Battleships could remain out of range of the Allied ships and pound them to pieces.

Fortunately, the sighting was in error and a few minutes later the British issued a correction. The ships were heavy cruisers, not battleships. Shortly thereafter, the *Houston* saw them too. "We saw these little sticks on the horizon," Bill Weissinger said, "and gradually they got larger, and then there were hulls underneath them."

Doorman issued orders for flank speed, making it even harder for the American and Dutch destroyers to keep up with the cruisers. The heading of the Allied fleet was the worst possible one to maintain, relative to the Japanese ships. If Doorman continued on the same course, the enemy would soon cross his T, the classic naval maneuver that would enable every Japanese ship to fire broadsides at the Allied column. At 4:21, Doorman altered course to a heading of 260°, roughly parallel to the enemy force.

The Japanese ships could be seen clearly. Their two heavy cruisers stood about 30° off the starboard bows of the Allied cruisers. To the left, bearing about 45° from Doorman's force, were a dozen destroyers in two groups of six each. A light cruiser headed each of these forces.

The Japanese opened fire. Shells splashed near the *Electra*. The *De Ruyter*, Admiral Doorman's flagship, came under fire, but the range was still too great and the shells fell some 3,000 yards short. The *Houston*'s new course brought her within 30,500 yards of the Japanese heavy cruisers. Up in the foretop, gunnery officer Maher got the range and bearing of the farther cruiser. The crews of his two forward turrets trained around and elevated the eight-inch gun barrels to give the proper trajectory to their shells. For most of the men, this would be the first time they had fired the big guns.

Maher gave the order to the turret officers and the six guns fired at the same instant. The ship lurched and shook, heeling over about four degrees, as though struck by a whip. Griff Douglas was sure that the *Houston* had been hit by enemy shells. It felt just like the time the bomb had struck turret three. "I ran out on the quarterdeck and there was a chief standing there. 'Chief,' I said, 'we've been hit somewhere.' And he said, 'Kid, that's the main battery firing.' He kind of made fun of me, but I'd never been aboard when that main battery had fired."

Douglas wasn't the only one who was surprised. "That was when we found out that our shells were loaded with dye," reported the gun boss. They left blood-red geysers when they struck the water. The purpose of the dye was to enable spotters to distinguish their own salvoes from those of other ships, but no one aboard the *Houston* had been informed, not even Captain Rooks. "It had been kept a secret," Commander Maher said. "The Navy Department had told us we were not to fire them before the war. What difference would it have made? Who would have seen it if we had used them in training exercises?"

Now they knew, and the dye not only terrified some of the younger officers aboard the Japanese cruiser that was the *Houston's* target, but it also helped in correcting the aim of the eight-inch guns. By the sixth salvo, the *Houston's* shells were straddling the target, causing huge eruptions of water on both sides of the enemy ship. The guns fired as rapidly as possible and on the tenth salvo scored a hit. In turret one, Lieutenant (jg) Harold S. Hamlin, Jr., the turret officer, watched through his periscope.

"I saw the dull red glow of bursting shells, so different from the orange flash of gunfire. From the waist of the Jap ship a cloud of smoke burst up, and then, back aft, a bright orange flash—not gunfire, but a burning turret."

Hamlin let out a shout and reached for the voice tube connecting him with the gun chamber. The crew working the shells into the guns couldn't see outside and he wanted to let them know of their success. "We've just kicked hell out of a ten-gun Jap cruiser!" he yelled.

The enemy cruiser slowed, ceased firing, and straggled out of line, but not before the *Houston's* turret guns scored a second hit, this one in the vicinity of the forward turrets. Now the Japanese ship was almost completely obscured by the smoke from the fires on her deck. On the *Houston*, the gunnery officer shifted the fire to the other Japanese heavy cruiser.

Hamlin's turret crew was putting forth a superhuman effort.

The fuse box for the automatic rammer of the starboard gun had stopped functioning. It had sustained some damage during the bombing of February 4, but the problem had not seemed to be serious then. After the fifth salvo, however, the fuse box fell off the bulkhead and the rammer refused to work. The only way to get the heavy shells into the gun was to ram them in by hand. Sixty-five times the turret crew did the job, managing to keep pace with the other two guns in the turret. Lieutenant Hamlin knew that such a feat was considered impossible. "No gun crew could ever do it—but they did."

Within 20 minutes, Japanese ships opened fire on the *Houston*. Salvoes of eight-inch shells landed perilously close to the ship, first on the starboard side, then on the port side, and finally exploding in a perfect straddle. A marine on an aft five-inch gun remarked coolly, "Those little bastards. If they're not careful, they're going to hurt somebody."

Everyone on deck could see the shells coming. To antiaircraft officer Galbraith, they looked like flocks of ducks, and as they got closer, he said they sounded like freight trains. "We weren't particularly scared," said Lloyd Willey. "It was just the fact that we had been lucky so many times . . . we'd just come to believe that we were almost unsinkable."

Captain Rooks began evasive action, ordering a zigzag course. As he turned to starboard, the shells splashed close to port, and when he hove to port, the shells fell on the starboard side. The black gang kept the engines turning over at maximum revolutions, and the ship maintained its place in column, slicing through the water at better than 30 knots.

At a little after five, the Japanese cruiser the *Houston* had damaged returned to action, though the men could see that she was still smoking. She resumed firing, but the rate of fire was considerably slower than before. Still, the splashes around the *Houston* came uncomfortably close, and each one sent spray over the decks.

A few minutes later the *Houston* took a hit. An eight-inch projectile struck the forecastle and plowed through the decks on the port side. After passing through the main deck it penetrated the second deck and emerged on the starboard side. It failed to explode but left a hole about 18-by-32 inches, letting several inches of water into the warrant officers' quarters forward.

John Bartz on his 1.1 gun saw it happen. "The shells came in threes, looking like red hot lava, and I watched one of them go through officers' country and right out the other side."

Then a second shell hit, exploding on the port side near the laundry, destroying all the laundry equipment. It buckled the deck about a foot and ruptured an oil tank below. It had also passed through the brig and set a mattress afire. Merritt Eddy and his damage-repair party beat out the fire and checked on the oil leak. He decided that it was not serious.

The *Exeter* had not been so lucky. At 5:10 an armor-piercing eight-inch shell crashed through an antiaircraft mount and exploded in the powder chamber below. The damage was severe and the cruiser rapidly lost speed, falling off to five knots. She swung out of the column to port. Behind her, the *Houston, Perth,* and *Java* followed, thinking that Doorman had ordered a turn. They bore down quickly on the stricken ship.

"Suddenly," said Hal Hamlin, "the *Houston* gave a lurch and began to heel and turn. The turret rumbled as it trained around, trying to keep on the target. Over the phone came the voice of the gunnery officer, Commander A. L. Maher, 'Check fire—*Exeter* has been hit.'

"The *Houston* heeled sharp over, the screws shaking her as they went astern. Six hundred yards ahead of us [lay] the *Exeter*. The *Houston* was maneuvering sharply to avoid ramming her. As the *Houston* turned, the *Perth,* farther behind and in no danger of ramming, swept past to lay a smoke screen around the *Exeter*. She charged past with her throttles wide open and a billowing cloud of white smoke streaming from her smoke generators. There was a beautiful snow-white bone in her teeth, and from the yardarms and the gaff, three battle flags streamed straight behind. She was firing rapid fire and was one of the finest sights I have ever seen."

"She had two big tanks on the bow that looked like acetylene tanks," said Bill Weissinger. "I could see the guys up there operating the valves. A thick plume of smoke came out and by the time it got back to the turrets, it had widened out and covered the whole after part of the ship."

The Allied force was in disarray. For a few minutes, Admiral Doorman on the *De Ruyter* was unaware of the confusion behind him. The smoke obscured his view and he was steaming ahead alone. When he saw that the cruisers were no longer in column, he turned the *De Ruyter* to port. The four American destroyers still on the original heading had to turn quickly to get out of the cruiser's path. It was a fiasco.

While this frantic maneuvering was taking place, the *Kortenaer* sustained a hit amidships from a torpedo meant for the *Houston.* The Dutch destroyer had turned into the torpedo's path as she tried to follow the *Houston,* no more than 100 yards away. "One minute [the *Kortenaer*] was speeding along and then there was a big splash and when the water cleared, the after part of the ship was turned upside down and the bow was coming up to meet it. It just jackknifed and went down in less than a minute."

"It was terrible," Commander Maher said. "I could see the propellers going around and the men going down." Dutch sailors were standing on each upright end of the ship during those awful last moments. "They had the guts to give us a thumbs-up as we went by," Q. C. Madson said, "then both pieces sank very quickly. Not nice to see."

The Allied ships could not stop for survivors, for suddenly the sea was alive with torpedoes. "The next thing you knew, these torpedoes were jumping out of the water," said Bill Weissinger. "You could see these big old white plumes coming up everywhere, from every direction. Captain Rooks took her right down between them. Everybody was hollering, 'Torpedoes!' and 'We're going to get hit.'

"Guys were yelling on both sides of the ship as the torpedo tracks went by us. They'd yell, 'Cleared by five yards,' and then on the other side somebody would yell, 'Cleared by ten yards.' I just knew there was no way they could miss us. There were so many of them."

Madson looked over the side. "A torpedo had overtaken us from astern and was steaming right alongside us. We were doing about thirty knots, so the torpedo must have been doing about forty-five. It was only about fifteen feet out from the side of the ship. Scared? Damn right I was scared!"

Several Allied ships were laying smoke screens around the stricken *Exeter* and there was so much smoke in the air that it obscured everyone's vision. The *Houston*'s gunners could no longer see the Japanese ships, and for a short time the rate of fire from all ships dropped considerably. Doorman ordered a course change for the cruisers.

He dispatched the American and British destroyers to repel a Japanese destroyer attack. They were successful, but before they could rejoin the cruisers, the *Electra* was hit at point-blank range and went down.

As the smoke around the *Houston* cleared momentarily, the crew saw the *Jupiter* bearing down on them. At a distance of only 1,000 yards she launched a torpedo. The men were horrified. "She couldn't miss at such close range," said Lieutenant Winslow. "The torpedo traveled about five hundred yards when a great explosion occurred and two large chunks of metal flew high in the air, tumbling end-over-end and back into the sea. A large oil slick bubbled to the surface along with considerable debris. *Jupiter* had put a very timely end to one Japanese submarine."

The *Jupiter* heeled sharply and passed close astern of the *Houston*, tracking a torpedo that had narrowly missed the cruiser. She raced back up the torpedo's wake, heading for its source, and began shooting depth charges from the Y-guns. A moment later, wreckage and oil spewed into the air. There was never any confirmation, but apparently the British destroyer had sunk a second submarine.

Admiral Doorman was trying to regroup his force but with little success. The *Exeter* had been able to build up speed to 15 knots. She steamed south, away from the battle, trailing heavy black smoke. Doorman had ordered her to Surabaja, escorted by the Dutch destroyer *Witte de With*.

During the brief lull engendered by the smoke screen, the *Houston* crew had to attend to a serious problem. Turrets one and two were running low on ammunition. Few shells and powder bags remained in the magazines. An all-hands working party was formed, drawing on every seaman who could be spared. Only the engineering personnel, the five-inch gun crews, and the turret crews remained at battle stations. Even the men in the five-inch magazines were detailed. Their job was to carry the 150-pound shells and 63-pound powder bags from the useless turret three all the way forward to turrets one and two.

The aft turret magazine contained 300 projectiles and 800 powder bags, and the men worked furiously to move them and distribute them between the forward turrets. Some of the junior officers joined them. Chaplain Rentz was there with a thermos of cold water, cookies, and words of encouragement. The work was backbreaking and dangerous, made all the more treacherous by the high speed of the ship and the sharp and frequent course changes. The temperature below decks was well over 100°, but the men kept at it. They knew what their fate would be if the turrets ran out of shells during the battle. One member of the working party suffered a crushed finger when he dropped a shell, and this turned out to be the *Houston*'s only casualty of the Battle of the Java Sea.

Although shielded from the enemy ships by the impenetrable smoke, the *Houston* was still visible from the air. A Japanese spotting plane flew overhead; the pilot would pass on their location to the enemy ships. Gunnery officer Maher clambered down to sky forward, the forward five-inch gun director, and pounded on the door. When Lieutenant Rogers opened it, Maher shouted, "Shoot down that goddamn airplane!" But the plane was too high and it continued to circle leisurely, safely beyond the range of the *Houston*'s guns.

Only 15 minutes had passed since the *Exeter* had been hit. The four remaining cruisers re-formed, and Admiral Doorman set a course eastward. They emerged from the smoke to confront the Japanese heavy cruisers in a battle line some 18,000 yards away, within easy range. The *Houston* commenced firing immediately.

The men were firing the guns so fast that the gun casings grew extremely hot. Anyone who touched them would burn his skin. It would take 24 hours for them to cool down. The lubricant on the gun slides melted from the heat, leaving the gun pits filled with grease to a depth of three inches. Every time the ship turned, the men in the turrets slipped and fell.

Conditions were also bad in the magazines and handling rooms below the turrets. The ventilation system for the spaces beneath the turrets was inadequate at the best of times. Men on the shell deck fainted from heat exhaustion, and replacements had to be summoned from the forward repair parties. In the powder circles, a pool of water one inch deep flooded the deck. Most of it came from perspiration. It made footing hazardous and also dampened the powder. This was a problem because moisture affected powder's explosive power and, in turn, the projectile's range.

Otto Schwarz was working on the shell deck below turret one. As he manhandled the greasy projectiles onto the hoist, he thought about the endless drills before the war. "We used to ask the oldtimers how we were ever going to get these shells off the shelf during battle, and they always told us, 'Don't worry about it, because there has never been a naval battle that lasted for more than twenty minutes and they'll never use up all the shells they've got up in the turret.' Now we began to joke about that. Here we were passing shells up hour after hour and we'd say to each other, 'Oh boy, these twenty-minute battles are really something.'"

In addition to the oppressive heat and the exhausting physical labor, being below decks during a battle had another drawback—little or no information about the fighting. "There's no doubt about it," Schwarz said, "it's frightening, especially when things get real hot and you know you're being hit and you know that any second a projectile could come through that wall that separates you from the sea. And when you're so busy in the middle of a battle, you get no information at all except the instructions on passing up the ammunition. So you really don't know what's going on, and your mind is left to wonder."

The men below decks during the Battle of the Java Sea had a long time to wonder about what was going on. In the forward engine room, Bob Fulton was bothered by the lack of information and the feeling of isolation. "The *Houston* had no formal system of broadcasting battle progress to those below decks. We would eavesdrop. We would hear word being passed from one gunnery station or one observer to the bridge. We'd pick up information that way and pass it on to those down there with us."

Engine-room personnel were also suffering from heat exhaustion. The fresh-water drinking supply had long since been used up and the men were "drinking boiler water, which is treated with compounds to prevent boilers from scaling up. The water the men were forced to drink had been all through the turbines and condensers and feed tanks." It tasted awful, but at least it was wet.

Like the men in the magazines and handling rooms, those in the firerooms and engine rooms had little respite throughout the battle, though men from the after damage-control parties were sometimes able to spell them.

Topside, conditions were a little better. Although the men could see the action, that may have been a mixed blessing. Many would rather not have seen the torpedo tracks straddling the ship or the shells heading for their position.

"The firing just went on and on," Lloyd Willey said. "The cotton had blown out of my ear from all the concussions. My left ear hemorrhaged, and it ruined my hearing in that ear." In sky forward, Lieutenant Rogers knew that "when those eight-inch guns went off, they'd just rattle your eyeteeth." The concussion blew in the door of the director. "Every time turret two fired, that door would pop open. I remember George Stoddard, one of my talkers, saying, 'I can't keep this goddamn door shut.'" The concussion also bounced the director off its track so that it would no longer train.

Back on gun number eight, Charley Pryor watched the shells and heard their whistling sound. "I know that one time that afternoon the Japanese fired a four-gun salvo, and three of them landed over and one landed short of us. Our marine captain, [Frederick] Ramsey, was sitting out in the open on top of the aft antiaircraft director when this thing went over and we all heard that tremendous swish. Captain Ramsey, who talked rather slowly and deliberately, looked around and said, 'You know, if they get much closer than that, I'm going to have to get down from here.'"

The Japanese shells did not get any closer during the afternoon, and by nightfall, a few minutes after six, the action ceased. Admiral Doorman broke off the engagement. He decided to head north and attack the Japanese transports. Several ships had reported sighting "a forest of topmasts" beyond the enemy cruisers and destroyers, but they had not been able to get at them through the fire of the Japanese covering force. Under cover of darkness, Doorman hoped to evade the Japanese warships and work his way in among the transports. What Doorman did not know, being without radar or air reconnaissance, was that the transports were already fleeing to the north as fast as they could go.

"The next six hours will, I am sure, remain a bitter memory to those of us who have survived," wrote Lieutenant Hamlin after the war. "On the four cruisers churning northward there was no radar available for searching. We had come north and sighted the convoy. We had fought and subdued the escort. Yet, in hours of straining our eyes through periscopes, range finders and binoculars, we never sighted a single transport. Around us trouble was building up in large batches. On the plotting board were shown 55 enemy surface warships in the east end of the Java Sea. There must have been many submarines as well. Opposing them were now four cruisers and half a dozen exhausted destroyers, low on fuel, ammunition, and torpedoes."

At 7:30 P.M., spotters reported two enemy warships off the port beam. The *Perth* fired star shells, but they failed to light up the sky and nothing more was seen of the ships, if, indeed, they had existed. Doorman, frustrated in his search for the Japanese transports, ordered a course change to the east.

Twenty minutes later, men on the *Houston* reported hearing aircraft. "We felt fairly safe after the sun went down," Bill Weissinger said, "until we heard those planes. We just couldn't believe they were flying over the water at night. Then they started dropping flares."

It was not difficult for the Japanese planes to spot the Allied ships. "They picked us up from the phosphorous wakes made by our speed," Ensign C. D. Smith explained. They "began dropping flares right alongside us, disclosing our identity to any Japanese ships in the area, telling them where we were, what course we were on, and almost how fast we were going. We maneuvered radically, but as long as we remained at high speed, it was impossible to shake these planes off."

The planes dropped eight flares, one at a time. Each one burst and hung in the air, suspended from a tiny parachute, before settling slowly into the water. After the last one, darkness again enveloped the ships. Everyone waited, hushed and tense, for the next flare, for the shells from the enemy cruisers, but nothing happened.

Doorman altered course again, to 180° due south, toward the Java coast. The American destroyers were dangerously low on fuel and had spent their torpedoes, so he sent them on to Surabaja. There was little they could do to help if Japanese ships attacked the cruisers, so it was better to try to get them to safety. The ABDA striking force was reduced to the four cruisers—*Houston, Java, Perth,* and *De Ruyter*—and the two British destroyers, *Encounter* and *Jupiter*.

Within an hour, the Houston crew could see the mountains of Java in the distance, and by 9:00 P.M. Admiral Doorman had swung his column of ships on a westerly course, paralleling the coast. Griff Douglas, who was leaning on the rail and looking over the side, remarked to a chief petty officer standing nearby that the water looked funny. "We're in shallow water," the chief said. The antiaircraft officer, Jack Galbraith, saw "this great big wave behind us. It must have been six or eight feet high. The ship began to vibrate and I reported to the bridge that I thought we were running into shoal water."

They were in imminent danger of running aground. Doorman had brought the ships too close to shore and to a minefield that had been laid the night before. Captain Rooks instantly swung the *Houston* out of column, without waiting for orders from the flagship, and headed away from the shore. Moments later, Doorman recognized the danger and brought the other ships around to a course of 000° and the *Houston* rejoined the column.

Last in line was the *Jupiter*. At 9:25, just before making the new course, she was ripped by a fiery explosion. "I am torpedoed," she signaled. The fleet was under orders to stop for no one, and when last seen, the *Jupiter* was still burning. She sank during the night with a heavy loss of life.

Apparently the *Jupiter* had been sunk by a Dutch mine. She had not been torpedoed; the Japanese later reported that they had no submarines or destroyers in the vicinity at the time. A Dutch historian wrote that the minefield "was not laid with the necessary accuracy," and so the mines were not precisely where Doorman had expected them to be. "Though it is perhaps wrong to jump to the conclusion that the [*Jupiter*] indeed struck a mine, the chances are that this *was* the case."

The five remaining ships continued steaming northward, with Doorman still hopeful that they would find the Japanese transports. With every course change the fleet made that night, flares illuminated them from above, dogging their every move. They always appeared directly over the flagship, but the men rarely heard the sound of aircraft engines.

Suddenly a string of floating lights bobbed up in the water alongside the ships, accurately tracing their course. "They resembled round smoke pots," said Windy Winslow, "with a yellowish oily flame such as used to light construction sites. No one could determine what they were or how they got there. Some considered them a form of mine while others concluded they were simply beacons to light our track. Either thought was depressing."

"That was a very eerie feeling," Jack Galbraith said, "not knowing what the source of those flares was and knowing that somehow the Japs knew exactly where we were, no matter which way we turned."

At 10:15 that night they heard shouting in the water. They had come across survivors of the Dutch destroyer *Kortenaer*. The Dutch seamen blew whistles and yelled and waved, but the cruisers slid past; they could not stop for survivors. The *Houston* came within 100 yards of some of the men. Finally, Doorman ordered the *Encounter* to pick them up and take them to Surabaja, leaving the cruisers without destroyer escort.

About 45 minutes later, two Japanese heavy cruisers were sighted off the port side. Air defense officer Galbraith saw them first. "I had a very good pair of binoculars, especially good for night work, and I picked up two large ships on the port side. I reported the sighting to the bridge, and the captain said to see if we could illuminate them with star shells. We fired four star shells out, and then another, increasing range until we got to our maximum range, which was fifteen thousand yards, and we were still short of the ships."

Even without the star shells, however, it was easy for the

men of the *Houston* to see the cruisers in the bright moonlight. The enemy ships were heading south. Captain Rooks ordered turret one to fire one salvo. It fell close to the first cruiser but not near enough to cause any damage. Because the *Houston* was low on eight-inch ammunition, turrets one and two were ordered to track the cruisers, but not to fire unless they were sure of getting a hit. The enemy ships fired three salvoes, one of which straddled the *Houston*'s stern. Then the Japanese reversed course and disappeared.

For 30 minutes more the Allied cruisers plowed on without sighting any other ships. The exhausted men were growing more tense, watching and waiting, wondering if they would see more action. A huge explosion 900 yards astern jolted their thoughts. The *Java* had been torpedoed.

"There was one hell of an explosion," Q. C. Madson said. "The entire aft part of the ship seemed covered with flames, and explosion followed explosion in rapid succession, with each one sending a tower of flame and debris a hundred feet in the air while the old *Java* just rocked and bucked. She didn't last long after that."

Charley Pryor happened to be looking at the *Java* when the torpedo struck her. "I was looking through binoculars and I could see in the glare of all the fire and flame people just visibly blown off the ship. You could see their bodies and other debris from the ship blown through the air, and all this fire was on the water. I thought, Oh, my gosh, those submarines have got us now."

The *Java* was finished, dead in the water, aflame from end to end. Pryor had to turn away from the sight. "The *De Ruyter* was ahead of us and slightly to our left and almost in the same instant that I looked around there, the *De Ruyter* was hit in the same way."

Bill Weissinger was watching the fire on the *Java* when he heard "another thump. I looked around and saw a ball of fire on the bow of the *De Ruyter*, and it just rolled back and then a big orange Christmas tree came up. It was completely mystifying. We didn't know where it was coming from. It was really eerie."

The *De Ruyter* was finished, too. Moments after the torpedo hit, the fire ignited all the antiaircraft ammunition. In seconds the entire ship was covered in flames.

On the bridge of the stricken *De Ruyter*, Admiral Doorman

had time to send a single radio message: "Do not stand by for survivors. Proceed to Batavia."

The *Houston* and the *Perth* could not have stopped anyway. They were in immediate danger of colliding with the flaming *De Ruyter* and of being torpedoed themselves. "We saw the tracks of torpedoes pass astern of us. They just went harmlessly on by." But Captain Rooks of the *Houston* and Captain Waller of the *Perth* had no time to think about the torpedoes. They were too busy trying to avoid the flagship and each other. Rooks turned the *Houston* quickly to starboard, to avoid running the *De Ruyter* down. Captain Waller, as the senior officer and now technically in command, charged ahead to take the lead. He approached the *Houston* on her starboard side, the direction in which she was turning, and the two ships were on a collision course.

On the *Houston*'s bridge, Ensign Herb Levitt, a communications officer, was the first to recognize the danger. He felt that they were only seconds away from disaster. He had no time to inform the captain so he pushed the helmsman aside, grabbed the wheel, and swung the *Houston* into a sharp turn to port. "The next thing I knew," said Weissinger from his aft five-inch gun, "was that I looked up and here's the *Perth*. We just barely missed her stern by about two feet. It was an exciting night."

Jim Gee, stationed for most of the day and evening in the five-inch magazine, was topside when the torpedoes struck the Dutch cruisers. "Here we were in a line formation and there's only four of us and you know there's nothing out there but the enemy. And the number-one ship in line goes, and the number-three ship in line goes. They just disintegrate and are gone in a matter of minutes. And there are not many more targets, just us and the *Perth*. And you sort of wonder, How much longer can we go on?"

The Battle of the Java Sea, that "forlorn battle," as Winston Churchill called it, was over. Half the ships of Admiral Doorman's fleet had been sunk and most of the others would be lost within 24 hours as they tried to flee. Doorman himself had gone down with his ship and the Allies' last chance to save Java from Japanese occupation had evaporated. The invasion of the island had been delayed by no more than a day. The enemy had not lost any ships, and their valuable convoy of troop transports had not even come under fire.

Admiral Helfrich later criticized Captain Waller for leading the *Perth* and the *Houston* back to Batavia. "The return of *Perth* and *Houston* was against my order. . . . I wanted the Combined Striking Force to continue action whatever the cost, and till the bitter end." Helfrich wanted the Allied ships to fight to the last man.

Three days after the Battle of the Java Sea and seven days before Java surrendered, Admiral Helfrich left by plane for Ceylon, by order of the Dutch governor-general.

10

I Think We've Got It Made

The men of the *Houston* spent another night—their third in a row—at their battle stations. With the *Perth* in the lead, the two ships steamed westward at a speed of 28 knots, zigzagging to evade any submarines that might be stalking them. The crew remained awake and alert, and the lookouts constantly swept the horizon with their binoculars, scanning the sea for any smudges in the darkness that might turn out to be enemy ships.

They saw nothing all night. Shortly after dawn, Captain Rooks secured from general quarters and set Condition Two in the antiaircraft batteries (half the guns manned). The off-duty crews dozed restlessly, close by their guns, ready to spring into action when needed. It was too hot to go to their bunks, and too dangerous as well. No one whose duty station was topside wanted to be caught below decks during an attack. Indeed, most of the men had not slept in their bunks for weeks.

At 11:00 A.M. the men were jolted awake by the air-defense bugle call. They raced to battle stations, expectant, watchful, hoping this would not be the final blow. It wasn't. The planes that had been spotted were Dutch patrol aircraft on a routine mission, and the off-duty crews once again tumbled into an uneasy sleep.

The exhaustion they felt was almost beyond the limit of physical endurance. In his official Navy report, Commander Maher, the senior surviving officer, described their state on that Sat-

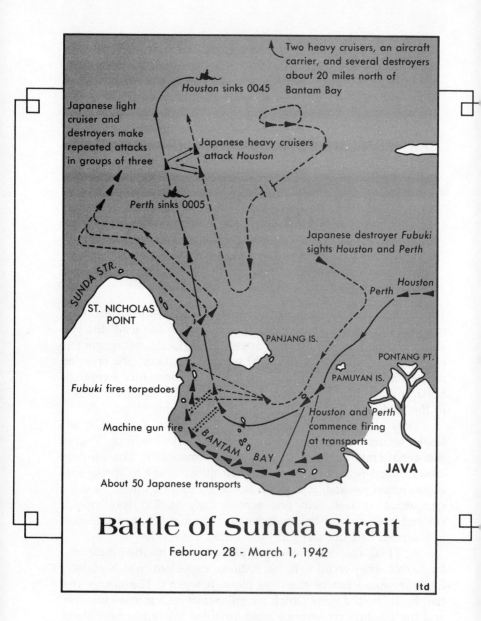

Two heavy cruisers, an aircraft carrier, and several destroyers about 20 miles north of Bantam Bay

Houston sinks 0045

Japanese light cruiser and destroyers make repeated attacks in groups of three

Japanese heavy cruisers attack *Houston*

Perth sinks 0005

Japanese destroyer *Fubuki* sights *Houston* and *Perth*

Perth   Houston

SUNDA STR.

ST. NICHOLAS POINT

PANJANG IS.

PONTANG PT.

PAMUYAN IS.

Fubuki fires torpedoes

Machine gun fire

Houston and *Perth* commence firing at transports

BANTAM BAY

JAVA

About 50 Japanese transports

Battle of Sunda Strait
February 28 - March 1, 1942

ltd

urday morning, February 28, the last day most of the *Houston* men would live:

> The physical condition of both officers and men was poor and in some cases treatment for exhaustion was necessary. More than four days had elapsed since most of the crew had received adequate rest. Battle stations had been manned for more than half of this time and freedom from surface contacts or air alarms never exceeded four hours at a time. Meals necessarily had been irregular and inadequate.
>
> The effect of this sustained effort was most serious among engineering personnel where approximately 70 cases of heat exhaustion had occurred, and among AA crews and ammunition supply parties where the most vigilance and physical exertion were required. For the past 24 hours, all men off watch had been engaged in moving ammunition from disabled Turret III to Turrets I and II.

Lieutenant Payne put it more succinctly. "Oh, Lord, we were just dead to the world. Everybody was just staggering around. Their energy was pretty low, about as low as you can get."

Yet despite the bone-deep tiredness, the weariness that made it an effort to keep their eyes open, the morale of the crew remained excellent. "Everybody was still gung ho," Howard Brooks said. "Our spirits were really high." They knew they had been lucky and that their ship had been lucky. They weren't at the bottom of the Java Sea like most of the ships of Admiral Doorman's striking force. But they had done more than merely survive. The *Houston* had performed well. The men could feel a deep sense of pride in themselves and their captain. They had carried out their duties with courage and efficiency. It was their ability and confidence, as well as some luck, that had kept them alive.

The *Houston* and the *Perth* were the only cruisers left in the Allied fleet, and the *Houston* was in no shape to go back into battle right away. She would have to leave the Java Sea and find a drydock, a well-equipped navy yard to undertake repairs.

The ship was a shambles. The shocks and concussions from the eight-inch guns had shaken loose everything that was not welded down and had even broken many things that had been secured. "The whole ship was falling apart," said Al Maher. "She was leaking at the seams, and the carpenter parties were working as fast as they could to plug up all those leaks." When Leon Rogers went down to his cabin that morning, he found that "the drawers were all popped out and stuff was strewn all over. There was an electric overhead fan hanging on by the wire. The fan was just blowing itself around and around."

"Clocks lay broken on the deck," Windy Winslow said, "furniture overturned, mirrors cracked, charts ripped from the bulkhead and large chunks of soundproofing jarred loose from the overhead added to the thick rubble underfoot." In addition, "the glass windows of the bridge were shattered. Fire hoses strung along the passageway were leaking, and minor floods made it sloppy underfoot." The *Houston* was "battle-scarred and battle-weary."

The eight-inch guns in turrets one and two were nearing the end of their life expectancy. Normally, an overhaul was required after 300 rounds. The *Houston*'s guns had fired more than 260 rounds, and they had been fired so rapidly that their liners were protruding at least an inch from the ends of the barrels. Thus, neither the guns, the ship, nor the crew would be combat-ready for a while.

Tanjong Priok, the port of Batavia, Java's capital city, looked and smelled of defeat, destruction, and death. As the *Houston* and the *Perth* entered the harbor, they passed the bombed-out hulk of a freighter lying on its side in the mud. Pieces of other ships peered from beneath the oily waves. Masts and superstructures were all that remained visible above the surface, and these were blackened by the fires that had sent the ships to the bottom.

The stench of burning oil rose in the humid air. Giant oil tanks spewed thick columns of smoke that stained the skyline. Along the waterfront, warehouses filled with millions of dollars of goods—Goldflake and Players cigarettes, fine Scotch whisky, crated aircraft, shells, torpedoes, military uniforms—lay open and ready for capture or burning with stiff, persistent flames.

The port was a ghost town, quiet and still. Gone were the noises of a busy Far Eastern anchorage, the cries of Javanese boatmen hawking their wares, the rhythmic chants of work gangs on the wharves. An odd silence settled over the water, broken occasionally by the crackling of new fires that spurted up along the piers. "Defeat was everywhere. It was something you could almost reach out and touch. It covered everything like the smoke from the splintered tanks half a mile away."

The *Houston* tied up to an undamaged dock at one in the afternoon. Captain Rooks and Captain Waller went ashore to see if ABDA headquarters had any orders for them. If Java was falling, surely the cruisers would be sent elsewhere. The *Houston*'s engineering officers, Gingras and Fulton, also left the ship, to try to obtain more fuel. Bob Fulton said there was "a lot of confusion on the go-down and the office to which I went, and it was pretty hard to figure out who knew what was going on."

At first the Dutch refused to allocate any fuel to the *Houston*, arguing that their supply was reserved for Dutch ships. Gingras and Fulton explained that most of the Dutch ships had been sunk. When the local officials finally relented, they allowed the *Houston* to take on only a modest amount of oil. "We got no more than a dribble," Fulton said.

The oil lines were connected to the ship and the engineers started pumping as rapidly as their equipment would work. There was no telling when Japanese planes might appear overhead or when they would be ordered to depart with all possible speed. They worked so quickly that one of the fuel lines broke, spilling more precious oil into the already oily harbor.

Late in the afternoon, Tommy Payne, ashore with his SOC in Surabaja, radioed the *Houston* that he was returning to the ship. He had been shuttling between Surabaja and Batavia since leaving the *Houston*. During the first night in Batavia, while asleep in the officers' lounge, he'd been caught in an air raid. "Then I figured, I'm getting the hell out of here and I went on back to Surabaja," he said. "The next day, I thought I'd give this thing another whirl, so I went back to Batavia again, still looking for the ship."

Payne flew about halfway up the coast when his oil line burst. He made a landing at sea, crawled out on the lower wing, and "pinched the line off. I had about a gallon of oil left and a good hour-and-a-half flight. That engine kept going. I don't know how in the heck it did. The temperatures kept going up, all the gauges went out of sight."

Back at the harbor at Tanjong Priok, about six that evening, a single-engine double-wing seaplane flew past the dock at an altitude of about 250 feet. The Dutch destroyer *Evertsen*, out in the harbor, opened fire. The *Perth*, which was tied up on the far side of the pier from the *Houston*, also opened up with her pom-poms. The plane banked steeply over the *Houston*'s bow, exposing the big red circles of the Japanese insignia beneath its wings. The *Houston* gunners joined in the fire, but they were too late. "Everything happened so fast," Q. C. Madson said, "that we all missed what should have been an easy shot." It was vivid testimony to the tiredness the men were experiencing to have missed an aircraft that was flying so slow and low.

About 15 minutes later, the plane came over again. Instantly the *Perth* and the *Evertsen* opened fire, but again the *Houston* gunners waited. The pilot was Tommy Payne.

"Oh, God," Payne said, "I don't know how they missed me. Those tracers looked like they were all going through the wings."

"You dumb bastards," he yelled over his radio. "Don't you know I'm one of you?"

Payne banked the flimsy SOC and scooted out to sea as fast as he could, with the tracers right on his tail. When he got beyond range, he set the plane down and began cautiously to taxi back in. A Dutch PT boat raced out to investigate, its gunners ready to fire. When they had identified the seaplane to their satisfaction, Payne brought it alongside the *Houston* and was hoisted aboard.

Captain Rooks returned from headquarters and called his senior officers together on the bridge. He informed them of their new orders. By telephone, Admiral Glassford had instructed Captains Rooks and Waller to take the *Houston* and the *Perth* through Sunda Strait that evening, to get out of the Java Sea. But they were not going to Australia for repairs. Instead, Glassford, under orders from Admiral Helfrich, had told Rooks to proceed to Tjilatjap. Helfrich was not ready to give up the fight. He planned to assemble his remaining naval forces in Tjilatjap and continue to resist the Japanese.

Glassford did not approve of Helfrich's decision, but his position was subordinate to the Dutch admiral. The *Houston's* officers were not enthusiastic about it either. "Tjilatjap!" Lieutenant Payne said. "My God, the war was over! There wasn't anything left to fight with. That was like going to your own funeral."

Captain Rooks seemed buoyed in spirits that evening and unusually talkative. "We're getting out of the bottleneck," he told his officers. "Now we can breathe easy and not worry about going to general quarters all night long."

The intelligence information Rooks had received from the Dutch that afternoon had certainly given him reason for confidence. "The straits are clear of Japanese ships," he reported. The enemy was not in Sunda Strait, nor anywhere near the western end of Java. The ABDA staff had told Rooks that the closest Japanese naval force was at least 10 hours sailing time away and thus posed no threat to the *Houston* and the *Perth.*

Gunnery Officer Maher asked if the ship shouldn't be at general quarters anyway, at least until they got through the strait. "No," Rooks said. "It isn't necessary and the men are too worn out." Maher knew that the captain had the crew's welfare in mind all the time, but he and some of the other officers felt uneasy about not having the battle stations manned while traversing the strait.

Payne questioned the Dutch intelligence information. "I told Captain Rooks it was wrong. I had seen a Jap cruiser seventy miles northeast of Batavia that afternoon. Also, the plane that came in just before I did had to come from somewhere, and it was a ship-based plane."

Captain Rooks agreed to set Condition Three; one-third of the guns would be manned during the passage that night. Captain Waller on the *Perth* also set a reduced state of readiness for the voyage. "The captain was just trying to be as lenient with the men as he could," Payne explained later, "in view of what they'd been through." But he hoped that the enemy cruiser he had seen was not heading toward Sunda Strait.

Dutch intelligence was dead wrong. The Japanese convoy that was supposed to be 10 hours away was a lot closer and its course was set for the northern end of Sunda Strait. If it maintained its present speed, it would arrive at 10:00 P.M., about the same time as the *Houston* and the *Perth*. The convoy was a major invasion force and included 5 cruisers, 11 destroyers, an aircraft carrier, 40 troop transports, and a number of PT boats. It was just the kind of enemy concentration Admiral Doorman had died seeking the day before.

At five that afternoon, about an hour before Captain Rooks returned to the *Houston* to inform his officers of their orders, the commander of the Netherlands East Indies Army, Major General Schilling, had been told of the existence of the Japanese invasion force. Schilling, at his headquarters in Batavia, did not pass the information on to naval authorities, even though the British naval liaison office was in the same building. No naval officer— American, British, Dutch, or Australian—was given this vital piece of intelligence. If the information had been properly disseminated, the *Houston* and the *Perth* would never have been ordered through Sunda Strait.

Sailors are a superstitious lot. Omens are not taken lightly or joked about. They can keep a man awake at night and ruin his appetite. That evening, the men of the *Perth* detected two bad omens. One involved their mascot, an undistinguished-looking cat that had been aboard since New Year's Eve of 1941. Named Red Lead, because the first thing it did when it was brought aboard was to upset a pot of red lead, the cat was a veteran of several battles in the Mediterranean Sea and had remained aboard in several ports of call. That day it tried to jump ship. Three times it crept down the gangway. Finally the master-at-arms put it in the "brig," a large can with air holes punched in it.

The second incident involved one of the passengers the *Perth* had taken aboard. These were Australian navy personnel who had been stranded in Tanjong Priok. One turned out to be a chaplain. The *Perth* already had a chaplain assigned to her, and now there were two aboard. To the Australian sailors, that was a bad sign. "One chaplain was enough, but two? That was lethal."

Aboard the *Houston*, however, the mood was quite the opposite. Most of the men were jubilant when the announcement came over the PA system that they were heading south through Sunda Strait. They had not been told that the destination was Tjilatjap, only that they were leaving the Java Sea. That was reason enough to celebrate. As to their next port once they passed through the strait, rumors, hopes, and fears charted the *Houston*'s course.

"We all thought we were finally through out there," Lloyd Willey said. "Our spirits were high. We thought we were going home." Lieutenant Rogers was optimistic about getting through the strait and away from the overwhelming Japanese forces. "Thank God," he thought, "we're going to get out of this Java Sea."

Jim Gee said, "They're bound to send us out of here now. Somewhere where we could get a good day's rest and some good food and relax a while. Our spirits were high. Everybody was dog-tired, but we thought we were going to get out and we were laughing and joking and settling down for some needed rest."

"The rumors were that we were going to the Indian Ocean and to safety," Howard Brooks said. "My main feeling was, Oh, boy, we're going to get out of here and we're going to be safe. We're going to be out of the range of those planes that have been harassing us for weeks. We're just going to be able to sit out on the deck in the sun without having to worry for a while. We're lucky," he added. "Just us and the *Perth* and a couple of others left out of all those ships."

Other rumors put their destination at Pearl Harbor; Australia; Bremerton, Washington; and Long Beach, California. A few of the men even mentioned Tjilatjap, but the scuttlebutt about that was that the *Houston* would stop just long enough to pick up whoever was standing on the dock. Griff Douglas was on duty in sick bay that afternoon when one of the radiomen, Jim Ballinger, came running in out of breath. "We're going to Norfolk, Virginia," he said. "Our orders are to get our butts out of here. We're not looking for anything else, nobody to jump. We got orders to get out of here."

That was good enough for all of them, just getting out of the Dutch East Indies for a time. Get some rest, get some food, get their ship back in fighting trim so they could take on the Japanese. It was a great feeling.

Back by sky aft, the after antiaircraft director, Shorty Gingras, the engineer, was talking with Jack Galbraith, the AA officer.

"You know," Gingras said, "I had no hope that we would ever get away from all this, but now I think we've got it made."

The *Houston* and the *Perth* were due to get under way at 6:30 in the evening, but they were delayed because the Dutch harbor pilot failed to show up. Dutch port authorities had promised them a pilot to lead them through the minefield, and the two ships waited for an hour. They were now well behind schedule and the delay meant that they would approach the strait some time after the Japanese convoy was due to arrive.

At 7:30, Captain Waller, as the senior officer, decided that they should depart without the pilot. With the *Perth* in the lead, he guided the ships through the nest of mines at the mouth of the harbor. As they passed the Dutch destroyer *Evertsen*, Waller radioed her captain that he should leave with them. The Dutch skipper said he had no orders. Waller replied that the *Evertsen* had better get out now while there was still a chance. "I cannot get under way for one hour," said her captain.

The *Evertsen* did not depart Tanjong Priok for two hours. At midnight, she sent a radio report of a sea battle taking place off St. Nicholas Point. It was the *Houston*'s last battle. The *Evertsen* slipped past and made it through Sunda Strait before being attacked by two enemy destroyers. She was forced to beach on Sabuko Island.

Once clear of the harbor, the *Perth* and the *Houston* headed west at a speed of 22 knots. Bill Weissinger said, "It really felt good to cross the bar and get into open water, to see that water turn blue. They put the ship in high gear and away we went. We had been tied up at the dock and it was so hot you could feel the heat coming off the decks. It felt good when we got out in the ocean breeze and the sun went down.

"The cooks were in the galley. They were busy making up sandwiches and coffee. We were going to have a big party about three in the morning. That was the time we were supposed to be through the strait and be in the Indian Ocean and be safe. We were going to have this big party with ham sandwiches and coffee, fresh bread and the whole bit. It was really going to be something."

The off-duty crews stretched out for some much-needed sleep. Bob Fulton turned in around ten. He bedded down on the quarterdeck beside the port catapult tower, where he had occasionally been able to grab a nap.

Charley Pryor was not scheduled for duty on the number-eight five-inch gun until eight the next morning. "For the first time in a month I went down below, got my mattress, brought it back up onto the gun deck, spread it out and took off my outer clothing. For the first time in ten days, I was actually going to get some sleep."

Jim Gee said, "We set a third of the crew on watch. The rest of us just lay down where we were. We were so tired and so weary that we just lay right down on the decks and went to sleep, because we felt that everything was calm for the night. We were heading home."

Griff Douglas left the sick bay and took his pillow and blanket up on the quarterdeck. "For the first night of that whole month I stretched out and really went to sleep, because I knew we weren't hunting to jump on anybody. We had heard the nearest Jap ship was sixty miles north."

Even those on watch felt they could afford to relax just a little. On duty in turret one, Otto Schwarz said that "we were at the ready, not at general quarters, but we were at our battle stations. We had the hatches open and we were sitting around on the deck."

Captain Rooks was on the bridge, along with Lieutenant Hamlin, the officer of the deck. They received word from the Dutch military headquarters in Batavia that the Japanese naval force thought to be 10 hours sailing time away was now on an easterly course. There was no way it would cause any problems for the *Houston* and the *Perth*.

Again the information was incorrect. By 10:30 that night, as the two cruisers were almost within sight of the entrance to the strait, a Japanese destroyer, the *Fubuki*, was shadowing them off their starboard beams. Although the sea was calm, the air still, and the cloudless sky and full moon provided visibility for up to six miles, neither the Americans nor the Australians spotted the enemy ship. Ahead of them, the convoy was already landing troops at Bantam Bay. Japanese cruisers and destroyers were patrolling offshore. The *Houston* and the *Perth* were heading right between the transports and their escorts.

At 11:00 P.M., Captain Waller on the *Perth* increased speed to 28 knots, preparing for the run through Sunda Strait. It would take about an hour. In two hours or less, they expected to be in the Indian Ocean, out of the trap. At 11:06, when they were five miles from St. Nicholas Point, the northwesternmost tip of the island of Java, lookouts on the *Perth* sighted a ship.

"Challenge," Waller ordered. "It's probably one of our corvettes patrolling the strait."

The chief yeoman signaled with his Aldis lamp, and the other ship responded, but her lamp was a strange pale green color and her code was unfamiliar.

"Repeat the challenge," Waller said.

As the yeoman did so, the other ship began to turn and make smoke. Waller recognized her shape. "Jap destroyer," he said. "Sound the rattles! Forward turrets open fire!"

Aboard the *Houston*, a few hundred yards astern of the *Perth*, Captain Rooks and Lieutenant Hamlin had their binoculars trained on the unidentified ship. "It appeared to be moving faster than could be expected of any patrol vessels that should be in the area," Hamlin said. "As I looked, she fired a red Very star."

No one saw that the enemy destroyer had fired nine torpedoes at a range of only 3,000 yards. Waller ordered a turn in the direction of the destroyer, and the torpedoes raced by. They struck several of the Japanese transports on the far side of the Allied cruisers.

Captain Rooks called for battle stations and ordered gunnery officer Maher to commence firing. Turret one, manned and ready, started shooting as the klaxon was sounding. As weary as the men were, they succeeded in manning their battle stations within one minute. Turret two was in action by the time turret one had fired its third salvo.

"Of course we were all worn out," Ray Sparks said, "but at the stroke of general quarters we were all up. It seemed like you forgot your tiredness then." Others agreed. Merritt Eddy had no recollection of fatigue at that moment. "Of course we were young and all excited. You're nervous and scared, and you suddenly don't feel tired anymore."

And their spirits remained high, even when they found themselves going into battle where there weren't supposed to be any Japanese ships. "Even at the last battle station everybody was gung ho," Howard Brooks said. "There was one big rush to the battle stations and in my mind I said, Oh, boy, we've gone through all these days. We can go through this one too. We never lost our confidence and our feeling of being able to handle whatever came along."

History books record these events as the Battle of Sunda Strait. It was a melee, a chaos of star shells and flares hanging overhead, a tangle of blinding searchlights piercing the night, the freight-train roar of eight-inch shells, the silent tracks of deadly torpedoes, the enemy destroyers racing so close to the cruisers that the men could hear their engine-room blowers whining. It was explosions and fires, machine-gun bullets slicing through steel and through flesh, and many good friends wounded and killed and two good cruisers shelled and torpedoed until there was nothing more that mind or muscle or steel could withstand.

The *Houston* and the *Perth* were surrounded by Japanese ships. As they maneuvered to take evasive action, they went from one trap to another. The eight-inch guns roared, the five-inchers boomed, and the pom-poms and machine guns chattered as men took aim at shadowy forms and bright pinpoint flashes from enemy guns. It was hard for them to tell what they were shooting at, but they knew they had to keep firing. Aboard the *Perth*, one seaman looked back at the *Houston*. From her dim shape "was pouring stream after stream of red and blue and amber tracers as though madmen were throwing electric light bulbs across the sky."

The guns were firing in every direction because the enemy targets were on all sides. The fat stationary transports were lined up against the shore, and the Allies' five-inch guns poured shell after shell into them. They hit four fully loaded transports, sinking one immediately. The others beached themselves to avoid going down. Two of these were headquarters ships. General Imamura, commander of the Japanese invasion force, had to jump overboard to save himself.

He floated for about 20 minutes, supporting himself on a piece of wood, before he was rescued by a small boat. The ship he had abandoned was listing. Its tanks, automobiles, and the rest of the cargo on deck slid into the water with a dreadful crash. Imamura was brought ashore, where he sat down on a pile of bamboo to dry off. His aide came over and congratulated him "on his successful landing." The general's reply was not recorded.

The Battle of Sunda Strait had no plan or form or pattern. Ships on both sides heeled over in tight turns to avoid incoming shells, torpedoes, and collisions. Hundreds of shells, thousands of bullets, raked the air. The Japanese launched a total of 87 torpedoes, some of which damaged their own ships. The distances between the enemy vessels ranged from 500 to 5,000 yards. A Japanese destroyer took a hit in her rudder, and a heavy cruiser had her electrical supply knocked out briefly by a shell from the *Houston*'s guns, but up to that point, the two Allied ships had suffered no damage.

At five minutes after midnight the *Perth* took four torpedoes deep in her bowels. As she slowed, eight-inch shells plowed into her from bow to stern.

"That's torn it," Captain Waller said. "Prepare to abandon ship."

The bridge emptied in minutes, except for Waller and two of his officers.

"Let's get off before she turns over," one urged.

Waller would not budge. "Get off the bridge," he ordered.

"I went down the starboard ladder," the officer said. "It was the last time I saw [Captain Waller]. He was not among the survivors."

Waller remained on the bridge, calmly looking down at his silent guns. Right after that the bridge was hit.

The *Houston* was alone, and the Japanese cruisers and destroyers closed in for the kill. But it was not to be a quick and easy victory for them. With so many ships circling in the narrow strait, it was not always clear which one was the *Houston*. It was easier for the *Houston*'s gunners to choose targets. Now that the *Perth* was gone, everything afloat was the enemy.

Destroyers raced in three at a time to fire torpedoes, only to be forced away by a wall of fire from the *Houston*. Captain Rooks maneuvered the ship with great skill, making rapid changes in course and speed. Commander Maher, up in the foretop directing the guns, spotted two torpedoes hurtling toward the stern. He recommended the course change to the bridge and Rooks took the ship right between their wakes. One torpedo passed 10 feet off the port side and the other about 10 yards off the starboard side.

The *Houston's* luck began to run out a few minutes later. A shell crashed into the forecastle and started a fire that burned for 15 minutes before the damage-control party could extinguish it. It lit up the *Houston* like a beacon, and the enemy was able to score several more hits, most of them forward around the blaze. Then something—no one knows if it was a shell or a torpedo—crashed into the after engine room, killing Lieutenant Commander Gingras and his crew instantly. (Forty years later, when Gingras's widow died in Annapolis, Maryland, her daughter carried the ashes to Indonesia and scattered them over the waters at the northern end of Sunda Strait.) Steam escaping through the rents in the deck forced the crews of the after directors and the five-inch gun crews on the boat deck to abandon their stations.

A torpedo struck the *Houston* on her starboard side, damaging the central gunnery plotting room and killing the fire control officer and most of the plotting room personnel. Turrets one and two were forced to go to local control. At 20 minutes past midnight, a shell hit turret two, igniting the powder. The flames that shot up reached higher than the bridge. The crew flooded the magazine for the forward turrets, leaving turret one with only the shells and powder already on hand. There was no more eight-inch ammunition.

Japanese shells struck the *Houston* again, starting a fire up forward. The five-inch guns had run out of shells. The crews loaded and fired the only thing they had left, the star shells. The intercom system was alive with voices, calmly reporting targets, fires, explosions, leaks, the dragging of the inboard prop, the growing devastation.

Gunnery officer Maher described the last moments in his official postwar report.

> The disposition of the enemy vessels was such as
> to completely encircle the *Houston* on all offshore
> bearings. Light patrol and torpedo boats operated

with the transports in Bantam Bay. Enemy planes were overhead. Enemy ships believed to be cruisers or carriers were firing at the *Houston* from about 12,000 yards to seaward. Having established hitting range, they were pouring fire into the ship and causing considerable damage. Destroyers operating in formations of three or four ships were making repeated attacks upon the bows and quarters of the *Houston,* using both guns and torpedoes.

The proximity of the ship to shoal water and the strong current running were additional hazards to maneuvering. . . . All communication systems which were still operative were hopelessly overloaded with reports of damage received, or approaching torpedoes, or new enemy attacks begun, or changes in targets engaged.

Dead and dying men covered the decks topside and jammed narrow passageways and cramped compartments below. A shell exploded in the bake shop, killing a large number of men in the passageway outside. Their bodies were stacked waist high. The forward paint locker was on fire, as was the sick bay and the marines' compartment. The starboard catapult collapsed, crashing across the quarterdeck. The number-two pom-pom received a direct hit, wiping out the entire crew. Flames reached toward the five-inch magazines. The ship was listing dangerously to starboard.

"The Japanese were still pouring shells into the *Houston* as though they feared she would escape them again," said Q. C. Madson. "But the *Houston* was dying. She could not run anymore. Her fight was finished."

At 12:25 on the morning of March 1, 1942, Captain Rooks gave the order to abandon ship.

No man aboard the *Houston* saw the battle as a whole. Combat is too intensely personal for that. It constricts and focuses the senses on only that small part of the fight that a man can see and hear and feel with clarity. Each man experiences the battle as though surrounded by fog. Only that which is close at hand takes on form and substance; the rest is a blur of shadows, sights, and sounds that cannot fully register in the mind.

The Battle of Sunda Strait was different for the throttleman in the engine room than it was for the loader on a five-inch gun, different for the officer in a turret than for the helmsman on the bridge, different for the damage-control parties and the talkers. Some fought the battle alone, others with their crews, but few knew what the last terrible night was like for someone 20 feet away or in a watertight compartment below or in the foretop above. Each man fought in his own world, immersed in his unique moments of courage and terror.

It was only later, when the survivors gathered to compare their recollections, when the officers wrote their reports, that the battle assumed a retrospective unity and cohesion. But while it was being fought, it was a thousand isolated battles.

"One thing I regret," Otto Schwarz said, "is that I never got to see all the things that were happening. All we knew was that we were in one hell of a battle, because we just started shooting everything. Being down where I was [in the eight-inch magazine], we didn't know what we were shooting at, or anything else. The talkers on the telephones could hear all kinds of things going on—'There's another cruiser over there' or 'We hit one over there.' It was really pandemonium. And then we got word to abandon ship. The talker just took his phones off and said, 'Let's get out of here.'"

To air defense officer Galbraith, the battle was all searchlights and targets. "When the Japs turned on a searchlight, we'd have that thing shot out in twenty or thirty seconds. The steam from the after engine room came up around me and I couldn't see anything for about five minutes. The exec came by and said they got one of the engine rooms. Then I got word that there was hardly any ammunition left in the boxes. I reported that to the bridge. Then turret two was hit. We had not been hit at all back where I was, so we were surprised when the word came to abandon ship. People around me said, 'Why in the world are we abandoning ship?' We just didn't know what was going on up forward."

Lieutenant Payne on the bridge saw "a lot of gunfire going off. We started out on the navigation bridge, then we came down to the conning tower. It was pretty damn hot and heavy. It was a case of trying to avoid collisions as much as anything else. When turret two got hit, there was a roaring inferno right there at the bridge for two or three minutes, even on the wings of the conning tower where I was. My God, that was so hot!

"Then we got the torpedo hits. The one back in the after engine room, that was the bad one. It started slowing us down. Then we got another torpedo hit up forward, and about that time we started taking on a list, and that got worse and worse until it was obvious that we weren't going to win this one. Captain Rooks gave the word to abandon ship."

Seaman First Class W. J. Stewart was on the shell deck of turret two when it was hit. "I felt a slight jar from it, and a second later I saw a spark come through where the overhead part of the turret rotates. We knew the turret was on fire then and that if we were to survive we had better start getting out. So all seven of us hit the door at the same time and we got it open. By the time we got the door open, the shell deck was full of fire. When we opened the door, the fire had tremendous pressure and it was just blowing out this door. It was like it was coming out of a blowtorch and it was bouncing off the bulkhead about eight feet in front of us.

"I got my dungarees caught on the door and I thought I wasn't going to make it. But I did get out and got clear. All seven of us got out. As soon as we got into the passageway, a corpsman said, 'Come this way and we'll fix you up.' He took us in one of those little offices where they had mattresses laid down and he gave us each a shot of morphine. I ended up burned black clear to my waist. I had about a third of each ear burned off. Of course my face was burned so that I could hardly open my mouth because my lips and everything were burned. My left arm apparently got burned a little bit worse than the other, but on the palms of both hands I had huge blisters.

"I was numb. I hurt, yes, but it wasn't an excruciating pain like it is if you were taking a knife and cutting a finger. Then about the time we got the morphine, the bugle sounded abandon ship. The medic said, 'You go right down this passageway to the quarterdeck, and you go over the side from there.' "

Far aft of turret two, Marine Pfc Marvin E. "Robbie" Robinson was in the ammunition hoist leading up from the five-inch magazine. "You don't know what's going on down there and you're absolutely so tired and so weary. And you sweat so much. You have no facilities and there's so much sweat and urine on the floor that it's actually measurable. We got down to star shells. That's all we had left. I was so tired. I wanted to lie down so bad, but I couldn't. Then came the call to abandon ship. I was on the phones when it came and I told the boys, 'We've had it.' And somebody said, 'Well, we might as well go topside.' And then we happened to think. We can't go topside. We were battened down there several decks below because the hatches are battened down as you go into your magazine."

Lieutenant Rogers, in charge of the forward five-inch director, got word from the air-defense officer to concentrate his fire on the side away from the main battery. "I tried to, but hell, I couldn't see anything. Occasionally, you'd see a flash of gunfire, but you couldn't get a real range and bearing on it. But we'd train around to where we thought it was and fire a few rounds. I don't know if the five-inch guns ever hit anything, but we did a lot of shooting that night.

"We were just fumbling around in the dark looking for something to shoot at and every now and then thinking we saw something—a shadow or a puff of smoke or a flash of a gun. When turret two was hit, I heard a loud metallic clang and saw a shower of sparks from somewhere on the turret. This was followed almost immediately by a flash of flame that rose higher than my position in sky forward. It didn't burn me or anybody in my director, but we could sure feel the heat of it. It never occurred to any of us to get out of the director. We stayed right there and continued to try to find a target. Then we got word over the phones to abandon ship."

For refusing to abandon his battle station, even though the bridge beneath the director had to be abandoned, Lieutenant Rogers was awarded the Silver Star.

Down in the number-four fireroom, George Detre was another seaman who did not know what was going on topside. "When that torpedo or shell hit in the after engine room, it caused giant sparks to fly into our section, because the engine room was immediately behind us. One of the men was wounded.

He had the habit of rolling his pants up. The paint blew off the bulkhead and it cut his legs just like a knife.

"Then the water disappeared out of the glasses in the boiler and I yelled at the watertender that the water was gone. I went down to the lower level and told them to start the emergency feed pump. The boilers were now white hot. The brick work was literally molten, and it would actually coast from side to side as the ship would roll. As soon as we lost water, there was no hope for that little pump pumping enough water up in there to keep those boilers from burning up. The boilers just melted inside.

"Then they passed the word to abandon ship. Another fellow and I had phones on and we were the last ones out. Believe it or not, we put the phones in the little boxes like we always did. They insisted that you take good care of those things."

Gus Forsman, a pointer on a five-inch gun on the flight deck, said, "The action was so close that you could see Japs on the decks. I know a destroyer went past us one time and we trained on it and I actually saw the people on the decks through the sights. We just fired at anything that came close. Searchlights would come on and we'd immediately train on them and fire on the searchlights. It just kept going like that all the time. It was invigorating to be in a battle line like that where you didn't wait for orders to fire. You just picked a target and fired at it.

"We ran out of ammunition at that time and I remember we had a ready box over there with some star shells in it. One of the crew members, E. C. Humphrey, backed up against this ready box. I remember asking him why he did it and he said, 'Well, I thought I was going to get it, and when I got it, I wanted to go all the way.' He figured that with a shell in his arms, well, he wouldn't be wounded, and he'd have gone all the way.

"We started firing star shells at point-blank range. Then shortly after that, the word was passed over the PA system to abandon ship. I couldn't believe it. It really didn't register. Maybe I was in shock or something, I don't know. I know I went down to the boat deck and I ran across my friend, E. L. McFadden, and he and I stood by the rail and lit up a cigarette."

"We were ready for whatever was going to come," said Bob Fulton, in command of the forward engine room. "When the after engine room got hit, all that really happened to us in the forward engine room was that the engine order telegraphs went haywire. It was like a man with a broken ankle just flopping in all directions. That's what was happening to the pointer on the telegraph. The signal was still for full speed from the bridge so we kept on making full. I tried to reach the after engine room on all three phone systems, but I couldn't get any answer.

"Two or three minutes later, word came down to abandon ship. I sent word back asking for a verification of that order and told the bridge that we were still making full power and that we were in perfectly good shape. After a minute or two, word came back again—yes, abandon ship."

Bill Weissinger was in the ammunition train, carrying shells from the hoist to five-inch gun number one. "I was going back for the third round when [Paul] Blake, the gun captain on gun number three, came over and said, 'Shippy hasn't shown up. I need you over here on gun three.' I jumped in the pointer's seat and started matching pointers. A guy by the name of Black was trainer on gun number one, my regular position, and I looked up and our barrel was pointed right over Black's head. Next thing I know a big orange blast comes out of our gun and I see something go tumbling off Black's shoulders. I hit the sightsetter and said, 'We shot Isaac Black's head off! We shot his head off!' It turned out to be his black flash helmet that was blown off. He couldn't hear for the next two days.

"Suddenly a destroyer was out there with a searchlight and [Robert] O'Brien—he's back there on his 1.1 mount—said, 'Get that son of a bitch.' He opened up, and those tracers just floated out and all of a sudden there was a big flash and you could see the smoke coming out of that searchlight.

"Then I felt someone beating me on the head and shoulders and pulling on me. 'Get off here, damn it. This is my station.' I look around and it's Clair Shippy and he's angry. 'Well, hell, you can have it,' I said, and I crawled off. I was just stepping off the platform onto the deck when this torpedo hit. My foot didn't quite get to the deck and the ship started sliding sideways. I went down on my knees and just when I started to get up, the water started coming down and it just mashed me flat. I thought it would never stop falling. I thought I was going to drown.

"It's funny what kind of reaction you have. I got up and

raised myself on my hands. It was the first time I had ever carried cigarettes on watch. I had just put a fresh pack in my pocket and as I came off the deck I looked down and said, 'Goddamn, my cigarettes got wet.' And that's when they sounded abandon ship."

For Joe Gans, the battle took place in a sealed compartment above the after engine room. "When that torpedo hit, we had nineteen people in our repair party. I don't know where they all went, but there were three of us left. The steam started coming up out of the engine room. We had this big crow's-foot—a big wrench six feet long—and we tried to get it on the steam line. There were two or three valves and we tried to shut them off. That would have kept the steam from going up on the deck. We pulled and pulled but we couldn't turn them, no matter how hard we tried.

"Then I went out of the blower room where these valves were and saw some people trying to open the after engine room watertight doors. 'Don't touch them!' I said. 'Leave them alone.' The people down there in the engine room were finished anyway and if we'd have opened those doors, we'd have killed everybody with all that live steam in there."

Commander Maher, the gunnery officer, had the best view of the battle. "The place was lit up like Times Square on New Year's Eve. The ship was pinpointed in all those searchlights. We were firing at everything, and then turret two was hit. The flames shot up as high as where I was in the foretop. I thought the ship was going to blow up right then and there.

"The directors went out on turret one, and I gave the order to go to local control. I tried to get some ammunition transferred from turret two to turret one, but it was too late for that. And then we had to flood turret one anyway, so that left only the five-inch guns and the 1.1s. I stayed in communication with Captain Rooks and with Galbraith, who was directing the five-inch guns, and stayed on the lookout for torpedoes.

"Then Captain Rooks ordered me down from the foretop. With the turrets gone, I had no more duties. I started down the open ladder and was hit in the neck by a piece of shrapnel, but I didn't think too much of it at the time. I was about halfway down when I saw a torpedo heading toward the ship from starboard. I didn't have time to go back up to the foretop or to get down to the bridge, so I just hung there and watched the torpedo hit directly underneath. I had a very good view of it. I was positive we were going then. The ship began to list heavily to starboard. The order to abandon ship came when I was still hanging on the ladder."

C. D. Smith, the officer in charge of turret two, saw the battle through the tiny slit of his periscope. "As we were loading for the twenty-eighth salvo, with the powder flaps open and the powder bags being passed into the gun chamber, we were hit in the face plate by a dud. The dud penetrated the face plate and broke up. Hot fragments struck the powder bags and set fire to the powder train.

"The fire swept through the gun chamber into the powder pockets and down into the powder circle, but the flameproof wall between the officer's booth and the gun chamber prevented damage to the range finder operators, the booth talker, and myself. After I turned on the sprinkler system, I looked through the glass port to see if I could identify anything, but there was just a red haze as if on a foggy night.

"I saw red particles flying through the air, traveling at high velocity. They struck the glass in the soundproof bulkhead and within ten seconds shattered it. This forced us to abandon the turret. We got clear, far enough to see that there was going to be no explosion. Within about ten seconds after I left, Seaman First Class [Henry S.] Grodzki, who was in the right powder pocket, pulled himself through the powder flap into the gun chamber, unbolted the door into the officer's booth, and came out under his own power. He fell on the communications deck just outside the turret in a badly burned condition. I carried him back into the lee of the radio shack.

"By this time, the flames had abated somewhat and, aided by Lieutenant [Harlan G.] Kirkpatrick, Pay Clerk [R. B.] Thompson, and Gunner's Mate First Class [John A.] Bonkoski, we got the fire hose from the front of radio one and went back into the officer's booth to try to put the fire out. The electrical circuits had not been damaged and the lights were still on. While I played the hose into the gun room, Bonkoski turned the lights out. Within three to four minutes, all the fire had burned down and the turret was dark.

"The fumes forced us to retreat back out through the same way. Reports from survivors indicated that six men from the gun chamber had evidently gotten out through the port door of the turret and escaped in life rafts when abandon ship was sounded. Every one of these men died when they got into the water. Out of the fifty-eight men in turret two, seven of us got to Java.

"There was not much for me to do after the fire was controlled so I made myself useful around the 1.1-inch mount, getting the empties out of the way and throwing them over the side. It might have been two minutes or it might have been a half hour, but shortly after turret two was hit, we received a torpedo hit under the catapult amidships on the starboard side. Then the ship took about a ten-degree list. The ship was listing much worse and losing speed when the captain ordered the ship to be abandoned."

A thousand different battles, most of which will never be known because two-thirds of the men who fought them had been killed or would die in the water or in Japanese prisoner-of-war camps. Most of those who remained alive had only one thought, to get off the ship before she went down.

But a few men seemed to have no intention of leaving the *Houston.* Captain Rooks, said Ensign Smith, "was evidently determined to stay with the ship, because when he came out of the conning tower, he passed several men, shook hands with them, and told them good-bye and good luck."

Back on the boat deck, Seaman First Class Seldon Reese was ready to abandon ship. With him was Boatswain's Mate First Class Theodore F. Sandercook. "I had a great amount of respect and admiration for Sandercook," Reese said, "but Sandercook had been on the Yangtze River and saw the Japanese when they took over there. I wanted to abandon ship with Sandercook and I said to him, 'Let's go, Sandy.' And he said, 'I'm not going to be taken prisoner of war.' He sat down in the gun cut with his headphones on. I was sorry to leave him there, but it was obvious that he was not going.

"There have been many, many times since then that I have wished I had sat right down there with Sandercook."

Leon W. Rogers, an officer in the forward antiaircraft director, reported aboard the USS *Houston* in September 1941. *(Courtesy Leon W. Rogers)*

Radioman Jerry Judson Bunch and his young son, taken in 1939. *(Courtesy Judy Bunch)*

William A. Epstein, the senior medical officer, taken in the early 1950s while serving at the naval hospital in Oakland, California. *(Courtesy Minna Epstein)*

Plan of the USS *Houston. (Courtesy Otto Schwarz)*

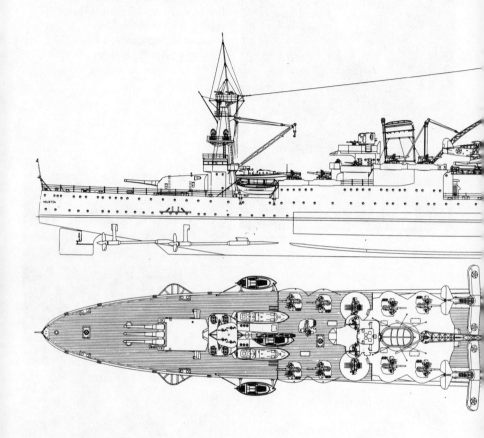

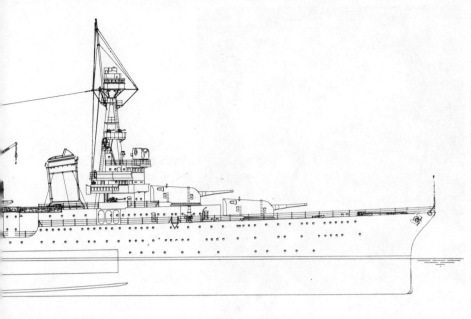

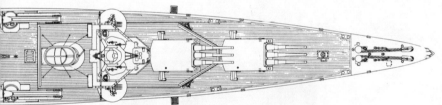

Recruiting poster, 1942. *(Courtesy Cruiser* Houston *Memorial Exhibit, M. D. Anderson Library, University of Houston)*

Vice-Admiral C. E. L.
Helfrich, Royal Netherlands
Navy, commander of allied
naval forces (ABDAFLOAT).
(National Archives)

Thomas B. Payne, the senior
aviator, U.S.N.A. 1931,
taken in 1953 while skipper
of the USS *Valley Forge*.
(Courtesy Thomas B. Payne)

Howard E. Brooks, one of two survivors of the after damage control party in the bombing raid of February 4, taken in 1946. (*Courtesy Howard E. Brooks*)

Jack D. Lamade, U.S.N.A. 1932, taken in 1948 while serving as Operations Officer aboard the carrier USS *Coral Sea*. (*Courtesy Jack D. Lamade*)

Merritt V. Eddy, carpenter's mate, age 22, taken in July 1938 on the forecastle of the USS *Farragut*. (*Courtesy Merritt V. Eddy*)

Lloyd V. Willey, U.S.M.C., taken in January 1946. Willey has been dubbed the *Houston*'s "poet laureate" for capturing in verse the people, events, and emotions of the time. *(Courtesy Lloyd V. Willey)*

James W. Gee, age 21, taken in September 1940 at the Sea School, San Diego Marine Corps Base. *(Courtesy James W. Gee)*

Robert B. Fulton, U.S.N.A. 1932, the assistant engineering officer. *(Courtesy Robert B. Fulton)*

John E. Bartz, pointer on a 1.1 antiaircraft gun, taken on his wedding day, March 12, 1946. *(Courtesy John E. Bartz)*

Philip T. "Joe" Gans, machinist's mate, joined the Navy in 1928 and served aboard a gunboat on the Yangtze River before the war. *(Courtesy Philip T. Gans)*

Lieutenant Payne as a prisoner-of-war in Zentsuji POW camp, August 1942, "before the food began running out." *(Courtesy Thomas B. Payne)*

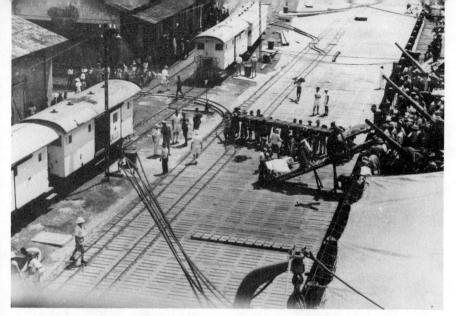

The USS *Marblehead* offloads wounded to a hospital train at Tjilatjap, February 6, 1942. *(National Archives)*

A group of USS *Houston* crewmen shortly after their release from captivity. *(Courtesy Leon W. Rogers)*

The bridge over the River Kwai. *(Courtesy Otto Schwarz)*

The ship's bell, salvaged by Indonesian divers in 1973. *(Courtesy Otto Schwarz)*

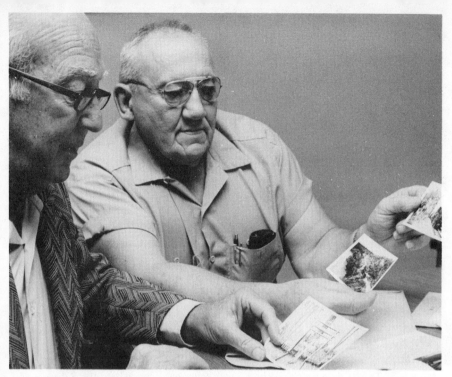

USS *Houston* survivors Leon W. Rogers and L. W. "Dutch" Kooper reminisce on Veterans Day 1982. *(Courtesy* San Diego Union; *Union-Tribune Publishing Company)*

Albert Rooks, the son of Captain Rooks, prepares to place a wreath in the waters of Sunda Strait at a 1981 memorial ceremony. On the right, wearing an American Ex-POW cap, is *Houston* survivor Otto Schwarz. *(Courtesy Otto Schwarz)*

11

The Colors Were Still Flying

The shell was one of hundreds that ripped the *Houston* that night. Like most of the other shells that struck the ship, it killed and maimed members of the crew. But this particular shell did more. This one killed Captain Rooks.

The captain was making his way down the ladder from the signal bridge to the communications deck. On the port side was a 1.1-inch mount. Its crew was firing rapidly at whatever targets they could distinguish in the darkness. Suddenly a shell tore into the gun mount and it exploded in a ball of fire. The crew died instantly. Pieces of steel, sharp, jagged, and deadly, flew through the air, cutting down everyone nearby. A second later, the ammunition in the 1.1 ready box exploded, adding to the carnage.

A piece of shrapnel struck Captain Rooks in the back. He staggered around to the port side of the communications deck and fell within 10 feet of Ensign C. D. Smith, a survivor of turret two. With Smith was Herb Levitt, an ensign in the communications division. They rushed to the captain's side and saw instantly that he would not make it. Blood covered his head, left shoulder, and chest.

"He was too far gone to talk to us," Smith said. "At that stage, I realized it was just a matter of time before he would die, so I injected two tubes of morphine from an emergency first-aid pack which I carried in my belt."

Captain Rooks died a few moments later in Ensign Levitt's arms.

They laid his head down gently on the deck. There was nothing more they could do for him, and there were many other wounded men who needed assistance. Smith and Levitt dressed the wounds of several men and helped them off the sinking ship. One of the Chinese mess stewards was more concerned about being captured by the Japanese than about his wounds, but the young officers found him a life jacket and put him over the side.

Commander David Roberts, the executive officer, and Commander John Hollowell, the ship's navigator, joined them, and a few moments later Commander Maher arrived. Levitt reported that the captain was dead. Maher told the exec that the ship had too much way on and that it was dangerous for the men to abandon ship while she was still moving so fast. Roberts agreed. He passed the word to belay the abandon-ship order and to man the battle stations again.

Some men had already gone overboard. When Charley Pryor had passed on the abandon-ship order to his number-eight five-inch gun crew, one man "jumped overboard immediately. The flight deck where we were is about thirty feet above the waterline. I never heard from him again and I never knew what happened to him."

Almost all of those who went over the side on the first abandon-ship order were lost. They weren't prepared for the swift current that flowed perpetually from the enclosed Java Sea to the Indian Ocean. It swept lifeboats, rafts, and swimmers helplessly through Sunda Strait and out into the ocean, to lingering deaths from heat and dehydration. It would also claim many of those who left the ship later, although they had a slightly better chance because the ship was then nearer to shore.

Minutes after the abandon-ship order was countermanded, a torpedo hit on the starboard side. The ship listed to starboard as much as 25°. The crew of the forward engine room had shut down the engines and left their battle stations in response to the original order, and the *Houston* was almost dead in the water.

The men from the magazines and the other stations below decks were beginning to come topside, and as more shells raked the ship the casualties mounted. Roberts saw that it was hopeless to continue, and he ordered abandon ship again.

"We had a bugler named Jack Lee, a marine," Lloyd Willey said. "I think Jack Lee sounded that second abandon ship. He never missed a note. He was just so clear."

Japanese destroyers were closing in, pouring shells and machine-gun fire into the dying ship. Searchlights illuminated the destruction.

Willey remembered "when the Japs turned all those searchlights on. I think that was the most horrifying moment of all, because you felt really naked." George Detre remarked on all the machine-gun fire topside. "I think we lost an awful lot of men this way. Out of the fireroom, which had probably eighteen men in it, only three of us survived. I had no report of any of them being in the water."

Bill Weissinger noticed something glistening and sparkling all over the water. "It was guys' faces. Two searchlights were being held steady and the other two were sweeping across the water, and the guys' wet faces were reflecting in these lights."

On the bridge, Commander Roberts told Commander Maher to proceed to the forecastle to make sure that all the men up there had life jackets and were getting off the ship. "I asked Roberts what he was going to do," Maher said, "and he told me he would proceed aft to see that all the men were off that part of the ship.

"Roberts said either 'I'll see you later' or 'I'll see you in the water.' I've never been sure, but I never saw him again. I think he may have intended to go down with the ship. Roberts was a fatalist and didn't want to be a prisoner. He was under no illusions regarding Japanese treatment of captured enemy. He had talked to me about it before."

Smith and Levitt finished tending to the men on the bridge, but before they left, they saw someone in the shadows, cradling the body of Captain Rooks. It was Tai Chi-Sah, the captain's Chinese steward, known to all hands as "Buda." Ensign Smith shook his shoulder and said, "Buda, you've got to come with us. The ship is going down." Buda did not seem to hear him. Smith shook him again. Buda gave a loud moan and began to rock the captain gently back and forth, as though he were comforting a sleeping child. He ignored the officers and repeated quietly to himself, "Captain die. *Houston* die. Buda die too."

Other men were determined to flee, but some of those below decks were having a difficult time getting topside. "We were in quite a predicament," Otto Schwarz said, describing his escape from the turret two magazine. "In theory, when you go to abandon ship, there's supposed to be a repair party to open the hatches to let you out. All those hatches are battened down very tightly. Well, no repair party was there to open our hatches. Either they'd been killed or were busy at something else or whatever. I never did find out.

"But we had a mallet which we could use in an emergency to undog the hatch from our side. We let the crew out of the powder magazine inside to our compartment, and then we decided to undog all the hatches and get out of there. I had the mallet in my hand and I opened up the dogs. Of course, when you open up the hatch, you don't know what's on the other side. Maybe that compartment has been hit and is on fire or maybe it's flooded. Each time you open up another hatch, you go through this trauma of not knowing whether you're going to be alive in the next instant.

"We got up okay on the next deck and we started to make our way forward. Everything was filled with smoke and you could hardly breathe. You couldn't see at all. Everything was pitch black with smoke and powder. I hollered back and said, 'Everybody put one hand over your nose and mouth and one hand on the shoulder of the guy in front of you and we'll try to get out.' And I led the way.

"I remember going up another deck. At that point, I felt the guy's hand behind me leave my shoulder. For what reason I don't know, the guy behind me went left toward the port side of the ship, and I continued going forward through those compartments on the starboard side. Then a torpedo hit on the port side and it knocked me unconscious. I found out later that the entire group behind me that had let their hands go off my shoulder were killed by that torpedo. When I came to I knew I was in the marine compartment, because I felt the bulkhead and I could feel their gun rack where they store their rifles. So I knew where I was then and I quickly made my way up topside.

"When I came out onto the deck it was like the Fourth of July at an amusement park. We were dead in the water and it seemed like the Japanese were out there ten feet away with searchlights on us. Stuff was coming at us like crazy. Shells were exploding all over the place. They were raking the decks with machine-gun fire. It was just a duck shoot. They had us surrounded and they were just sitting out there shooting.

"Pieces of teakwood deck were flying in the air and the hot steel was flying all around. I remember a guy named Barrett from my division who knocked me down to the deck and fell on top of me. He had his life jacket on and I guess he figured he could protect me from all this hot shrapnel. When I got up, a guy ran past me and said, 'Here, take this life jacket,' and I took it and put it on."

In the after damage control party, Howard Brooks started to go up on deck when he remembered that his good friend Steve Feuchak was way down in the after steering room. "Steve and another guy had to come up through a manhole from the bottom, at least three decks down. It was just a round thing with a wheel on top of it. So I went back there and whirled that thing and I opened it up and there was Steve just ready to come out." If Brooks had not gone aft to help, Feuchak would not have survived.

Two marines, Jim Gee and Robbie Robinson, were trapped in the after five-inch magazine. Six other men were with them. The hatch was battened down and the man who was supposed to open it from above hadn't come. "Had it not been for a marine corporal, Hugh Faulk," Robinson said, "we would probably have never come out of that magazine. It was not his duty; it was a chief's duty [but] he didn't make it. Hugh Faulk, gun captain on number-seven starboard gun, happened to think of us marines down there. Marines have got a pretty close feeling toward each other."

"He came over and he released us," Jim Gee said. "I'll never forget him sitting up and saying, 'Y'all come on out, and hurry.' He was sitting with his feet in water and this was the second deck of the ship. So we climbed out of the hatch in this five-inch magazine, and there was a water fountain just across from us. I had never been so thirsty in my life because we had been fighting like demons for the last hour. I went over and I said to myself, 'Well, there's not a chance this thing'll work, but I'm going to try it. This may be the last drink I'll ever have.' And the best-tasting, coldest water I've ever had came out of that drinking fountain and that was the last good drink of water I had for a long time.

"Someone yelled, 'Go forward and help with the ammunition.' By the time we got to the first compartment ahead of us, it was nearly waist deep in water and we just backed out, went up on deck, and went on to the forecastle. Two or three of us just stood there and watched for a minute. We were at a tremendous list at the time. Someone had put the flag up on the mast, and the ship was sitting at about a forty-five-degree angle with the front part of her going down. The forecastle was nearly under water."

From all parts of the ship, men were preparing to go into the water, but a few had to attend to some unfinished business first. "I had a good buddy on gun number five," Bill Weissinger said, "and I wanted to find out if he was still alive. The steam was still coming up out of these vents and everything was obscured aft of there. I went through the steam and nearly to the port side and I looked and I didn't recognize anything. I thought I was in a foreign place. I'd spent many an hour on that boat deck scraping and painting, but now it was like no place I'd ever seen before. All our boats were gone and they had thrown empty brass and shell cans there and it was just a big stack of debris. The guns were sitting at all sorts of angles." He never found his buddy.

Lieutenant Leon Rogers and his sky forward crew made their way to the communications deck. Their assigned life raft, number 13, was lashed to the side of the forward stack. "We went down and got the life raft down and were trying to get it over the side and it got hung up. The rope net and slat in the bottom of the raft got caught on an awning stanchion. It must have been thirty feet up in the air on this deck and I wasn't sure what we were going to do with it if we did get it over the side.

"While we were fussing with the thing, I saw a torpedo wake approaching, heading right for us, directly underneath us. It hit, and I don't know whether it knocked me to my knees or I got down on my knees first, standing by for the thing to hit, but I lost interest in that part of the ship. Then we got word for all hands to move aft. We were getting a lot of hits up forward, so I went across the port catapult back to the flight deck, then down one more level to the boat deck. It was time to think about getting off the ship."

Lieutenant Payne, the senior pilot, was trying to go below while everyone else was trying to get topside. His life jacket was in his room. "When I got down to my room, I saw Dr. Burroughs in the next stateroom aft with a couple of very badly wounded people. I went in there to see him and he said, 'My God, I wish I could get some water.' 'I'll try to get you some,' I said, and I went down to the wardroom to see if I could get any from there.

"I overlooked the fact that the stewards always locked up the wardroom whenever they went to battle stations because they didn't want anybody stealing their rice. When I came back to the stateroom, they were all gone. I don't know what happened to them. So I got my life jacket and went back up and walked across the catapult and got the rubber boat out of the airplane.

"As I was on the catapult, a whole salvo of shells came through beneath the catapult, between the catapult and the quarterdeck. There were people there coming out of the watertight door on the starboard side and it just wiped out the whole mess of them. They were all over the place, arms and legs flying through the air. It was awful.

"But there was this one fellow back there on this five-inch gun on the starboard side, all by himself. I yelled at him. 'Hey, you know they've given the word to abandon ship.' And he looked at me and said, 'Goddamn it, Lieutenant, I've got one shell left and I'm gonna fire it.' And he did."

Charley Pryor was heading down to the hangar on the port side looking for a life jacket. They always had a lot of spares there. He reached the passageway just aft of the bake shop and the galley. "Just as I started forward on the starboard side, a salvo of shells came through. I don't know if it was two or three of them, but there was more than one. They ripped through, and of course there was no armor up there, [it was] just like sheet iron. That salvo hit with such force that it knocked me to the deck. When I got up, I thought, Well, a dead man doesn't need a life jacket, and I jumped into the water without one."

*   *   *

Captain Rooks had issued the first order to abandon ship at 12:25. It was countermanded by Commander Roberts four minutes later. The second order to abandon ship was given by the exec at 12:33. Those who waited for the second order had 12 minutes in which to leave the *Houston* safely, for that was all the time she remained afloat.

"There was no point in staying," said assistant engineering officer Bob Fulton. "We might as well get off the ship. We went over on the port side just aft of the catapult tower. Some cargo nets had been rigged there and we just climbed down them and dropped off into the water. I paddled out about a hundred yards from the ship and turned around. It was so bright you could see the ship clearly.

"She was really a beautiful sight. The colors were still flying, flapping in the breeze. I was tempted to go back. She looked so big and she'd been such a good home for so long, so sturdy compared to being out here in the dark in the water, not knowing where you are.

"I actually started back, but I didn't take more than two or three strokes when another salvo hit the ship and the water around her. The shocks from those shells shook me up, so I turned around and started swimming away again until I joined a group of about a dozen people. Ensign Levitt was in the group and I heard him say that the captain had sent out a message to the effect that we were hopelessly engaged. Therefore, the word had gotten out as to what had happened to us and so tomorrow morning we could look for help to arrive. The smart thing to do was to stay and wait. Some people agreed with that and others didn't, but I decided to head for the shore."

Howard Brooks found a life jacket when he got up on deck. "I put that thing on and then I made a big mistake. I took my shoes off. I shouldn't have done that." All the men who removed their shoes regretted it later. They would pay dearly for it in the coming days.

Joe Gans climbed down a rope ladder back on the fantail. "I kept thinking, What the hell am I doing, going in that water? What am I going to do out there? The damn Japs are out there. They're going to kill me anyway. Then I decided to take a chance, but when I got in that water, I wished I'd stayed back on board. The Japs were shooting all over the place. People were screaming and hollering. I watched the ship go down. It was the most beautiful sight I've ever seen with that flag flying. She looked good, but it was really a sorry day for all of us."

Otto Schwarz went over on the port side of the bow. "I knew there was a boat boom there a few feet below the deck level, so I lowered myself onto the boom and jumped in from there. I started to swim as rapidly as I could away from the ship. I remember the sensation of shells exploding in the water. It was like your stomach hitting your backbone. I had one objective in mind and that was to get away from the ship, because the suction would take me down with it. I didn't even look back at it. A lot of guys can tell you vividly of their last glimpse of the ship going under. I can't. I just kept going."

Ray Sparks and Q. C. Madson stood on the starboard side of the quarterdeck. The water was ankle deep on the deck. Madson took off his shoes, placed them at a neat 45° regulation angle, laid his flashlight next to them, and looked at Sparks. "Let's go, kid," he said.

"We floated out there in the water," Madson said, "and watched some of our men on the ship still firing at the Nips. High atop the mainmast, the marine gun crews were still firing their fifty-caliber machine guns. The ship glided off with the searchlights still on her and the Nips still shooting at the old girl. Finally, the stern lifted up high and she slid down so smoothly it surprised us all.

"So we turned around and struck out for a life raft about a quarter of a mile away. Nip shells were still striking the water and exploding, which caused a feeling similar to stomach cramps. It caused us to double up and it hurt like hell in the guts."

Lieutenant Hal Hamlin, turret officer in turret one, went off the *Houston* from the bow. "I was able to slide down without any difficulty because we were listing so far, and when I reached the waterline, I was able to stand on the ship's bottom. As I walked down the bottom toward the keel, I found myself rising out of the water to get over the bulge that the *Houston*'s bow had. I hit the water on the other side of the bulge and gave the best imitation of a torpedo that I could, trying to get away from suction.

"I swam a couple of hundred feet away and turned back to take a look at her. She was full of holes all through the side.

Those close-range destroyer shells had gone right through one side and out the other. Her guns were askew, one turret pointing one way, and another the other, and five-inch guns pointing in all directions.

"There was a big bright flame coming up just about the main-mast and she was listing way over. I couldn't help think what she looked like when I first joined her, when she was the President's yacht. She shone from end to end. As I watched her, she just lay down to die, she just rolled over on her side and the fire went out with a big hiss. I looked at her for a couple of seconds and then began to think of suction and swam for all I was worth."

Jack Smith dove overboard from the starboard side of turret three. "I just dove over headfirst. I had to wait awhile because there were so many people jumping over from there. After I got in the water, the ship went ahead just a little bit, then the Japs started shooting again. There were some slight swells and we were right between the ship and the guy who was shooting, and those shells were hitting the tops of those swells. I kept thinking of my head being up in front of one of those big projectiles."

John Bartz removed his shoes and, like so many others, placed them on deck at the proper angle. "You'd think they were going to come back, the way they were placing their shoes. Then here we were in the water and all of a sudden you hear these guys singing 'California, Here We Come.' And look how far we are out there! This was right after the ship went down and it was just as quiet as a tomb and then we heard this singing. I looked back at the ship and I just could not believe that they could ever sink her. I was crying. I don't know if from fear or from seeing that glorious thing go down like that. We'd been on her a long time and it was our home."

Griff Douglas found that it wasn't easy to jump overboard. "It was pretty black. Just as I jumped, I thought, I'm not sup-posed to jump with a life jacket on. It can break your neck. We were always warned against that in drills. But it was too late then. I'd already jumped. My head just went under and my first-aid bag was wrapped around and it kept my head under so I let it go. I should have held on to it. I needed it later.

"The Japs were still firing. They were shooting over us in the water, but there were some short rounds that hit too close. The ship was on fire and she was listing to starboard and drifting away from me. I just lay there in my life jacket and looked at her. A hell of a sight. People were being blown up in the water and screaming and hollering and trying to get away from her.

"The concussions were awful. They hit close enough to me that I thought I was hit several times. It felt like a bunch of fingers hitting you all at the same time right in the stomach. I didn't know if I was hit or not. Then one shell hit right by me but it didn't go off. I don't know how large it was, but it went *plomp* and I doubled up. If it had gone off, it would have killed me."

George Detre made it topside from the number-four fire-room, found a life jacket, and went to his abandon-ship station on the port side of turret three. "Being a regulation man, I took off my shoes. They used to tell us to always be careful about jumping in the water with a life jacket on, so I jumped in with mine in my arms and I lost it. It stayed on the surface and I went down.

"When I came up, there was a big raft floating there and they had men three or four deep around it. But then I figured that the raft wasn't for me. It was too close to the ship and those shells were hitting the water and creating a tremendous pounding in my body. So I took off until I got out of that area. I said to myself, 'You'd better turn around and watch this. You don't see this every day.' It was just like watching a motion picture. You could see those shells coming and sparks flying. The ship was listed way over. I treaded water for a long time watching until I thought that I'd better do something about survival. By this time there was no one around me. I was all alone in the dark."

Gus Forsman and E. L. McFadden stood for a while by the rail on the boat deck having a cigarette. "When you hit the water," McFadden said, "swim like hell. Get away from the ship."

"We went up to the flight deck," Forsman said, "which was about forty feet above the water, and jumped. When I came up to the surface I lost McFadden. He wasn't anywhere near and I didn't know what happened to him. But I kept swimming like he told me and I heard people in the water. One man hollered out, 'Which way is Long Beach?' Another man asked what time it was.

"There was no panic. The only thing was getting away from the ship and those shells. The first time a shell hit the water I thought I had been hit. I cautiously put my hand down to my stomach to see if I could feel any holes. I kept swimming and I came onto one raft that was really crowded. They had wounded in the inside and people hanging on the outside. I thought that I'd be better off swimming than hanging on to that thing, so I just started swimming toward Java."

Dutch Kooper went off the *Houston* from the boat deck on the port side, just aft of the ladder from the flight deck. "It was hard to believe when I hit that water. It all seemed so unreal. I mean, that ship was my home. So I turned around for one last look and there's my ship. She had a little bit of way on her. I turned around and saw a few heads behind me. The Japs were still shelling the ship and some of the shells were dropping short and suddenly one of them went off and flipped end over end. When I came back to the surface those three heads I had seen bobbing behind me were no longer there.

"The machine guns started firing at us while we were in the water. Every time they'd fire, I'd dive down and I'd look up until the searchlights had passed. There was oil on the surface and I got it all over my eyes and clothes. I didn't look back at the ship again. I was really making knots getting away from her."

Charley Pryor jumped off the port side aft, where the propeller guard was. "Somebody jumped in on top of me and I swallowed fuel oil and saltwater. I was never sicker in all my life than I was most of that night. I vomited and retched and got dry retches after a little while. I couldn't see because of the oil in my eyes.

"Then I had sense enough to ask if there was anybody around who could give me a hand. A couple of guys came to help me. One of them, [Seaman First Class Marvin L.] Bain, swam along with me. He helped me along to a life raft and I hung on to it. Like a fool, I thought I could swim better without my shoes and so I kicked them off. If you ever abandon ship, don't ever kick your shoes off. Keep them. I wish I had."

When Bill Weissinger jumped overboard, he "kept going down and down and down. I never did know when I started up. All of a sudden I broke out of the water and there's a destroyer right there. I looked around, got my bearings, and saw some fellows I recognized in a raft. I started swimming for them. There were thirty-five to forty guys on that thing and there was nothing coordinated. Everybody was jerking and pushing and shoving and finally, through all this commotion, I heard a voice calling out, 'Stroke one two, stroke one two.' It was Henry Nickel, a boatswain's mate. He was out on the end of that raft calling cadence and had them all just about in order when the shells started hitting around us.

"You could see the splashes and feel the concussions. We scattered like a bunch of wild chickens. I swam away from the ship, but I stopped and looked back and they were still firing at her. I saw red rings where the shells went through the hangar deck and no answering fire coming from the *Houston*. I started yelling and cussing. At that time a searchlight came on again and showed the flag on the mainmast still fluttering up there.

"Some more shells fell nearby and I put my head down again and swam for about thirty seconds. When I stopped and looked around it was black. I could hear no one. I could see no one. God, I thought, I'm here by myself. I went into panic. I knew what I was doing, but I couldn't control myself. Then I felt a push on my head and somebody said, 'It's okay, sailor. It's okay.' I straightened up and there's Ensign [Frederick J.] Bourgeois, a real strict guy, but there he was and he was so gentle and nice. He kept saying, 'Take it easy. Everything's going to be okay.'

"A few other people came by and we drifted along, talking about what we were going to do next. Off to one side, we saw a little bit of land, just barely out of the water. It was about a half mile away. The others said, 'Let's head for that.' I saw this big tall mountain over on Java and I said, 'That's where I'm going.' I wanted the big one. We said our farewells and they took off and I never saw any of them again."

Bill Stewart, the badly burned seaman who had survived the hit on turret two, was on the quarterdeck by the port catapult tower. "Me and a bunch of others started climbing down this cargo net somebody had hung over the side. I was pretty close to the bottom, but since the ship was still going toward land, I hung on. Then the ship took another hit and it was a pretty heavy explosion that shook the ship a lot. Everybody hanging on that net was torn loose and went in the water.

"As soon as I hit the water, it seemed like a hundred people landed on top of me. When I got back to the surface, I started swimming away from the ship, and a few minutes later I was by myself out in the water. At that point, I had considerable doubts in my mind whether it was worth trying to go on or whether just to forget about the deal and give up and drown. I knew that with the burns I had, even if I managed to get ashore safely, within the next day or two I would probably give out from what was called at the time 'recurring shock.' But finally I decided that I would keep on going, because if I stayed there, there would not be any doubt about what would happen. So I kept on and started swimming."

Stewart wasn't the only man who considered whether the effort was worth it. Jim Gee took that drink of the best-tasting, coldest water he'd ever had and jumped overboard from the forecastle. With him was Marine Private Floyd I. Owens—"Sheep" Owens everybody called him, because he was from Montana.

"We stayed real close together," Gee said, "and tried to get away from the ship as quickly as possible. After we got far enough away, we just sat in the water and watched the ship go down. And we stayed like that for quite a while, but the Japs kept playing searchlights on the area. We treaded water for I guess an hour until I really became exhausted. I didn't think I could go on any farther.

"The most vivid thing that I remember is the fact that I finally decided mentally that it would be better to go ahead and drown at that point. It would be better to do that than to have the Japs take me. I thought, Well, a lot of them have already gone. There's no need for me to do otherwise. I didn't want to be captured, because so many of my friends were not going to be there. So I decided to just let down right there. And I shall never forget, I did try. I let my head stay under water I don't know how long. My life flashed in front of me just like a kaleidoscope. I saw my mom and dad. And suddenly I had a spurt of energy and I shot out of that water like a torpedo.

"From then on, I never gave up the thought that I had a round-trip ticket home. That really and truly was what I intended to do. I was going back home. From that point, I never wavered one minute in believing that I would make it, and I started looking desperately for a life jacket, a board, anything that would float."

We do not know how many men of the *Houston* survived the actual sinking of the ship, only to die later of burns or injuries in the water, of exhaustion or lack of hope, or from the treacherous currents that bore them through Sunda Strait and abandoned them in the Indian Ocean.

Those who did survive that night spent hours of darkness in the water, with the mountains of Java and the sanctuary they represented appearing tantalizingly close in the moonlight. The brutally swift current swept them across the narrows and back again, bringing some so near to shore that they could count the palm trees. Just as they thought they would be able to reach land, the current carried them out into open water.

Some men spent the entire night alone; others joined fellow survivors hanging on to rafts, fighting off the sleep that could loosen their hold on life. Some were fired on by the Japanese. Others floated so close to enemy ships that they could see the Japanese on deck shouting at them. Some swam away from the ship with their buddies, only to turn around and find them gone. Others greeted friends in the water, passing in opposite directions, as calmly as if they were meeting on a street corner back home.

Some left an overcrowded raft to strike out on their own and in many cases they never saw those in the raft again. Others in rafts watched sailors leave that relative safety to swim for shore, never to be seen again. Some stayed in the water until dawn; others until dusk of the following day. Some were captured in the water, others as soon as they hit the beach, and still others hid out for several days. A small group with Commander William Epstein, the *Houston*'s senior surgeon, reached a small island in the strait and held out for more than three weeks before being taken prisoner.

Despite the random pattern of death and survival, one constant hovered over them all: capture by the Japanese. No one who survived the sinking, the water, or the burns and injuries escaped the enemy. Of 1,064 members of the crew of the USS *Houston*, 368 were captured by the Japanese. These survivors had won their battle of Sunda Strait, but lost their freedom on Java.

The men of the *Houston* remember how tired they were, how hard it was to keep going. "I was exhausted," Charley Pryor said. "We'd been swimming in the water I guess eleven hours. You're just completely beyond exhaustion but you still go on. At a time like that, you've got some reservoir of strength you never know you have until you have to use it. You feel like you can't swim another stroke, but then eleven hours later you're still going."

Bill Stewart recalled "a couple of times while I was swimming—of course, I had had a shot of morphine—I got sleepy and I went to sleep in the water. I don't know how long it was before I woke up and started paddling again. My life jacket held my face up out of the water. I didn't get any water in my lungs and I just kept on swimming."

"I swam," Robbie Robinson said. "How long, I have no way of knowing, because at that point I was already tired, and it wasn't long before I was exhausted. But under those circumstances you've got strength that you don't realize you have. I guess I got my second wind."

They thought about how they were going to be rescued. Some believed that the Dutch military authorities would send rescue boats for them in the morning to take them to land. Others weren't depending on the Dutch but on themselves. "Our intention was to get to the beach as quickly as possible," Q. C. Madson said, "to go to Batavia and get a boat by hook or by crook and get out of there fast."

Commander Maher had the same idea. He and a 19-year-old seaman, R. W. Elam, were heading for shore. "We could see land. Mountains. We kept the mountains in view and we alternated swimming on our backs and doing the crawl. Elam asked what was going to happen to us. I said, 'Forget it. We won't be prisoners. We'll get up in the hills. The Dutch have two hundred and fifty thousand troops. We'll get behind the lines and be in Australia in a couple of days.' This psychological ploy of mine worked for both of us to keep up our morale, but we never saw one Dutch soldier when we got ashore. Nobody did."

Some of the men remember the sound of gunfire after the

ship went down. "Several times in the next couple of hours," said Madson, "we heard the chatter of a machine gun, and a few times in the now bright moonlight we saw a Japanese float plane. Someone on our raft said, 'The dirty bastards are shooting at our men in the water.'"

When Otto Schwarz saw a boat approaching him, he became "very frightened. I knew from what I could hear that the Japanese were machine-gunning men in the water. I decided that the only thing I could do would be to attempt to make them think I was dead already. I tucked my face up underneath the collar of my life jacket and got an air pocket there, and I just bobbed up and down in the water.

"I heard that boat coming up to me. They shut the motors down, just to an idle. I could hear them jabbering away. Then I had the strangest sensation. I could feel a searchlight on me. I felt myself being poked with some sort of hook or pole, then I felt the searchlight go out. The boat started up again and took off and left me.

"Scared? I prayed a lot that night to seek help, but I didn't feel that it did any good. I mean, I really prayed. My life jacket started to cut into my armpits, but I was afraid to let go of it. It was my only, my last hold on life."

The men remember those who died in the water that night. "We had guys on my raft who were severely injured," Howard Brooks said. "Shrapnel wounds and burns. Two or three of the most severely injured went out of their heads. I remember one guy saying, 'Well, I'm gonna go down to the sick bay now,' and he let go and disappeared."

Seldon Reese saw one fellow come by who was screaming and shouting. "I started to swim over to him, but Lieutenant Hamlin told me, 'It's hopeless. He's hysterical. You have very little chance of saving yourself. Let him go.'"

"I came upon an old buddy of mine," Gus Forsman said, "named Joe Dillon. He was from right near my home town and he swam with me for a while. He was behind me and you didn't talk too much in the water like that. I know the next time I talked to him, he wasn't there. I have never known what happened to him, but he wasn't wounded. I don't know whether he got hit by one of the boats that were running back and forth or maybe a shark got him."

Bill Weissinger was hanging on to a raft. "The next thing I know I wake up and it's daylight. You could see for miles and the water was just as slick as a slate top. Here and there we saw islands and we finally figured out they were fuel oil and debris, crates and capsized lifeboats all covered in oil. Isaac Black said, 'Look at that stuff over there. Isn't that a man in there?' It was about two hundred feet away at the edge of one of these islands of debris. He swam over there and we saw him lift the guy's head up. He dropped it and came back to the raft. 'It's [Seaman First Class Alfred] Martinez,' he said. 'He's dead.'"

Chaplain George Rentz died that night, and no one who was on the raft with him will ever forget it. Their makeshift raft, an airplane pontoon, was jammed with wounded men and many others hung on the sides. It was dangerously overloaded and riding too low in the water. More than once, Rentz told the men he would leave so that younger, stronger men would have a better chance. He let go several times and drifted away, but each time someone grabbed him and brought him back.

"He was gasping for breath from exhaustion. He looked around at those closest to him and said, 'You men are young, with your lives ahead of you. I am an old man and I am willing to go.' Before anyone could stop him, he uttered a brief prayer for the others, slipped out of his life jacket, and disappeared."

Jim Gee saw the chaplain remove his life jacket. "He was an older man; he had only about a year before retiring from the Navy. And he did let himself drown. He went under and did not come up. And no one realized what had happened. One minute he was there, and the next minute you look around and you take a head count, and sure enough, he wasn't there. But his life jacket was there, so we knew what had happened. One of the fellows who had been wounded quite badly put it on and we stayed together the rest of the night."

Commander Rentz was awarded a posthumous Navy Cross, for "extraordinary heroism." In June of 1984, a guided missile frigate named the USS *Rentz* was commissioned at Long Beach Naval Station, California, and many *Houston* survivors attended the ceremonies.

The men of the *Houston* remember floating past Japanese ships during the night and the early morning hours. "Sometime during the night," said Q. C. Madson, "three invasion barges full of troops passed us so close that we could hear them talking. Each time they passed us we stopped and kept very still so they would not get us."

At dawn, Lieutenant Rogers found himself alone in the water. He "drifted right down a column of Jap transports that were anchored and sending troops ashore. I was close enough to see the sentries on deck, close enough to see that they were wearing light-colored overalls. I didn't wave and they didn't shoot, so I let it go at that. I was making like a dead man, not moving a muscle, just low in the water."

Griff Douglas was on a raft that was swept "right down through those transports, right alongside of them. Some of our guys left the raft to get hold of their Jacob's ladder, but the Japs would shake them off. They wouldn't let them come aboard."

On Bill Weissinger's raft someone warned about a merchant ship that was bearing down at about 20 knots. "It looked like a mountain. We all scattered and [J. H.] Ben Whaley and I stuck together. After we swam a few strokes, I heard a noise and I saw they had the paravanes strung off this ship. I tried to figure out if that cable was going to miss us and by the time I figured out that it was, it did. The ship passed alongside and it was full of Jap troops standing on the hatches and singing. We cussed them out pretty good as they went by, but I don't guess they heard us."

They remember the deadly current too. Swimming alone, Otto Schwarz heard surf toward morning. "Every time I'd take one stroke forward, I'd go back two strokes because the currents were extremely swift. I just couldn't get anywhere. The best I could do was to stay at one point. This struggle went on for hours."

"We kept trying to make the beach," Seldon Reese said. "We'd look up one minute and we'd be just a slight distance from Java and we knew we were going to make it. The next time we'd look up—there was a little lighthouse out in the center of the strait—and we'd be just a little piece from there. And then we'd go like hell trying to get to that lighthouse. The next time we'd look up, we were just about that close to Sumatra. It was just like a giant whirlpool we were in."

Lieutenant Fulton and a young sailor from the forward engine room "swam all through the night. As it began to get light, we could see how the current was taking us away from where we wanted to head. By midmorning, we finally reached a point about one hundred yards from shore. There was only one more point of land ahead of us. After that, the land receded in a big way. Against my advice, the sailor with me started swimming straight for that point. I never saw him again. I swam to the left to compensate for the current."

During the next day the survivors from Bill Weissinger's raft found themselves close to the beach. "We'd swim in and get about eight hundred feet from the beach and we'd be stopped like there was a fence there. We could not get through that barrier. The current just moved us along down the coast. We just couldn't make it. We started drifting right toward Sumatra on the other side. We came across a crate of onions and managed to break it open and everybody grabbed a couple of onions. They tasted like apples. I never tasted anything so good.

"Our raft floated in toward the beach and then the current caught it and took us out into the strait once again. We crossed that strait three times, back and forth. About five in the afternoon we knew we couldn't make it through another night. Our energy was just giving out."

By dawn of the first morning, many of the men had already been captured, taken in the water. Otto Schwarz was picked up by a Japanese landing barge. "At that point, I was glad to get out of the water. They didn't mistreat us. They just threw us down into the bottom of the barge. We didn't understand what they were saying. We just sat there wondering what was going to happen next.

"I thought I was being brought somewhere to be chopped into pieces. I figured that we had bought it. We were so exhausted that that was it. We had been at battle stations for months, we hadn't had any food, we had fought some fierce battles, and we had just fought the ocean for six or eight hours. I mean, there wasn't another ounce left.

"They took us to the beach and placed us with about sixteen

other survivors. I came out of the water and got rid of my life jacket and I couldn't stand up. I was so exhausted. I spotted a box with Japanese writing on it. I didn't know what it was, but I went over and sat down on it. When I did, a Jap came over and started clobbering me. He beat me and knocked me right off the box."

Jack Smith was taken prisoner about four in the morning. "A landing barge went by me and I hollered, 'Ahoy.' They pulled alongside and I started to get in and one of them knocked the hell out of me. I recognized that they weren't Dutch and they recognized that I wasn't a Jap, so I fought free and jumped back in the water. I figured that was it. I ducked my life jacket and tried to swim under water, but they had the boat hooks out. They looked like spears. And they had a thirty-caliber machine gun on the bow trained on me. I couldn't lose them and they wouldn't leave me, and I got to thinking that they might practice with that thirty, so I swam back in and this time they were real nice to me."

Another landing barge approached Griff Douglas's raft. "There were four or five soldiers with rifles pointed at us and a guy with a machine gun. We believed they'd been sent out there to kill us, because we thought they did not take prisoners. I thought that we didn't have a chance, but they just laughed like hell and went on.

"Then another barge came out and hooked on to us and tried to pull us to the beach. That current was so strong that they couldn't tow us in. They took most of the guys into the barge, and me and about five others stayed on the raft. This time they pulled us to the beach. They lined us up and there was a bunch of Jap soldiers standing out there with rifles. We thought again they were going to kill us, but some Jap officer or sergeant stepped up and said, 'Do not be afraid. You are not going to be killed. You are now prisoners of the Great Dai Nippon Army.'"

Some *Houston* sailors were captured in the water and freed. "The Japanese picked up a whole bunch of us in a motor whale-boat," Seldon Reese said, "then they took us aboard a Japanese transport. They gave us a cigarette and then they kicked us all back over the side."

In Bill Weissinger's group, "Everybody sat down in this barge and the Jap engineer—he was just grinning from ear to ear—came among us and offered us cigarettes. Another Jap yelled out, 'What's your nationality?' Lieutenant [J. F.] Dalton said we were American. 'No,' the Jap said. 'No American. You English. No America. America—boom, boom! San Francisco—boom, boom!'

"He pulled up to one of the transports and motioned for us to stay seated. He went up the gangway and talked to a guy on the ship. Then he came back down, rang the bell, and away we went. We went over to another ship and we did the same thing. This happened four times and the fourth time he came back down and he started yelling. Lieutenant Dalton thought he was talking to him so he stood up, and the other Jap whacked him in the back of his head with a rag. They cut our raft loose and we got the idea right quick that we were supposed to go back to the raft. And that was the last we saw of those Japs."

About 9:30 that morning a landing barge picked up 18 *Houston* survivors, including Jim Gee. "They took us to a Japanese merchant ship and they gave us a bowl of rice and some tea, and that tasted just about like ice cream and cake would now. It was good and we appreciated that. They let us go up into one of the holds of the ship and we lay there and rested and slept. Later they gave us another hot meal and we talked about what they were going to do with us. Were they going to send us back to Japan? Were they going to keep us aboard ship? We figured that the war was not going to last all that long.

"We thought that we were going to have a short stay on that ship and that the Americans were just around the corner. They'd be there any minute and they'd take back that island and we would get out of there free and head back home. It didn't work out that way."

Some of the men of the *Houston* were captured on the beach in the morning. Bill Stewart had reached shore during the night, despite his serious burns, and had fallen asleep on the sand. "Just after daylight I woke up and started looking around me and I saw a rock about fifty feet out in the water. One of our men was sleeping on top of that rock. He woke up shortly after I did and he came ashore and we decided that we had best see if we could get to Batavia and get a ship or an airplane to Australia.

"We started walking down a little road. I would guess the time at around eight or eight-thirty in the morning. We were walking down this road and around the corner and up ahead of us comes a platoon of Japanese soldiers, about twenty or twenty-four of them. We knew there was no point in trying to run. I couldn't run anyway. I did well to stay on my feet. They stopped us there and one of the officers came forward and pulled out his little pistol. He questioned us about the *Houston*. He didn't ask me any questions because I was in pretty bad shape. Then we started marching on down the road."

Gus Forsman and John E. "Pee Wee" Forrester finally reached shore on a little island 100 yards off the Java coast. It was hard work beating the current, and the only way they could keep from being swept back out to sea was to let the incoming waves bring them in, then to dive down and grab hold of a chunk of coral when the waves went out.

"I finally got in to where I could stand up," Forsman said, "and I waded in a little ways. I remember sitting down on a little piece of coral, knee-deep in the water. I sat down there resting and the Japanese jumped out of the bushes and trained their rifles at me. There were about a half dozen of them. I just sat there and they motioned me to come in.

"It was still another twenty or thirty yards into the beach. I happened to think that I had this sheath knife, so I turned my side toward them and slipped it out of my sheath and let it drop in the water. I figured that if they were going to cut my throat, they weren't going to use my knife. They kept motioning me to come in, so finally I went on in. Pee Wee was already lying on the sand there. A Japanese said something to me. Of course, I couldn't understand him, so he bashed me alongside my head with his hand. I have to say that they were very menacing-looking. That was one of the first times I got scared."

Others from the *Houston* reached Java and evaded capture, some for a few hours, some for days. Lieutenant Tommy Payne reached shore shortly after daybreak. "Finally I got to the point where I could stand up, or at least touch ground, because by then I couldn't stand up. My legs were absolutely useless. I had to crawl out of the water. And I looked back and there was Bob Fulton out there and he was having the same trouble. I wanted to go out and help him, but I just couldn't get up. Fulton came in and after we had rested a bit we tried to figure out what to do. There were about nine of us there on the beach."

"We headed for high ground," Fulton said. "We were trying to get to the Dutch lines, wherever they might be. We went about a half mile and saw a group of maybe thirty soldiers across a rice paddy. They were beckoning to us with their fingers pointing down instead of up, the way we would do it, so we flopped down on the ground thinking they were going to shoot us. Nothing happened, so we stood up again. They beckoned downwards again and we laid down again. This went on three or four times.

"Finally I told Tommy that if it was all right with him, I'd go over to the Dutchmen and explain who we were. He said, 'Okay. Go ahead.' I trotted across this rice paddy waving my white undershirt over my head, with my eyes on the ground watching where I was putting my feet. I got right up in front of them, and instead of Dutch faces I found Oriental faces staring at me. The thing that had fooled us was the fact that they wore these pieces of cloth hanging down from the backs of their hats to protect the backs of their necks from sunburn. I'd only seen them in the Dutch army.

"They asked who was out there and if they had any weapons and I told them no. They told me to order them to come in. So I turned and called out to Tommy. 'Tommy, the Japanese says for you to surrender.' I said it real loud and real slow so he would know what was going on."

"They took us back along this road to Bantam Bay," Payne said, "and we could see some of the ships that had been sunk. Since I was the senior officer they took me to interview this Jap general, the commander of the landing force. He was sitting on the side of a hill with his legs crossed, looking like a little Buddha. He started asking me questions about where the battleships were and I told him that there weren't any battleships, and this kept bouncing back and forth, with the general getting madder and madder.

"Finally, I thought he was going to blow up. He was red in the face, just livid. He was yelling and screaming and he told the interpreter to take me away and that they were going to execute me at five in the morning. I figured, Well, that's been a lot of fun, but that's the way it is. The next morning they gave me a shovel and told me to start digging a trench. I thought I was digging my grave. It turned out to be a latrine."

Commander Maher and Seaman Elam landed on a coral reef that morning, a good bit west of where most of the survivors came ashore. After resting for a half hour, they headed inland, looking for the Dutch army troops. They were on the move for three days, climbing higher and higher into the hills. Occasionally, a Javanese native gave them a bit of rice, and then motioned for them to get away quickly. Once they heard the sound of a drum and saw a column of Japanese troops, but they were not spotted.

By the third day they were too exhausted to continue. They came upon some nipa huts, Al Maher said, "and it was getting dark. There was no one there so we went into a hut and fell asleep on the ground. The next thing we knew, the hut was on fire. We got out and sank down on the ground. We were just all in. The natives who had set the hut on fire came at us with machetes and started making whacking motions at me, particularly at my Hamilton wristwatch. I'd had it since the thirties. It was a gift from my wife. I didn't want to give it up, but Elam said they would kill us if I didn't. It wasn't waterproof anyway.

"I thought then maybe the natives would leave us alone, but now they wanted my class ring and they kept whacking at my arm. I said no, and they got madder. Elam said, 'Give them the damn ring, Commander,' and after they got the ring, they left. We rested a bit and then moved on and ran into a group of six or seven *Houston* survivors."

The group included Ensign Herb Levitt. They too had been heading inland and had evaded several Japanese patrols. "The wound in the back of Commander Maher's neck was badly festered," Levitt said, "and he was suffering from fever, but we kept going. In the afternoon—hungry, thirsty, and exhausted—we sat down to rest and were suddenly surrounded by a horde of Jap soldiers."

"The Javanese natives had turned us in," Maher said. "We watched the Japs pay them in money printed for Java. The going rate was one guilder for enlisted men and five for officers."

A Japanese soldier approached Commander Maher. "Do not

be afraid," he said. "We will not harm you. There is plenty of food and cigarettes in the village for you."

"We were bound to each other by a line," Levitt said, "and taken to a village below. When Commander Maher protested about our bonds, he was hit in the face—our first sample of what we were to expect for the next three and a half years."

Lieutenant Leon Rogers reached shore at sunset the next day, with a group of a dozen other *Houston* men. "We found ourselves bending our knees as we waded in because those life jackets had become waterlogged. We saw some natives and they took us to a little nipa hut and gave us some cold tea and a handful of rice. In exhaustion, we laid down in this shack and went to sleep. The next morning, the natives indicated that they would really rather we didn't hang around. So we left and got up on the road and began to see some other stragglers congregating in little groups. We milled around a while and finally decided to go up the road and try to catch up with the Dutch army. The Dutch had felled trees as obstacles for vehicles. They were also damn good obstacles for barefoot survivors trying to get along.

"So we straggled out—about fifty of us by now—and kept fairly well together most of the night. We heard drums, and I remember thinking, This is just like the movies. We went on for three days, losing people who couldn't keep up or who decided to go off in a different direction. Now and then we passed a native shack and motioned for food and water. We'd get a rice ball or a handful of beans, but none of them wanted us to hang around.

"On the fourth of March, a few of us came into this village of Pandeglang. The natives started gathering around us, jabbering amongst themselves and pointing at us. They had bolos and knives and they put us in a pony cart—me and two Australians from the *Perth*—and took us to the Pandeglang city jail. The warden bowed us in, closed the door behind us, and showed us over to cell number one. Within an hour, other stragglers were turned in, among them the ship's bandmaster, George Galyean. Over the next day or two, they kept coming in a few at a time, and pretty soon we had about twenty Americans and thirty Australians.

"The first day in that jail, we saw our first Jap combat soldiers. They came by and looked in our cells. They pointed at us and asked, 'Englander? Hollander? American?' 'Yeah, American,' we said. They got all excited. 'American!' they shouted. 'Baseball! Joe Dimag! Lefty O'Toole! Babe Ruth!' "

Bill Weissinger made a long trek into the mountains, coming across groups of *Houston* and *Perth* survivors. At one time there were nearly 200 of them; at other times he was almost alone. At noon of the second day after the sinking, a few of them reached the top of a mountain where they could look out over Bantam Bay. "We tried to guess where our ship was sunk and we looked at it for a while. I was wishing I had a camera. The only photograph I took was with my eyes. I looked at that scene for a long time."

They wandered from village to village and noticed that the natives were becoming increasingly hostile. In one village they saw about 50 Javanese standing around. "We started walking out of town and we looked out across the rice paddies, and about a quarter of a mile away were some bamboo huts and in front of them was a tall pole with a flag on it. It was a big white banner with a red circle on it. We had never seen a Jap flag before.

"[Seaman Second Class A. J.] Wolos said, 'Hell, I know what that is. That means the Dutch high command is holding a meeting up there.' And one of us said, 'Since you know what it is, you go on up there and tell the Dutchmen we're out here.' So he took off and we sat down and by now a crowd of almost a hundred Javanese had gathered around. They weren't smiling, just murmuring among themselves.

"About twenty minutes later, Wolos comes strolling along like he didn't have a care in the world. He was just walking along, kicking stones. When he got up to us he said, 'It's the Japs and they said if we value our lives we better come in and give ourselves up.' We couldn't go back the other way because the Javanese were there in the road and they weren't friendly at all. There was no way out. The only thing we could do was to give ourselves up."

A petty officer, Lanson H. Harris, said, "Well, this is a military operation and we'll do it in military style. We'll form up in a squad and march in."

"And that's what we did," Weissinger said. "'Hut, two,

three, four' all the way. Ben Whaley and I threw our pocket knives away. Harris had a forty-five. He took that apart and threw the pieces out in the rice paddy. As we marched up, we saw a squad of soldiers up ahead with rifles at port arms. A guy in a gray uniform was standing in the middle of the road with his legs apart and a shiny revolver aimed at us. We got to within twenty feet and Harris called out, 'Detail, halt.' It was just like we were on a parade ground.

"'What nationality are you?' the Jap officer asked. 'American,' Harris answered. 'Are any of you from California?' It turned out the Jap had gone to school at Berkeley. 'How about so-and-so's old gin mill down on such-and-such street?' he wanted to know. 'Is that still there?' They had a regular old home week there for a little bit. Then the Jap said he was going to have to search us.

"Harris called out, 'Detail, open rank,' and the Jap came through and searched us all. When he came to me he reached down in my watch pocket and pulled out a twenty-dollar bill. I didn't even know I had it. I had forgotten all about it. He pulled it out and unrolled it. 'It's been a long time since I've seen one of these,' he said. He rolled it back up and put it back in my pocket. He never took anything from us, and some of us even had watches on.

"He pointed to some trucks and told us to get into one of them. As we got near the trucks, the Jap soldiers were lined up. One of them was a real little fellow and he was fighting with his bolt and his clip, trying to get the thing in. He looked like he'd never had a rifle in his hands before. So Wolos walked over to him, grabbed the rifle out of his hand, put the clip down in the magazine and put a round up in the chamber, handed it back to him and climbed in the truck.

"As I passed the Jap officer, he said he was sorry. I believe he was sincere."

There was no consistency to the way in which the men of the *Houston* were treated when they were captured. Some were beaten and starved from the beginning. Others were given food and cigarettes and treated kindly. Some even received expressions of concern from their captors. But in the years to come, consideration, compassion, and mercy became as rare as decent food and medical treatment.

Even those who were treated well at first faced the shock of becoming prisoners, of seeing their ship go down, and of no longer being free men. That was difficult to accept. Sergeant Pryor was lined up on the beach with several other survivors. "You are prisoners of war," a Japanese officer told them. "Your lives will be spared." Pryor never forgot those words.

"I wouldn't have cared if he had lined me up and shot me then. I'm not brave. I was just so dadblamed disheartened that no matter what they would have done, it wouldn't have bothered me a whole lot.

"All I could see was that I was destroyed. My liberty was gone. Am I really in command of my fate? I thought. Until a man is confronted with a thing like that, he has no conception of what it is. I was heartsick to the point that if they had shot me, I don't think I'd have protested a nickel's worth. I've never felt so miserable and so low in all my life."

12

The Japanese Put
Them There to Die

The survivors of the *Houston* began their captivity in the same
way they would end it three and a half years later, working as
slave laborers for the Japanese. On the first day, March 1, while
some crew members were still in the water trying to reach land
and others were heading inland toward the mountains, at least
half of the survivors were already prisoners. Some, captured in
the water, had been taken aboard Japanese transports in Bantam
Bay. They were the more fortunate ones.

They were put to work right away, unloading gasoline, ammunition, and other supplies from the ships onto barges, but
generally they were treated well. "It wasn't hard work," Jim Gee
said. "They didn't beat us, they didn't push us. Every now and
then they'd give us a break and we'd rest, and they'd give us
some hot tea. We began to think that this really was not going to
be too difficult. We could live like this until our break came. We
kept thinking that it wouldn't be long and we'd be free again."
Most of these men remained aboard the transports for eight days
before their trial of captivity formally began.

The majority of those already captured were not so lucky.
Their ordeal began immediately, on the beach, where they were
forced to unload the barges. They carried heavy boxes, bags, barrels, drums, and crates. The sacks of rice alone weighed 220
pounds each, and the Japanese guards made it clear at the start

that only one man—not two or three—would carry a bag. This was a backbreaking chore for the weary, hungry, dispirited men. They were given no food and little water, and they were not permitted to stop even at sunset. Torches were lit so that they could work well into the night.

The markings on some of the crates and other materiel they were hauling onto the beach made them angry—medical supplies designated "American Red Cross 1922" and Nissan trucks with Goodyear tires. Bob Fulton remembers also carrying cases of newly printed money. "It was impressive to us to see this invading army arrive with currency already printed to replace the Dutch money."

Lieutenant Commander Jack Galbraith protested to the Japanese that the men were "prisoners of war, and as such were not supposed to work for the enemy and contribute to their military effort. I got a poke in the ribs with a bayonet and was told to go back to work." One evening an officer showed up and made a speech saying, "We have decided to sacrifice your lives." Fulton asked if he didn't mean "spare our lives," and he said yes. "We all felt a little bit relieved."

Some of the sailors and marines from the *Houston* were on the beach offloading supplies for three days and nights without being given food and water, although they soon found that they could pilfer a little food from boxes and sacks that had already been damaged. Some got leftovers from the Japanese combat troops. Charley Pryor said that these troops usually broke open their C-rations as soon as they came ashore and ate before they formed up and marched inland. "They'd eat whatever they wanted, and then as they passed by, they'd give us some. That was all we had for that day."

Once the supplies had been brought ashore, the survivors were pressed into service as horses and mules, to replace the animals that had been lost when the transports were sunk. The men loaded the supplies in two-wheeled carts designed to be pulled by horses. A prisoner was placed between the long poles that extended from the front of each cart and ordered to start pulling.

Some carts were a lot heavier than others. George Detre said, "The Japs threw all their packs in there, so this thing was really heaped up. They had ideas of me pulling this cart, so they put me in the shafts and they said, 'Go!' Everybody who was holding the cart let go and I went right up in the air, it was loaded so heavy. I was hanging up there on these bars and that Jap sergeant just laughed. Finally it took eight of them to move that cart."

It was midafternoon when they started out from the beach. The sun beat down mercilessly. The temperature rose well over 100°. The prisoners had few clothes and almost no one was wearing shoes. The surface of the road was macadam.

They hauled the carts for 30 miles with no food, no water, and no rest, for nearly 24 hours. Bob Fulton had been paired with a captured Dutch officer to pull one overloaded cart. "That Dutchman must have weighed two hundred and eighty pounds. It was awfully tough going for him. One time he begged the Japanese guard to shoot him. The Japanese was disgusted with him and made him stand aside, and the Jap and I took turns pulling that cart. The thing rolled smoothly on a paved surface, but the Dutch [army] had destroyed all the bridges, and every time we came to water we had to detour around a rough path. Without shoes, that really hurt the most, because we were walking on sharp stubble."

"There were long periods," Otto Schwarz said, "where we were just at the end of our rope. We'd had only a couple of hours' rest on the beach and no food. The only reason we could continue was because a Jap was prodding us with a bayonet and making very free use of his rifle butt. Every time you looked like you were staggering or stopping, you'd get hit on the head or in the backs of the legs with the rifle butt, or you got poked with the bayonet.

"This went on day and night. We didn't stop, except when the guards got tired, and that would only be for five or ten minutes. At one point I lost consciousness and my last recollection was that I was falling and the Jap was beating me with his rifle butt. I apparently passed out, but he got me going on my feet because later in the morning, I came up to my group again. I had fallen way behind. When they saw me, they said that they thought he had killed me, because they saw me fall and they passed me and then they heard a rifle shot."

Mile after mile the men staggered on. Hour after hour, fading in and out of consciousness. The hot tar burned the soles of their feet, the sun scorched their unprotected bodies, hunger and thirst gnawed at them, and the ever-present bayonets and rifle butts prodded them. Sometimes they passed natives along the roadside. The Javanese would run out in their path and hit them with their fists or with sticks and stones. Rarely did the Japanese guards protect them from these attacks.

The road ended in the town of Serang, about 50 miles west of Batavia, but the nightmare did not end there. The men were taken to an old motion picture house, the Banton Park Theater, and shoved inside. All the seats had been removed. Over 1,000 men—*Houston* and *Perth* survivors, RAF personnel, Dutch naval officers and soldiers, British troops who had escaped from Singapore—were crammed into the building to squat on the concrete floor.

A *Perth* survivor described "the filthy stone floor of the cinema where fifteen hundred men, mostly naked and all near starving, existed in space designed for perhaps five hundred; the reek of wounds and vomit and dry fuel oil and unwashed bodies, and the gray smell of polluted cement; the flies rising like brass bands every time the men used the open-pit latrine in the enclosed courtyard at one side of the cinema; the machine gun watching from the theater balcony; the Japanese officer kicking wounded men and bashing others, and strutting with drawn revolver among the helpless whites, chattering and threatening, like a malignant frog."

The Japanese guards forced the men to sit cross-legged and in silence throughout their waking hours, from 8:00 A.M. to 8:00 P.M. If they moved or talked, they were beaten. Muscles and joints stiffened and skin sores developed as the men were jammed against one another. At night they were allowed to stretch out flat, but the floor was so crowded that they were lying almost one on top of another.

No medical treatment was provided for the burned and wounded men, and the Allied doctors were forbidden to help them. Bill Stewart, the burned survivor of the *Houston*'s turret two, was aided by a doctor from the *Perth* who had managed to obtain some cod liver oil to apply to the burns and help alleviate Stewart's suffering. Stewart felt fortunate in one respect. "I never did get to the point where I couldn't get up and walk outside to go to the privy. One thing that bolstered my courage was the fact that up in one end of the building, there were several men off the *Perth* who had arms and legs badly mangled, and they couldn't get up and walk. They couldn't move and had to be carried. Looking at them, I was glad I wasn't in their shape."

The only consolation to be found in the theater was that there was plenty of water to drink, but there was very little food. Once a day each man received a loaf of bread that measured two-by-two-by-four inches and a one-ounce bowl of rice. Javanese civilians did the cooking, and the food was filthy, full of bugs and dirt, but it was all the survivors had.

Ugliness, misery, and death pervaded the theater, hovering over them like the smell of their own bodies. One night when two *Houston* survivors went to the latrine, an open pit eight feet deep with bamboo slats across it, with legions of flies and an aroma so pungent it made them gag, "one of the guards was on the toilet and he fell in. We left him there. Those people were short anyway and there was no way he could get up. And we weren't about to reach down there and get him."

The *Houston* men lost one of their own in that theater, Marine Corps Private Donald W. Hill. "I hate to say it," fellow marine Robbie Robinson said, "but I guess Don wanted to die. They were feeding us rice and, in between, a small loaf of bread. The bread was pretty ragged, rough stuff. It even had worms in it. Don, on a couple of occasions, remarked, 'This is not the way my mother made bread.' He was right, and of course we marines attempted to huddle close to each other. He was right in the midst of us, and we talked to him and talked to him. But it did no good. He died."

The death of Hill affected the *Houston* men deeply. "He was a nice kid," Q. C. Madson said, "and we wondered how many more of us would go the same way before conditions might improve."

Hill's death turned out to help another *Houston* survivor, Ray Sparks. "I had dysentery and the only thing that saved me was the fact that they wanted a burial party and [Seaman First Class Ross M.] Glover and I were on it. We buried Hill in the mud and water and where we went to bury him, the Dutch gave us some bread and bananas that were constipating. That was great. I was really in bad shape before that."

The survivors endured the awful conditions of the theater for a week before they were moved across town to the Serang city jail. They looked forward to the change, believing that anything would be an improvement. They were wrong.

About conditions at the jail, another *Perth* survivor said, "If I ever go to hell, I don't expect to find anything new there, after Serang." Its gray stone walls were high, water-stained, and spotted with thick moss. The huge rectangular courtyard had a well in the center and sickly, stunted cypress trees at the corners. The cells, which enclosed the courtyard, had thick wooden doors with iron grilles. To this day, the men remember the "twenty, thirty and more exhausted, sick men packed into space for six and eight; the sweet death smell of dried blood and pus and sweat; their own excreta in a cut-down barrel, their only latrine, which they poured through the cell bars into a gutter, already full, which edged the cobbles of the courtyard; the rice, gray and hard and cold, heaped like dirty snow on the cobbles among the fly-blacked filth; the decapitated fish heads among the rice leering up at them with cold glazed eyes; the cup of water daily from the green and almost empty well."

The well in the center of the courtyard quickly became tainted by the excrement that ran into it from the gutters. Dysentery and malaria began to crop up among the men, and by the time they left the Serang jail, 42 days later, most of them had lost anywhere from 20 to 60 pounds. At least one-third had developed crippling dysentery. The Japanese still denied them any medical treatment.

The well was Serang's only source of water. The prisoners repeatedly requested that the water be boiled, but the Japanese refused. No water was available for washing and some of the men were still covered with the heavy, sticky fuel oil from the night the *Houston* had sunk. There was no way to remove it without soap and water.

Javanese convicts in the Serang jail did the cooking. "They mixed raw rice in a concrete bin with a shovel," said Ensign C. D. Smith. "By the time it got to us, it was so sticky that you could turn the plate upside down and not a grain of it would drop out on the floor."

"The Japs fed us twice a day," Sergeant Charley Pryor said, "less than half a canteen cup of rice, which was augmented by a small amount of moldy sweet potato. We had meat once in the forty-two days we were there. The Japs tried to stretch it to make it last over a period of three days, but after the second day it rotted. So on the third day they put it over our rice and made us eat it."

Commander Maher, confined to a cell with 39 other officers—Americans, British, Dutch, and Australians—was suffering from dysentery and the festering neck wound he had received while climbing down from the foretop on the *Houston*'s last night. Lieutenant Payne was also ill. "Here we were," he said, "expected to get well on the same food that made us sick in the first place." The entire jail smelled of disease and death, but it seemed worse in the officers' cell. "Everybody began to complain about the smell of a dead rat," Jack Galbraith said, and finally they realized that the foul odor was from Maher's shrapnel wound. It had become gangrenous. Tommy Payne scrounged an old, rusty razor blade, made an incision in Maher's neck, and dug out the piece of shrapnel.

Maher's condition continued to deteriorate and eventually even the Japanese admitted that he was critically ill. They took him and two others from the cell and marched them through the streets of Serang. The men were so weak that they had to stop to rest every block. They were led to separate cells in a Dutch jail and given a loaf of bread and a couple of pills, the nature of which no one knew. Maher stretched out flat on his back on the concrete floor, all alone.

Some time later, a Japanese doctor visited his cell. "We cannot take care of you," he said. "The military hospital is only for our own wounded." Then he asked if there were someone who could take care of him. Maher remembered seeing Marco Su, one of the *Houston*'s mess stewards, in the Serang jail, and the Japanese brought Su to Maher's cell. They had no additional food or medicine, but Maher had a fifty-cent piece that Jack Galbraith had given him just before he was removed from Serang. "What am I going to do with this?" Maher had asked him. "You never know when you might need it," Galbraith had said. Now, with that fifty-cent piece, Marco Su was able to buy some food. He fashioned a stove from a five-gallon gasoline can and perched outside the cell door to cook. "I can't eat anything," Maher said weakly when Su brought him some chicken. "You'll eat this," Su said. Galbraith's coin saved Commander Maher's life. The two sick men in the other cells died.

On Sunday, April 5, a number of officers were taken from the Serang jail. Fulton was one of those singled out and told he would be leaving. "'Get ready to leave,' the Japs said. Of course there wasn't anything to do to get ready, because we didn't have anything but the clothes we had on." Thirteen officers were assembled, five from the *Perth* and eight from the *Houston*, including Fulton, Maher, Galbraith, Payne, Winslow, Kirkpatrick, Gallagher, and Dalton. They were driven to Batavia, where they were kept for the night in the Black Cat Cafe, and the following morning they were lodged in the forward hold of a ship. This would be their home for the month it would take to reach Japan.

It was on this ship that the *Houston* men encountered a rare instance of humanity and compassion. The Japanese purser, an older man named Masao Nishimura, tried to help them. "He was a good guy," Payne said. "He came down at night to bring us food. He was very much opposed to the war. If it hadn't been for him, our health would have been a lot worse." Maher was so sick that he was not expected to live, but the food brought by the purser helped him regain some strength.

When the ship docked in Saigon, the purser went ashore and bought a little notebook for each of the prisoners. Every day for the rest of the voyage, during the hours the other prisoners were up on deck, said Maher, "he helped teach me Japanese, and I used the notebook to make a Japanese dictionary. The purser said I should learn, because we were going to an interrogation camp where no one spoke English."

At the same time her husband was aboard the ship bound for Japan, Jack Galbraith's wife Gracious was trying to get to see the President of the United States. In Washington, D.C., the spunky Mrs. Galbraith, a reporter for the Knoxville, Tennessee, *Journal*, wanted to straighten out a problem that had arisen over her husband's allotment checks. When she asked Navy Department officials if she could speak with Roosevelt, they refused. She went to the main gate of the White House and asked the guards for an audience with the President, explaining that her husband had served on the *Houston*. She hoped to find out if President Roosevelt could offer her any news, any hope about the fate of the ship and her crew. The White House guards told her it would be impossible to see the President.

With that, Mrs. Galbraith marched across the street to a drugstore and, for the price of a nickel telephone call to Stephen Early, Roosevelt's press secretary, she obtained an appointment. The next morning she was shown into the Oval Office. "The President shook my hand very dramatically, held it for a long time, and kept me for a good ten minutes. He looked dreadful. His eyes were so sunken.

"'Oh, my dear ship,' he said. 'I lost so many good friends aboard her.'

"He asked me what I had heard from my husband before the ship was lost and I said, 'Mr. President, he didn't have time to write a decent letter, just tiny little snatches of notes. He just wrote me to keep my chin up and to get some help for them out there. "We don't have radar and we don't have anything to work with," he wrote. "For goodness sake, get us something out here so we can do something."'

"'That was my favorite ship,' President Roosevelt said. 'Now you be a brave girl. There were over a thousand men on that ship and I have the feeling that some of them are bound to be safe. But if we know the Japanese, you're not going to hear anything for a long time. It's going to be tough, and don't you expect to hear for a long time.'"

Mrs. Galbraith also went to see Admiral Glassford, who had recently returned to the States from Java. "It shouldn't have been," he said. "It shouldn't have been." The Red Cross was not encouraging either. "You might as well face it," she was told. "The ship was against overwhelming odds. There's no hope."

Finally Mrs. Galbraith visited Admiral Hart at his estate in Connecticut. "He walked me around that farm so hard I was ready to drop," she said. "And people said he was sick and that

was why he had to be relieved!" The admiral was extremely solic-
itous and he also revealed how greatly the loss of the *Houston* and
the rest of the Asiatic Fleet had affected him personally.

"You know, Gracious," he said, "I'm an old man. I've had a
good life. I've had a good run in the Navy. But those young fellows—that's what nearly kills me. To leave those young fellows
out there."

On April 15, 1942, the men of the *Houston* were transported
from the Serang jail to a camp in the heart of the city of Batavia. It
was called the Bicycle Camp, because it had previously housed
the Tenth Battalion Bicycle Force of the Netherlands East Indies
Army. It was now a prison camp—there was no mistaking that—
a square city block area surrounded by nine-foot-high stone walls
with broken glass embedded in the top.

Because it had been an army base, however, the surroundings and the seven long barracks were neat and clean. The buildings offered running water and electricity. Compared to Serang,
Bicycle Camp was paradise. Otto Schwarz called it "a Hilton of
prison camps." The quarters had been solidly constructed of masonry. Inside, each cubicle housed four men. The latrines were
also modern and clean and each barracks contained bathing facilities. For the first time since their capture, the men could attempt
to clean the oil off their bodies.

About 200 prisoners were already established in Bicycle
Camp before the group from Serang arrived. Most of these were
Australian soldiers, but there were a few *Houston* survivors
among them. As Q. C. Madson climbed down from the truck that
had brought him to Bicycle Camp, the first person he saw was
Ray Sparks. "Sparks was crying and I asked him what the matter
was. The reason, he said, was because we all looked so skinny,
pale, sick, and dirty. He gave me his mess gear and showed me
where I could get something to eat."

The Australian prisoners were also generous to the arrivals
from Serang. They shared their clothing and all the other items
essential to prison camp life such as spoons, forks, and mess kits.
The men soon began to feel like human beings again.

Despite their weakened condition, the *Houston* men immediately set about to make themselves comfortable in their new

surroundings. The barracks were indeed clean, but they were also empty of furniture. There were no beds or chairs or tables. With ingenuity and surprising energy, they worked and scrounged to make their lives a little better.

"For the next three days," Madson said, "the barracks was a bedlam of noise and a beehive of activity, with everyone building bunks and tables and chairs." Schwarz said, "It was amazing what human beings can do and are capable of learning to do under adverse conditions."

"Upon our arrival," Madson added, "there was a fairly new car parked in front of our barracks and gradually it disintegrated until all that was left were the chassis, engine, and a few body parts. The disintegration process took only three days. The first parts to go were the reflectors in the headlights and the hub caps. They made very serviceable mess tins, deep enough to hold plenty of rice. The car windows were used as table tops. With bamboo frames and legs, they were very serviceable. Doors were removed and frying pans, plates, and spoons were cut from the metal with hammer and chisel, then hammered into the desired shape. The car seats, of course, were moved into our cubicles for comfort. The car mirrors were taken to simplify shaving, and the rubber tires were made into sandals, with straps cut from the inner tubes. Oil drained from the engine and transmission was used as fuel for homemade lamps.

"A few days after our arrival, a stake-body truck pulled into the camp and ran out of gas in front of our barracks. The driver made it known that he would be back the next morning to move it. By the time he arrived the following morning, the truck was so far gone that he just shrugged his shoulders and walked out of the camp."

Everyone had become increasingly optimistic that the war would end soon and they would be freed. "The war's going to be over in nothing flat," John Bartz said. "Our attitude was that we weren't going to be here very long," Merritt Eddy said. Rumors passed that the Americans had already landed in Java and would be coming through the prison camp gate any day now.

And sure enough, three weeks later, the main gate opened and there stood a battalion of American troops in full uniform.

They were the Second Battalion, 131st Field Artillery, a National Guard outfit from Texas.

It was like Christmas, a festival, when these fresh, well-provisioned prisoners arrived. They endeared themselves forever to the Bicycle Camp captives. They immediately sized up the situation and distributed their extra supplies and equipment among the men. The soldiers offered shoes, uniforms, hats, even money for the extra food that was available on the black market flourishing outside the camp gates. In many cases, their generosity meant the difference between life and death for the prisoners.

Back home in Texas, the 131st came to be known as the "Lost Battalion." It was an antiaircraft unit that had been landed in Java by mistake and had been captured intact, while its men were still in good condition. The Texans and the *Houston* survivors became so close in Bicycle Camp that their special relationship continues today. The annual reunions of their survivors' associations are held jointly in Texas. These men formed an unbreakable bond, based on their shared experiences in captivity.

Life became more bearable and a daily routine was forged. The Japanese camp commandant, Colonel Suzuki, was keen on sports, and he gave the men volleyballs and nets. The Aussies and the Yanks organized a tournament and Suzuki provided a trophy. A theater group called the "Pow-wows" sprang up and performed monthly shows featuring dancing girls. "How could eight blond wigs be found in a prisoner-of-war camp," Q. C. Madson said, "or dresses for those beauties, or brassieres and panties? Somehow they always came up with the items they needed to put on a show complete with lighting, scenery, and curtains on the stage." The camp commandant and his staff enjoyed the shows as much as did the prisoners.

The men instituted courses on a wide range of topics—navigation, higher mathematics, Spanish, French, basic electricity, even dancing. Lieutenants Leon Rogers and Hal Hamlin compiled action reports of the *Houston*'s last battle.

Formal naval organization was established and discipline was maintained. Two courts-martial were held for minor offenses such as disobedience of orders. Rogers overheard some *Houston* seamen talking shortly after the proceedings. "Hey, can they do that?" one asked. "Damn right they can," the other said. "You're still in the United States Navy."

"When we came out at the end of the war," Rogers said, "we were still a military organization, not just a bunch of rabble. This was the USS *Houston* detachment."

Life in Bicycle Camp was an oasis in time that enabled the men to recover their strength after the weeks at battle stations, the sinking, and the deplorable conditions at Serang. They would soon need to call upon this strength. But while life may have been tolerable, they remained prisoners of war, and the Japanese never let them forget it. They were expected to come to attention and bow whenever a Japanese guard walked by. If they did not, or if they responded too slowly or in what the guard regarded as an improper manner, they were beaten.

Sometimes the guards wandered into the barracks and chose men at random for a beating. A particularly brutal guard, nicknamed "Brown Bomber," carried a bamboo rod or an iron pipe and would hit anyone he found lying in a bunk. When an Australian sailor once failed to salute him, the Brown Bomber beat the man unconscious with his rifle butt.

On the 14th of June, the Japanese guards informed the prisoners that they would have to sign an oath swearing that they would not attempt to escape. All the men refused and nothing more was said about it for three weeks. On July 3, the Japanese reacted. Rations were cut by one-third. The camp canteen, where the men had been able to buy extra food, was closed. Purchases of food and medical supplies outside the camp were stopped. The guards became more brutal, striking the prisoners with fists, rifle butts, and hobnailed boots much more frequently than before.

The next day, all the senior officers were led away and locked in the guardhouse. Then the junior officers were marched out of camp, to be imprisoned in a garage. Ensign C. D. Smith said that "the Japanese made a great show of loading their rifles and cocking their pieces as if they thought they could bully us into doing things by force."

With the officers out of the way, Colonel Suzuki assembled the enlisted prisoners and told them that their officers would be shot unless the enlisted men signed the oath by seven that night. The senior warrant officers met and decided that, since the signing of the oath was being forced upon them under duress, it would not be binding. Therefore, it was all right for the men to sign it. By 6:30 the officers were informed that the men had signed the oath. The senior Allied officer, Australian Army Brigadier A. S. Blackman, advised the officers to go ahead and sign also, agreeing that it would not be binding because it had been signed under pressure.

A number of the prisoners volunteered for work parties outside the camp. This provided an excellent opportunity to scrounge for food and other supplies, although anyone who was caught was severely punished. One *Houston* marine and four Australian soldiers who were found to have liquor in their possession when they returned to camp were beaten with bamboo clubs and made to stand at attention for an entire day. Signs were pinned on their clothes: "These men have stolen many things from working parties." If they fell, they were beaten until they stood up again.

Late in the summer, Colonel Suzuki was replaced, and the new commandant's approach was much harsher. But in the middle of October, the *Houston* sailors and marines and the other Bicycle Camp prisoners were taken to the port of Batavia and loaded on a ship for Singapore. Although the men were curious and a little apprehensive about their next stop, no one imagined how much worse it would be.

The people in the United States had not forgotten the *Houston*. Families and friends anxiously awaited word of their men, but none came. Meanwhile, the city of Houston, Texas, and the Navy prepared to honor the ship and her crew.

On Memorial Day 1942, a crowd of 150,000 people gathered outside the Loew's Theater in downtown Houston before a 60-foot-long replica of the USS *Houston*. The citizens had come to pay homage to the fallen ship and crew and to help launch a new one. A light cruiser already under construction had been designated as the new USS *Houston*. Texans had purchased $85 million worth of war bonds to pay for her. The amount thus raised also funded a new aircraft carrier, the USS *San Jacinto*.

The people of Houston assembled on Memorial Day not only to contribute their money; they were giving their sons as well. A

19-day drive to recruit 1,000 men for the Navy to replace those lost on the *Houston* brought a response from 1,600 young Texans who were sworn in during the Memorial Day ceremonies. More had tried to volunteer, but the Navy recruiters were so overwhelmed with the paperwork that the applications could not all be processed in time.

Six newsreel companies covered the proceedings, capturing Admiral Glassford on film as his emotions overcame him at the end of his speech. "The last admiral of the *Houston* salutes you," he said in a choking voice. The events were broadcast over 115 radio stations in the United States and carried by CBS over shortwave to the armed forces overseas.

The high point came when Glassford read a letter from President Roosevelt:

"On this Memorial Day, all America joins with you who are gathered in proud tribute to a great ship and a gallant company of American officers and men. That fighting ship and those fighting Americans shall live forever in our hearts.

"I knew that ship and loved her. Her officers and men were my friends.

"When men and ship went down, still fighting, they did not go down in defeat. . . . The officers and men of the USS *Houston* drove a hard bargain. They sold their liberty and their lives most dearly.

"The spirit of these officers and men is still alive. That is being proved today in Houston, in all of Texas, in all of America. Not one of us doubts that the thousand volunteers of recruits, sworn in today, will carry on with the same determined spirit shown by the gallant men who have gone before them. Not one of us doubts that every true Texan, and every true American, will back up these new fighting men, and all our fighting men, with all our hearts and with all our efforts.

"Our enemies have given us the chance to prove that there will be another *Houston*—and yet another *Houston*, if that becomes necessary, and still another *Houston*, as long as American ideals are in jeopardy. . . .

"The officers and men of the USS *Houston* have placed us all in their debt by winning a part of the victory which is our common goal. Reverently, and with all humility, we acknowledge this debt. To those officers and men, wherever they may be, we give our solemn pledge that this debt will be paid in full."

Following the ceremonies, the new recruits marched through the city to the train station to board five special trains bound for the Naval Training Station at San Diego, California.

President Roosevelt issued a Presidential Unit Citation to the USS *Houston*, and on June 24, Secretary of the Navy Frank Knox awarded the Medal of Honor posthumously to Captain Rooks, "for extraordinary heroism, outstanding courage, gallantry in action, and distinguished service in the line of his profession." The medal was given to the captain's elder son, Harold. The memory of the *Houston* was very much alive.

The new USS *Houston* was formally launched on June 19, 1943, at Newport News, Virginia. Captain Rooks's widow, Edith Redfield Rooks, attended the reception along with a number of officials from the embassy of the Netherlands. In conversation with the Dutch representatives, she said that she thought it was a shame that so many well-trained officers and men had been sacrificed against such superior odds in the fighting around Java. A Dutch official took offense. "It is never a sacrifice to give one's life in defense of Dutch territory," he snapped.

Upon Mrs. Rooks's return to her home in Seattle, Washington, she received a letter from the Dutch ambassador in Washington requesting that she return the Queen Wilhelmina Cross that the Dutch government had earlier bestowed on Captain Rooks.

The prisoners reached Singapore after a harrowing five-day voyage from Java, cooped up in the holds of a Japanese freighter, the *Dai Nichi Maru*. They had been issued little water and two meager meals of rice and stew each day. Sleep was difficult because the men were so tightly packed together that they could not all lie down at the same time. The holds were filthy, infested with rats and other vermin, and most of the men developed skin rashes by the time they reached port.

For nearly three months, their camp would be Changi Barracks, a former British army post on the southern end of the island. Thousands of British troops were interned there. The food was poor and the men soon showed symptoms of dysentery and malnutrition.

What annoyed the men of the *Houston* more during their time at Changi was the attitude and behavior of the British. They were in charge of the administration of the camp, under the supervision of the Japanese. The Englishmen "created an intensely unfavorable impression with the Americans due to their overbearing, egotistical manner," said Charley Pryor. They referred to the new arrivals as "the Java rabble."

"There was plenty of food," said Robbie Robinson, "but we were not given our share by the English who were in charge. We were a minority all the way through, and the English always had the say. Our ration was two pints of rice a day cooked by the English."

Some of the *Houston* marines were invited to attend a party hosted by the Royal Marines. They were amazed to be served European-style food, things they had not seen in months. And when Lloyd Willey was hospitalized to have his eyes treated, he was brought dinner by an English major. The tray contained meat, bread, and cheese, none of which the other American prisoners ever received during their months in Singapore.

Red Cross shipments arrived at Changi, but the British withheld them from the Americans. The British explanation was that the *Houston* men would be leaving soon, so their Red Cross packages had been forwarded to Burma. The senior American officers of "the Java rabble" protested to the British leaders about this unfair treatment, but it did no good.

Similar inequities applied to work, which involved clearing a rubber plantation, under British supervision, to plant vegetables. The labor was compulsory for the American prisoners of war, but not for the British. "Many a morning," Charley Pryor said, "as we passed the English barracks on our way to work, we saw their troops just getting up."

The friction that developed between the two groups of prisoners occasionally erupted in fistfights. Once, some in the Java contingent shot rocks at the British officers' barracks with slingshots. They were caught and put in chains, but were released later after vociferous protest.

John Bartz recalls that the *Houston* men stole some of

"General Percival's chickens. We'd tear the heads off and leave them there. The British would come running up to our camp and want to know which one of the bloody Yanks took the general's chickens."

For the most part, the Japanese left the Java contingent alone while they were at Changi. That was fortunate. The *Houston* men and the rest of the Java prisoners had enough trouble dealing with their British allies.

The eight *Houston* officers who had been taken by ship from Serang arrived in a little town outside of Tokyo, Japan, called Ofuna. It was also known as the "Hollywood" of Japan because it had been the home of a fledgling movie industry. Their camp was about 100 yards square, encircled by a high board fence. It was not a prisoner-of-war camp. That was made explicit on their first day.

The Japanese lined the men up and confiscated the notebook-dictionaries they had so carefully compiled during the voyage north. The commandant said, "You are not prisoners of war as long as you are in this camp. We picked you up out of the water and we can throw you back any time we want to." The men were placed in individual cells and instructed not to talk to one another. The penalty for disobedience was a beating.

Ofuna was an interrogation camp. "Questioners came down from Tokyo," said Lieutenant Tommy Payne, the *Houston*'s senior aviator, "and asked all these funny questions, like what our future plans were for winning the war. None of us knew anything, so it was sort of a futile exercise. But they would go through this same set of questions over and over again, and if there was the slightest divergence in your answers from one time to the next, they'd beat the hell out of you. Of course, sometimes they figured it was a good idea to beat you up anyway.

"They wanted me to tell them about the fortifications on Midway. I said there was nothing on Midway, just a bunch of sand and a whole bunch of gooney birds. Then I started talking about how the gooney birds fly and about the little crabs and the big crabs, and they got disenchanted with that after a while. I was only questioned that one time, and they must have decided that I was such a disappointment that there was no point in continuing. Still, I stayed there about three months."

Lieutenant Bob Fulton, the *Houston's* assistant engineering officer, was kept at Ofuna for more than 100 days before being questioned. "They wanted to know the engineering characteristics of the ship. Well, I had had nothing to do for day after day but lie there and cook up phony sets of figures. That's what saved me when I was finally questioned, because if you appeared unresponsive, they'd beat you up and throw you into solitary for a week, then drag you back and ask you the same questions."

The camp was run by a tough Japanese navy warrant officer who was contemptuous of the Americans for having allowed themselves to be captured. He took particular delight in describing the number of Chinese he had decapitated. To the *Houston's* gunnery officer, Al Maher, the commandant was a "tough SOB who wanted to be out to sea, but he did help me with my Japanese. He returned my notebook when he saw the Japanese writing in it. Many afternoons he would sit outside my cell with his arms folded. He would never look at me. He would say a word in Japanese and I would respond with the English word. I learned maybe one word each session."

One by one the prisoners were sent from Ofuna to regular prisoner-of-war camps elsewhere in Japan. Finally, of the original group, only Commander Maher remained. Questioned and beaten regularly and kept essentially in solitary confinement, he was held captive at Ofuna for 19 months without adequate food, clothing, or medical attention. Maher suffered from severe malnutrition and dysentery and his weight dropped to no more than 100 pounds.

During this time, Maher made extraordinary efforts to help each new prisoner brought to the camp for questioning. Because of his diligence in learning the Japanese language, he became the liaison officer between the prisoners and the Japanese at Ofuna and later at Omori, another camp near Tokyo where he spent the rest of the war. Despite frequent beatings, Maher continued to press the Japanese to improve the awful living conditions, and sometimes he succeeded. As senior officer at Omori, he was responsible for maintaining order among some 600 American, British, Dutch, Australian, Norwegian, and Javanese prisoners of war. He also attempted to persuade the Japanese that the prisoners could administer the camp themselves, under Japanese supervision.

After the war, Maher was awarded the Legion of Merit and the Navy and Marine Corps Medal for his actions in improving the lot of his fellow prisoners. He has said that of all his awards and decorations in a long career in the Navy, "I am proudest of the medals I got for being in command of the prison camps."

The other *Houston* officers who had been at Ofuna were sent to the Zentsuji prisoner-of-war camp, where most of them remained for the duration of the war. The *Houston's* air defense officer, Lieutenant Commander Jack Galbraith, assumed command of the American prisoner contingent. He was later awarded the Bronze Star for his "heroic service in persuading the Japanese to alleviate the situation for all prisoners." Lieutenant Tommy Payne received the Commendation Ribbon for his actions in helping a group of officers from Bataan, who arrived at the camp in wretched condition, "covered with vermin and afflicted with various diseases." Payne "voluntarily quarantined himself to assist the doctors in rendering medical treatment. With no thought for his own safety, he served as a nurse throughout the entire quarantine period."

The majority of the *Houston* survivors departed Changi prison in Singapore on January 16, 1943, bound for Burma, to help build a railroad that would later become well known because its route took it across a river called the Kwai. The rail line stretched from Burma to Thailand and was constructed at the cost of a staggering number of lives. Working with no tools save shovels and axes, and baskets to haul away the dirt, 61,000 Allied prisoners of war and 300,000 native laborers completed this most complex of construction projects through one of the world's most inhospitable terrains.

The conditions were appalling—little food and medical treatment, temperatures in excess of 100°, muddy monsoon weather, malarial swamps. The men worked 12- to 18-hour days, hacking out the trail, laying the rails, and building the bridges by hand. The Japanese and Korean guards regularly beat them, almost to the point of death, forcing them on a foot at a time, a yard at a time, through the jungle, over the fast-flowing rivers and deep crevices.

The railway project took a little over one year. For each of the 250 miles of track laid, 400 men died. Up to 90,000 native workers and 12,399 American, British, Dutch, and Australian prisoners of war never came out of the jungle alive.

The *Houston* men, the soldiers of the Lost Battalion, and a large contingent of Dutch and Australian prisoners from Changi were sent to join the builders of this infamous railroad. The *Houston* group numbered 220 officers and men. Some, too ill to be moved, were left at Changi. Others, the skilled workers such as carpenters and electricians, had already been taken to Japan.

The group had a difficult time reaching Burma. Two freighters laden with the prisoners were attacked 50 miles off the Burma coast by four U.S. B-24 Liberator bombers. The planes sank one ship, killing 40 Dutch prisoners and about 500 Japanese troops, but they did not hit the ship with the *Houston* prisoners.

The transport docked at Moulmein on January 27 and the men were confined to a jail reminiscent of the one at Serang. The facilities were deplorable and it was not long before dysentery was rampant again. After a week they were moved to the town of Thanbuyzat, about 25 miles to the south, the base camp for the railroad, and from there went immediately to the first work camp, the 18 Kilo Camp (it was 18 kilometers from the base camp).

The Japanese made known their intention to complete the railway regardless of the human cost. When work had started in October 1942, Lieutenant Colonel Nagatomo had delivered a long speech to the first batch of prisoner-slaves at Thanbuyzat. "We will build the railroad if we have to build it over the white man's body. It gives me great pleasure to have a fast-moving defeated nation in my power. You are merely rubble . . . and there will be many of you who will not see your homes again. Work cheerfully at my command. . . . By the hand of the Nippon Army Railway Construction Corps to connect Thailand and Burma, the work has started, to the great interest of the world. There are deep jungles where no man has ever come to clear them by cutting the trees. There are also countless difficulties and suffering, but you shall have the honor to join in this great work which was never done before, and you shall also do your best effort. I shall investigate and check carefully."

The *Houston* survivors were thrust into the "great work" as soon as they reached the 18 Kilo Camp. Each man was required to dig 1.2 cubic meters of earth per day. To Lieutenant Leon Rogers, "the backbreaking days of labor merged together in a blur. We'd have rice and stew—with meat sometimes—for breakfast. Then about seven every morning we'd be marched out of camp to the construction site. Each man was given a work allocation for the day. We stayed there—sometimes up to eighteen hours a day in a hundred-and-seventeen-degree heat—until everyone was finished. Then we'd march back to camp for another bowl of rice and stew or occasionally dried fish heads and cooked seaweed."

Using rudimentary spades and picks, the men had to build up the roadbeds and level them by tearing down the high ground and filling up the low ground. Tons of earth were carried in small baskets or on stretchers made out of rice sacks tied to long bamboo poles. The men crawled through ravines, up mountain slopes, across raging rivers.

Dutch Kooper marvels that he ever got out of those jungles alive. Death was all around him. He saw close friends die from disease and brutal treatment and he suffered, as most of them did, the often fatal combination of malaria, dysentery, and yellow jaundice. But like the others, he staggered on, hauling dirt, felling trees, and laying track.

Any man who stopped was slapped or hit in the head with a rifle butt. When he had been a loader on the *Houston*'s five-inch guns, Kooper had weighed 220 pounds. Now he weighed 160, and finally one day he slumped to the ground. He was allowed to stay in camp for five days. No extra food, no medicine except for a little bit of quinine, and then he was back on the line. "I was given the job of making little rocks out of big rocks that first day back. The rocks were splintering and cutting me on the arms and chest. Because of the quinine I was sweating excessively, so much that by the middle of the day, I was beginning to sweat blood." In a rare gesture of kindness, a Japanese sergeant offered Kooper a cigarette and the chance to rest. "The sergeant left and I sat down and smoked a bit. After a few minutes, a soldier walked around the bend and saw me. He thought I was loafing and he came up behind me and I got a rifle butt in the back and the head."

The work camps were primitive. The prisoners of war often had to build their own shelters, huts of bamboo, dry twigs, and leaves that offered little protection against the elements. In the dry season, the men had virtually no water for cooking or washing. Fine powdery dust settled over everything, accumulating up to eight inches. During the wet season the dust became a sticky mud that made walking difficult and tiring. The daily trip from camp to the work site would exhaust the chronically sick men. The latrines were long, open ditches, teeming with grubs and flies.

The railway project included the construction of 688 bridges. One of these, 80 feet high and 400 yards long, they called the "Pack of Cards" bridge because it collapsed three times while they were building it. It was being constructed out of green timber fastened with wooden wedges, spikes, bamboo ties, rattan or cane rope, and wooden dowels.

"Three weeks ago there was nothing there at all," said an Australian prisoner. "Now there is not only this vast bridge, but steam engines bumping slowly over it. . . . Two thousand predynastic slaves . . . had built the entire thing in seventeen days! It was characteristically Japanese, not only because it was a crazy wooden bridge that nevertheless functioned, but because no other nation in the world in 1943 would have bashed and bullied, and sweated and slaved prisoners to such fantastic lengths for such an object."

Thirty-one men fell to their deaths from the bridge during its construction. Twenty-nine others were beaten to death by the guards.

By mid-March of 1943, so many of the *Houston* men were seriously ill that the Japanese agreed that something had to be done. The men had reached the 85 Kilo Camp and it was decided to move the sick to a makeshift hospital back at the 80 Kilo Camp. The few trucks available were insufficient to transport all the sick men. A Japanese officer decided who would ride and who would walk. "He lined up the sick prisoners," said C. D. Smith, "and struck each man with his sword. Those who got to their feet again were judged able to march. Those who could not get up were carried by truck."

Waiting at the 80 Kilo Camp were one doctor and two Dutch orderlies, but no kitchen personnel, no able-bodied men to dig latrines or graves, and no one to maintain the quarters. The sick men had to take care of themselves as best they could. The Japanese put them there to die, not to get well. "The sick were of no use to Nippon," said Lieutenant Rogers, "and the Japanese commander announced that he was leaving them behind in this camp to die." Rogers said that the diet was so poor that many patients crawled out into the jungle to pick leaves or anything else that appeared edible.

"We only got rice twice a day," Charley Pryor said, "and it was a half ration of about eight ounces. We had the very worst living conditions, with no form of sanitation, and most of the men were bedridden. I was the only one on my feet, and I took care of some of them, but I wasn't able to do everything. About all I could do was bring them their food, and I could only stay up a few minutes at a time."

The most frequent and persistent form of illness at the 80 Kilo Camp was leg ulcers. The men had only shorts or G-strings to wear and the smallest scratch could easily develop into a tropical ulcer. Some men with these sores could not even stand up, although the Japanese forced them to work anyway. They were borne to the construction site on stretchers and given a hammer with which to break rocks while lying down.

In one camp, 150 men a day were operated on for leg ulcers. Little could be attempted beyond scraping out the ulcer with a spoon. There was no chloroform to deaden the excruciating pain. For many men, this treatment was ineffective and the only remedy was amputation, without anesthesia, using a hacksaw made from a barrel stave. No more than half of those operated on survived.

Lieutenant Rogers's ulcer in his right leg kept him flat on his back for 14 months in various hospital camps. "It got so bad," he said, "that the shin bone was exposed. We had hundreds of people lose their legs from these tropical ulcers. If we had had even rubbing alcohol, any kind of antiseptic, we could have saved those people."

Rogers was lucky. He was given some sulfa pills by Ensign John Stivers, one of the *Houston*'s pilots. Stivers had obtained the pills in Bicycle Camp. "I cut the pills in half," Rogers said, "and sprinkled in half a pill every other day and I know that's what saved my leg. An Australian doctor had looked at it one day and said to [Raymond] Rainy Day, our corpsman from the ship, 'Well, that leg will go in the pot.'"

Rogers did not lose his leg, but after the war he underwent a series of skin grafts and months of hospitalization. Ensign Stivers developed a brain lesion, probably as a result of the beatings he suffered at the hands of the Japanese. "The doctors opened his head up in the camps," Rogers said, "but took one look and knew there was nothing they could do. They sewed him back up again, but because the bone had been taken out, the tumor could expand outside the skull. Eventually, the tumor got as large as his head. He did not survive."

Simple rubbing alcohol would have saved so many lives. That was what was so maddening and frustrating to all the men working on the railway line. The Japanese could have saved most of the sick men with medicines that were readily available to them. Besides beatings, the major killers were beri-beri, dysentery, malaria, pneumonia, tropical ulcers, and the aftereffects of amputation. None of these conditions was fatal if properly treated, but the Japanese consistently refused to provide basic medical assistance.

The Japanese viewed illness among their prisoners as something shameful. They withheld treatment—and even deliberately mistreated them—in the belief that this would discourage them from falling ill. Japanese commanders had ordered that rations would be given only to those who were working. It did not matter to them if the sick men died.

This policy soon became self-defeating. Japanese maltreatment led to greater numbers of men who were too ill to work, and thus it became increasingly difficult for the Japanese to maintain their construction schedule. Guards put increased pressure upon the sick to return to work, often to the point of what an Australian prisoner called "frenzied, sadistic brutality. Work parades ultimately became a deplorable spectacle with men tottering with the support of sticks and carried piggyback onto a parade ground, unable to work, in order that fixed [quotas of workers] could be met. [Stretcher] cases were frequently carried to the engineers' lines and ordered to work with hammer and axe in a sitting position. The sick were frequently treated with special savagery."

A *Houston* sailor and a Lost Battalion soldier suffering from blindness caused by malnutrition were beaten mercilessly with rifle butts because they did not salute the Japanese guards whom they could not see. The beating was particularly ugly because the men also could not see to protect themselves, to ward off the blows.

If the daily quotas of men for the working parties were not filled at the morning work parade, the Japanese and Korean guards would enter the prisoners' huts and select those whom they felt were fit enough to work, disregarding the doctors' pleas. If the men did not fall in on the guards' orders, they were beaten until they did, or until they died.

The *Houston's* senior surgeon, Commander William Epstein, often confronted the Japanese on behalf of his men. "Dr. Epstein was a fabulous man in those camps," John Bartz said. "You had to have so many people go out for the work parade, but if you were in bad shape, the doc would go in to the Japs and say so. He'd stand right up to them. He'd take beatings for those guys."

The Japanese were especially fearful of cholera. Men who caught it were left where they fell. If a cholera victim could be carried back to camp he had to be isolated, usually in a low-lying area, which in the rainy season might be covered with several inches of water. Prisoners suffering from diarrhea and dysentery were not permitted to leave the line to relieve themselves. A group of 50 seriously ill men were taken from the hospital and forced to roll 40-gallon oil drums over rough track and down a steep hill for several miles. Those who allowed the drums to get out of control were beaten. Men were soon dying in such large numbers that graves could not be dug fast enough; sometimes two or three bodies were buried in the same hole.

Lloyd Willey remembered one *Houston* marine who died, First Sergeant Harley H. Dupler, "the kind of marine you'd want to put on the cover of a magazine. He was big and husky, weighing a hundred and ninety pounds, and had a Marine Corps emblem tattooed on his upper arm. When he flexed his muscles that emblem was huge.

"Out on the railroad line, he got a bad attack of malaria and told the Japs he couldn't work. They threw him in a hut and left him there with no food or water for three days. He was burning up with fever and the flesh just melted off him. One day I saw this man being brought into the hospital camp on a stretcher and his arm was hanging over the side. He was a skeleton; he weighed no more than sixty-five pounds. The only way I recognized who it was was when I saw that Marine Corps emblem on his arm. It was no bigger than a quarter.

"I went over to see him. His wife was pregnant at the time and he said, 'I know my wife is going to die carrying this child, and I know it's going to be a girl.' He lost his will to live because he thought she was going to die. He died in just a few days."

In 1960, Lloyd Willey was a guest on Art Linkletter's television program. Linkletter asked Willey who he would like to get in touch with if he could call any three people he chose. Willey said, "I'd like to get in touch with the wife of our first sergeant," and he did. "Sergeant Dupler couldn't have been more wrong. His wife had had no trouble in childbirth and had had a son. Some time after that I met him and at first I thought it was his father walking into the room. He looked so much like him."

Approximately one out of every four men from the USS *Houston* who were sent to Burma died building the Burma railway for the Japanese, 61 out of the 220, and several others died later of complications from illness and injuries received on the line. The American cemetery plot at the camps had to be extended three times.

One day it ended. "We were out digging up new ground to put in a garden," said Lieutenant Bob Fulton, describing his situation in late August 1945, at a prisoner-of-war camp in Japan. "Suddenly we noticed a heavy dust cloud moving over us. It covered the whole area and half obscured the sun. The sun appeared red-looking through this cloud. We had no idea what it was.

"A couple of days later one of the interpreters at the camp

told us that our country had done something of which we would be thoroughly ashamed, but he could not tell us about it. A day or so later the camp commandant lined us up and told us that as a result of a conference on a warship, we were now free. That was it. That was how the end of the war came to us."

The men of the *Houston*, the survivors, were going home.

Epilogue

The man pauses for a moment, putting his thoughts and memories in order before answering the interviewer's questions. He looks out the window at the deep blue water. A U.S. Navy guided missile frigate glides by, heading out to sea. It is November 1982, more than 40 years after the *Houston* went down, and he is sitting in a hotel room in San Diego, where he trained to be a marine in 1941.

It is a long way and a long time from Bantam Bay and a burning ship and the dark waters of the Java Sea, from the horrors of the prison camps in Java and Burma and Thailand, from the beatings and starvation, from near-blindness due to malnutrition, from dysentery and malaria and tropical ulcers, from rice with worms in it, from wrapping dead friends in rice bags before burying them in shallow jungle graves, from wondering if he would live to see the sun rise.

A long way and a long time, but in his mind it is not so distant. He is there now as he patiently, and with intense emotion, describes what it was like. The session is almost over. He has been reliving the past for two hours. There is one last question: How does he feel about the Japanese?

He looks away from the water and the passing warship and begins to speak. The tape recorder captures the pain in his voice. It will stay unchanged on that tape just as long as it will remain in his mind. The tape recorder is a Japanese machine.

"Most of the animosity is gone," he says slowly, "but it took a long time for that to happen." His voice quickens. "Back in Montana, I was driving a city bus not long after the war. One day, an elderly Japanese man who had lived in that town all his life, and who had been strongly anti-Japanese throughout the war, was crossing the street up ahead. Before I knew what was happening, I was heading that busload of people right toward that Jap. I was going to kill him. I caught myself in time.

"After that, I tried to school myself in another way of thinking. I kept telling myself that we're all human beings. We've got to live together."

Another memory forces its way onto the tape. "When I first got home, I went into my mother's kitchen and I got a bag of rice she kept there and I took it out in the yard." He stops. Tears run down his cheeks. "I threw it as far as I could. I wouldn't eat rice for a year, and then I started to crave it again.

"When I took that long bus trip home from Washington, D.C., to Montana, we stopped in a little town and I went into a nice restaurant. I ordered a steak, which I hadn't had in a long time. When I finished, the man brought over some dessert. It was rice pudding. I gave it a shove and it went all the way down the long counter.

" 'What's the matter with you?' the man asked. 'I've had over thirteen hundred meals of that stuff,' I said, 'and I don't ever want to see rice again.' He asked me where I'd been and I told him and he went in the back and came out with a big lemon pie. He cut it in four pieces and he wouldn't take a thing for the meal.

"We have rice at home all the time now.

"I got into Salt Lake City on that trip home and I was sitting there in that big bus terminal and here comes a busload of Nisei soldiers, the 442nd Regimental Combat Team. They were in uniforms, just like the guards had been. I knew they were just as American as I was. I knew they fought as hard as I had." He is silent for a couple of moments.

"That was one of the most traumatic things I ever went

through, sitting in that bus station and seeing those Nisei in uniforms. I knew I had to re-evaluate, even right then, so soon after it all happened."

Another survivor sits in his living room and answers the same question. "My last duty in the Navy took me back to Japan. That was in 1953. The first time I told a Jap to do something he didn't do it, and before I knew what was happening, I had a two-by-four in my hand. I didn't hit him, but I came awfully close."

He laughs sarcastically and takes another puff on his cigarette. "I had one act of kindness from them in three and a half years. It happened in Serang. As hungry as everyone was, as starved, one time when the Japs got through eating, they let me eat their scraps!" He tries to smile, but he cannot.

During the Korean War, in the early 1950s, several other *Houston* survivors found themselves face to face with the Japanese. "The first time I went ashore in Japan and saw Jap sentries checking me in to American bases, it was like a flashback," one said. "It was pure hatred. I could have killed them all."

"I got sent back to Japan, and the first day off ship, I tried to kill a Jap," another said. "I don't even remember doing it. All I remember is the shore patrol pulling me off this guy and saying I tried to kill him. I must have gone out of my mind."

"When I just got back from the war," said a career officer, "honest to God, I was bitter." Another officer, assigned to an American naval base in Japan eight years after the end of the war, said, "I went ashore and the first thing I saw were Japanese who had been hired by the United States as security guards for the base. These guys were still wearing the same brown uniforms and carrying rifles. It was like I was right back in the camps. I damn near turned around and got back on the boat. It was two or three days before I was able to get used to it and to overcome my resentment."

Most of the men of the *Houston* have come to terms with their experiences, but it has taken half a lifetime. They are practical men, realists. "I just had to put all that stuff out of my head," one said. "I thought about it a lot before I went ashore in Japan again," another explained, "and I decided it was no use being resentful. It was history. I had to put it behind me and get on with my life. I did, but, by God, it was hard."

Not everyone has gotten over it, of course. Some men still cannot talk about their treatment in the prison camps, but most are eager to do so. They need to, to help put the bitterness and anger aside and to help remind the rest of us of what they endured and survived.

The one thing they cannot do is forget. The war will stay with them until the end of their days. One survivor's wife is asked, while her husband is out of the room, if it is difficult for him to talk about his experiences.

"No," she says, "but he'll have nightmares tonight. He'll be back in the camps again and he'll cry out in his sleep. And when he does, he'll cry out in Japanese."

If you listen carefully to the tape recording, you can hear the sound of the two small native fishing boats banging together. You can hear the gentle rippling of the waves. Sunda Strait was very still on October 12, 1981. The group of men and women in those primitive little boats only three feet wide, with no seats and no cover from the steaming sun, can see the silhouettes of the mountains in the distance, just as the men could the night their ship went down. The trip from Bantam Bay has taken two hours. Now they sit in silence.

Otto Schwarz keeps staring at Java, at "the mountain range I had kept in sight that night when I swam so many hours alone and frightened. I could not help thanking God for allowing me to come back to this spot." His wife Gertrude calls it "one of the most emotional moments" of her life.

Captain Rooks's younger son, Albert, seems overwhelmed. His wife Janet carries bundles wrapped in palm leaves. She breaks them open and distributes handfuls of white flower petals to the others.

Judy Bunch and her sister Susie think of their father, Radioman First Class Jerry Bunch, and of the letters they have read so often, letters Bunch wrote from the USS *Houston* to his folks back home in North Carolina. Bunch survived the sinking and the prisoner of war camps, but has since died.

"I tried to visualize the water black with oil," Judy Bunch

says, "and the struggling men trying to make it to the shore I could see in the distance. I wished so much that my father could have been there. . . . I wondered what he would have felt. It was terribly sad that he was not there—or was he?"

The trip has been a pilgrimage for *Houston* and Lost Battalion survivors. Manila, Bangkok, the railway of death. A wreath laid at the memorial to the Allied dead. A quiet lunch at the River Kwai Restaurant and a slow walk across the bridge.

Singapore and Changi prison. A short flight to Jakarta, which they had known as Batavia. A stay at the Borobudur Inter-Continental Hotel, built on the site of the Bicycle Camp. They find a portion of one of the masonry pillars that had held the main gate, all that remains of the camp.

Serang, unchanged from 1942. The warden escorts them through the jail. Up the dirt road to the theater. People are lined up for the matinee, but the Americans are permitted to enter. As they walk around, you can hear the muffled voices.

"That's where I sat for six weeks on the concrete floor." "That's where they had the machine gun mounted on the balcony." "That was the only place to go to the toilet."

Then Bantam Bay, in two little boats.

The survivors place two wreaths in the water and scatter the white flower petals. Schwarz offers a prayer.

"Dear Lord. It is with the greatest humility and thankfulness that we find ourselves here in this spot at this time. We shall never forget the deeds of our great ship and our great shipmates, and our captain, who live forever in our memories. We appreciate that we can once more come back to this very spot and give them honor, for they are the real heroes. They are the ones who went to sea in ships, and they are the ones who, to the very last moment, never gave up the mission that they had been sent to do. It is with great honor and humility that we travel here today to pay honor to those shipmates who lie beneath us now.

"Well done, *Houston*. Well done, men of the *Houston*."

Presidential Unit Citation

The President of the United States takes pleasure in presenting the Presidential Unit Citation to the UNITED STATES SHIP *Houston* for service as set forth in the following citation:

"For outstanding performance against enemy Japanese forces in the Southwest Pacific from December 4, 1941, to February 28, 1942. At sea almost constantly, often damaged but self-maintaining, the *Houston* kept the sea. She maneuvered superbly and with deadly anti-aircraft fire repulsed the nine-plane Japanese Bombing Squadrons attacking a troop convoy under her escort. Later, in company with other Allied ships, she engaged a powerful enemy force, carried the brunt of the action with her two remaining 8" turrets and aided in damaging and routing two enemy heavy cruisers from the line of battle. On February 28, the *Houston* went down, gallantly fighting to the last against overwhelming odds. She leaves behind her an inspiring record of valiant and distinguished service."

Acknowledgments

It is a pleasure to acknowledge the unstinting support of the many individuals who gave freely of their time to help me tell the story of the *Houston*'s valiant crew. The survivors and their families welcomed us in their homes, where with both tears and laughter they shared the memories of their wartime years. They patiently and carefully answered our questions and provided us with books, diaries, letters, snapshots, unpublished manuscripts, scrapbooks compiled by wives and mothers, and the official narratives and logs in which they long ago recorded their exploits. Some chose to express their views off the record. Thus, the following *Houston* survivors, among others, contributed material to the book, either in person, by letter or telephone, or by tape recording: John Bartz, Howard Brooks, Merritt V. Eddy, Robert Fulton, W. J. Galbraith, P. T. Gans, James Gee, Shun Ching Kei, L. W. Kooper, J. D. Lamade, Q. C. Madson, Arthur L. Maher, Thomas B. Payne, Charley Pryor, Leon W. Rogers, Otto C. Schwarz, J. D. Smith, Ray Sparks, William Weissinger, Lloyd Willey.

Special thanks are due to Otto and Gertrude Schwarz, who fortified us with a hearty breakfast on their patio each morning so we could spend hours in Otto's basement office, the headquarters of the USS *Houston* Survivors Association. Otto made available to us the wealth of material he has amassed through years of dedicated effort to keep the men of the *Houston* together and the spirit of the ship alive. They have responded freely and promptly to the many requests we have made of them during the writing of the book. They arranged meetings with other *Houston* personnel and provided a complete roster of survivors. Otto and Gertrude are rare and generous people. This book could not have been written without their help.

Rear Admiral Arthur L. "Al" Maher, the *Houston*'s senior surviving officer, is a gracious, patient, and gentle man who received us in his home time after time and recounted his experiences for us. He provided an enormous file of official and personal papers, including his action reports, recommendations for awards and citations, and correspondence with the family of every *Houston* crew member. He also read the entire manuscript, his keen eyes ferreting out historical and technical errors that a landlubber author can easily make.

I would also like to thank Judy Bunch for writing to me about her father, J. J. Bunch, and for providing copies of the letters he wrote to his family from the *Houston*. Rear Admiral Robert Fulton sent many hours of tape recordings and detailed diagrams of the *Houston*'s engine rooms, and Q. C. Madson provided a fascinating manuscript about his experiences.

Colonel John R. Vance, USA (retired), an astute historian of both World War I and World War II, and a prisoner of war following the fall of Corregidor, also read the manuscript. I am grateful for his always insightful comments.

Elizabeth Wachendorfer of the M. D. Anderson Library, University of Houston, and curator of the Cruiser *Houston* Memorial Collection there, was generous with her time and resources, supplying deck logs, *Blue Bonnet*s, photographs, newspaper clippings, magazine articles, letters, and other materials that exist nowhere else.

Dr. Ronald E. Marcello of North Texas State University (NTSU) is responsible for an extensive oral history program there that includes his interviews with several *Houston* survivors. I am grateful to Dr. Marcello for making the transcripts available and for the skill with which he conducted the interviews. The NTSU archivist, Richard Himmel, kindly facilitated our work while at the university. The *Houston* survivors whose recollections have thus contributed to the book include Donald Brain, J. O. Burge, George E. Detre, Griff L. Douglas, Melford L. Forsman, James W. Gee, Charley L. Pryor, Seldon D. Reese, Marvin E. Robinson, Otto Schwarz, and William J. Stewart.

"The Reminiscences of Thomas C. Hart" in the Oral History Collection of Columbia University is copyright by The Trustees of Columbia University in the City of New York, 1972, and is used with their permission.

The map of the battles for Java has been adapted from John Toland, *But Not in Shame*, p. 235; the map of the Battle of Sunda Strait has been adapted from Samuel Eliot Morison, *The Rising Sun in the Pacific*, p. 367.

No project involving naval history could be undertaken without the resources of the Operational Archives Branch of the Naval Historical Center (NHC) in Washington, D.C., and the expertise of its head, Dr. Dean Allard. During our several visits there we were also ably assisted by Richard M. Walker and Martha Crawley. At the History and Museums Division of the U.S. Marine Corps, Dan J. Crawford dug into classified files to find the survivors' reports of the *Houston*'s marine detachment and arranged to have them declassified for us in record time.

The book would not have advanced beyond the idea stage were it not for my wife, Sydney Ellen, who remained diligent and cheerful through the interviews and research; the editing, proofreading, and indexing; and the endless cups of Navy coffee that went along with the memorable hospitality that was extended to us.

Chapter Notes

Chapter 1. Overdue and Presumed Lost

Author interviews with Kooper, Payne, Rogers, Fulton, Gee, Eddy, Weissinger, Pryor, Schwarz, Brooks, Bartz. NTSU interviews with Detre, Pryor, Schwarz. Bunch letters courtesy of Judy Bunch.

Hamlin's comments in "Narrative of Lt. (jg) H. S. Hamlin, Jr., USN: USS *Houston* in Battle of Java Sea," NHC. Additional survivor stories in J. Royce, "The *Houston*'s Last Fight," *Our Navy*, December 1945.

Bartlett story in *Chicago Daily Tribune* and *Chicago Sun*, August 29, 1945.

Radio message to Corregidor in Maher, "Action Report of the USS *Houston* (CA-30) in the Battle of Sunda Strait, 28 February 1942," NHC.

Morison on the prewar Navy and the Asiatic Fleet in Samuel Eliot Morison, *The Rising Sun in the Pacific: 1931–April 1942*, Vol. 3 (Boston: Atlantic-Little, Brown, 1948), pp. 6–10, 380.

Chapter 2. We'll Be Shooting in a Few Days

Author interviews with Weissinger, Fulton, Lamade, Galbraith, Payne, Rogers, J. D. Smith, Maher, Schwarz. NTSU interviews with Schwarz, Gee, Robinson. Bunch letters courtesy of Judy Bunch.

Deck logs, USS *Houston*, in Cruiser *Houston* Memorial Exhibit, George R. Brown Room, University of Houston Library.

Winslow's comments in W. G. Winslow, *The Ghost of the Java Coast: Saga of the USS* Houston (Satellite Beach, FL: Coral Reef Publications, 1974), p. 40; by permission of W. G. Winslow.

Captain Albert H. Rooks's prewar report in "Estimate of the Situation, Far East Area, 18 November 1941," NHC.

Information on the equipment of the Asiatic Fleet in Kemp Tolley, *Cruise of the Lanikai* (Annapolis, MD: Naval Institute Press, 1973), pp. ix, 193–194.

Comments of the USS *California* sailor in Theodore C. Mason, *Battleship Sailor* (Annapolis, MD: Naval Institute Press, 1982), p. 16.

Information on Admiral Hart in James Leutze, *A Different Kind of Victory: A Biography of Admiral Thomas C. Hart* (Annapolis, MD: Naval Institute Press, 1981); and on Admiral Hart's preparations for war in Gordon W. Prange, *At Dawn We Slept: The Untold Story of Pearl Harbor* (New York: McGraw-Hill, 1981), p. 406.

Chapter 3. Prepare the Ship for War

Author interviews with Maher, Galbraith, Kooper, Eddy, Weissinger, Gans, Gee, Pryor, J. D. Smith, Schwarz, Sparks, Brooks, Payne, Lamade, Fulton, Bartz. NTSU interviews with Pryor, Schwarz, Burge, Gee.

Winslow's comments in Winslow, *The Ghost of the Java Coast*, p. 39. Additional comments on service in the Asiatic Fleet in Mason, *Battleship Sailor*, pp. 126–129.

Deck logs, USS *Houston*; Orders for the Day, USS *Houston*; the *Blue Bonnet*, USS *Houston*; *The Third Presidential Cruise of the USS* Houston, *14 July to 9 August 1938*; and the William A. Bernrieder Collection; all in the University of Houston Library. Additional information on the presidential cruises in Harold L. Ickes, *The Secret Diary of Harold L. Ickes: The First Thousand Days* (New York: Simon & Schuster, 1953), pp. 449, 452.

Information on the gifts from the city of Houston, Texas, to the USS *Houston* in various issues of the *Houston Post*.

General Stilwell's comments in Leutze, *A Different Kind of Victory*, p. 150.

Description of Shanghai in Kemp Tolley, *Yangtze Patrol: The U.S. Navy in China* (Annapolis, MD: Naval Institute Press, 1971), pp. 207–208.

Information on Admiral Hart in Leutze, *A Different Kind of Victory*. Also "The Reminiscences of Thomas C. Hart," Oral History Research Office, Columbia University, 1962 (Privileged Manuscript Collection, CNOF-0334. Conducted by Dr. John T. Mason, Jr.). Cited by permission.

Chapter 4. It's for Keeps Now

Author interviews with Galbraith, Rogers, Maher, Eddy, Lamade, Payne, Gee, Schwarz, Weissinger, Kooper, Fulton, Brooks, Sparks, J. D. Smith. NTSU interviews with Pryor, Burge, Detre, Schwarz. Bunch letters courtesy of Judy Bunch.

Madson's comments in his diary, courtesy of Q. C. Madson.

Winslow's comments in Winslow, *The Ghost of the Java Coast*, pp. 39–45, 59.

Deck logs, USS *Houston*, in the University of Houston Library.

Additional description of Surabaja in George Sessions Perry and Isabel Leighton, *Where Away: A Modern Odyssey* (New York: Whittlesey House, 1944), p. 50.

Information on the USS *Langley* in Dwight R. Messimer, *Pawns of War: The Loss of the USS* Langley *and the USS* Pecos (Annapolis, MD: Naval Institute Press, 1983).

Information on Admiral Hart in Leutze, *A Different Kind of Victory*, especially pp. 233–235. Also Admiral Hart's comments in his diary, NHC, and in Walter Karig and Welbourn Kelley, *Battle Report: Pearl Harbor to Coral Sea*, Vol. 1 (New York: Rinehart, 1944), p. 145.

Admiral Glassford's remarks in "Confidential War Diary of Rear Admiral William A. Glassford, Jr., USN, from 29 November 1941 to 15 March 1942," NHC.

Chapter 5. A Strange Way to Fight a War

Author interviews with Willey, Lamade, Brooks, Bartz, Fulton, Galbraith. NTSU interviews with Douglas.

Madson's comments in his diary, courtesy of Q. C. Madson.
Winslow's comments in Winslow, *The Ghost of the Java Coast*,
pp. 69–70, 81, 94.
Deck logs, USS *Houston*, in the University of Houston Library.
Description of the ABDA command structure in Karig and Kelley,
Battle Report, pp. 165–170; Morison, *The Rising Sun in the Pa-
cific*, Chapter 14; David Thomas, *The Battle of the Java Sea*
(New York: Stein & Day, 1969), p. 108; Tolley, *Cruise of the
Lanikai*, p. 190.
Information on Admiral Hart in Leutze, *A Different Kind of Victory*,
especially Chapter 10; also Admiral Hart's diary, NHC.
Comments on Admiral Doorman in F. C. Van Oosten, *The Battle
of the Java Sea* (Annapolis, MD: Naval Institute Press, 1976),
p. 45.

Chapter 6. Man Your Battle Stations

Author interviews with Weissinger, Maher, Galbraith, Rogers,
Bartz, Willey, J. D. Smith, Lamade, Fulton, Sparks, Kooper,
Payne, Gans, Gee. NTSU interviews with Schwarz, Douglas,
Detre, Brain.
Winslow's comments in Winslow, *The Ghost of the Java Coast*, pp.
30–31, 94–95, 102.
Battle report in Maher, "Action Report of the USS *Houston*
(CA-30) on 4 February 1942 Against Enemy Aircraft," NHC.
Additional information on the USS *Marblehead* in Morison, *The
Rising Sun in the Pacific*, pp. 300–301.

Chapter 7. Fire in Turret Three

Author interviews with Brooks, J. D. Smith, Eddy, Weissinger,
Bartz, Willey, Fulton, Maher, Lamade, Pryor, Schwarz,
Payne, Gee, Gans. NTSU interviews with Pryor, Douglas,
Brain, Schwarz, Detre. Additional information from Lamade
in "USS *Houston*: From December 8, 1942 Until She Was Re-
ported Missing February 28, 1942" (privately printed), cour-
tesy of J. D. Lamade. Various letters from USS *Houston*
survivors and from Mrs. C. E. Reddingius-Soeters courtesy of
A. L. Maher.
Madson's comments in his diary, courtesy of Q. C. Madson.
Winslow's comments in Winslow, *The Ghost of the Java Coast*,
pp. 99, 102.

Battle report in Maher, "Action Report of the USS *Houston* (CA-30) on 4 February 1942 Against Enemy Aircraft," NHC. Also Asiatic Fleet Dispatches, NHC.

Information on the USS *Marblehead* in Perry and Leighton, *Where Away*; also Karig and Kelley, *Battle Report*, p. 197; Morison, *The Rising Sun in the Pacific*, pp. 306, 379; Tolley, *Cruise of the Lanikai*, p. 186.

Information on Admiral Hart in Admiral Hart's diary, NHC; Admiral Hart's "Narrative of Events, Asiatic Fleet, Leading Up to War and from 8 December 1941 to 15 February 1942," and "Supplement of Narrative," NHC; "The Reminiscences of Thomas C. Hart," Oral History Research Office, Columbia University; the *Blue Bonnet* (Union, NJ: USS *Houston* Survivors Association, Otto Schwarz, Ed.). Also Leutze, *A Different Kind of Victory*; Thomas, *The Battle of the Java Sea*, pp. 126–127; Tolley, *Cruise of the Lanikai*, p. 184.

Chapter 8. We're Going to Hell

Author interviews with Lamade, Bartz, Pryor, Maher, Schwarz, Fulton, Eddy, Rogers, Payne. NTSU interviews with Schwarz, Douglas, Pryor, Forsman, Brain.

Madson's comments in his diary, courtesy of Q. C. Madson. Winslow's comments in Winslow, *The Ghost of the Java Coast*, pp. 110, 114, 115. C. D. Smith's comments in "Narrative of Ensign Charles D. Smith, USN: USS *Houston* (CA-30) and Experiences in Japanese Prison Camp," NHC.

Battle report in Maher, "Action Report of the USS *Houston* (CA-30) in Defense of Convoy off Darwin, Australia, 16 February 1942," NHC.

Description of the bombing of Darwin in Morison, *The Rising Sun in the Pacific*, p. 320; of the bombing of Surabaja in Thomas, *The Battle of the Java Sea*, p. 155.

Information on Admiral Hart and on the ABDA command structure in Karig and Kelley, *Battle Report*, pp. 200–202; Leutze, *A Different Kind of Victory*, especially Chapters 10–11; Morison, *The Rising Sun in the Pacific*, pp. 330–338; Thomas, *The Battle of the Java Sea*, pp. 132, 148–149; Tolley, *Cruise of the Lanikai*, pp. 189, 207; Lionel Wigmore, *The Japanese Thrust* (Adelaide, Australia: Griffin Press, 1957), p. 495.

Chapter 9. Follow Me

Author interviews with Weissinger, Galbraith, Maher, Willey, Bartz, Eddy, Schwarz, Fulton, Rogers, Pryor. NTSU interviews with Douglas, Schwarz, Pryor, Gee. Additional information from Rogers in "Statement of Experience During Battle of Java Sea," courtesy of L. W. Rogers.

Madson's comments in his diary, courtesy of Q. C. Madson. Winslow's comments in Winslow, *The Ghost of the Java Coast*, pp. 116, 117, 120, 126, 130, 132. C. D. Smith's comments in his "Narrative," NHC. Hamlin's comments in his "Narrative," NHC; also "The *Houston*'s Last Battles," *Shipmate*, May 1946.

Battle report in Maher, "Action Report of the USS *Houston* (CA-30) in the Battle of the Java Sea, 27 February 1942," NHC. Additional information on the Battle of the Java Sea in Karig and Kelley, *Battle Report*, pp. 224–242; Morison, *The Rising Sun in the Pacific*, Chapter 18; Van Oosten, *The Battle of the Java Sea*, pp. 43, 68–73.

Assessment of ABDA and Japanese fleets in H. P. Willmott, *Empires in the Balance: Japanese and Allied Pacific Strategies to April 1942* (Annapolis, MD: Naval Institute Press, 1982).

Australian historian's comments on Admiral Doorman in Ronald McKie, *The Survivors* (Indianapolis, IN: Bobbs-Merrill, 1953), p. 15. Admiral Helfrich's comments on Captain Waller (HMAS *Perth*) in G. Hermon Gill, *Australia in the War of 1939–1945*, Vol. 1: *Royal Australian Navy, 1939–1942* (Canberra, Australia: Australian War Memorial, 1957), p. 616.

Chapter 10. I Think We've Got It Made

Author interviews with Payne, Brooks, Maher, Rogers, Fulton, Sparks, Willey, Gee, Galbraith, Weissinger, Pryor, Schwarz, Eddy, Gans. NTSU interviews with Douglas, Pryor, Schwarz, Stewart, Robinson, Detre, Forsman, Reese.

Madson's comments in his dairy; also unpublished manuscript, "Once We Built a Railroad," courtesy of Q. C. Madson. Winslow's comments in Winslow, *The Ghost of the Java Coast*, pp. 135, 138. C. D. Smith's comments in his "Narrative," NHC. Hamlin's comments in his "Narrative," NHC; also

"Personal Experiences in Night Action, 28 February–1 March," handwritten copy courtesy of W. J. Galbraith.

Battle report in Maher, "Action Report of the USS *Houston* (CA-30) in the Battle of Sunda Strait, 28 February 1942," NHC.

On HMAS *Perth* in the Battle of Sunda Strait see Gill, *Royal Australian Navy*, p. 619; McKie, *The Survivors*, pp. 26–28, 64–73; Alan Payne, *HMAS Perth* (Garden Island, NSW, Australia: Naval Historical Society of Australia, 1978), pp. 89–95; Thomas, *The Battle of the Java Sea*, p. 220.

Description of Tanjong Priok in McKie, *The Survivors*, p. 22; Payne, *HMAS Perth*, p. 87.

Comments on General Imamura in Morison, *The Rising Sun in the Pacific*, p. 366.

Chapter 11. *The Colors Were Still Flying*

Author interviews with Maher, Pryor, Willey, Weissinger, Schwarz, Brooks, Gee, Rogers, Payne, Fulton, Gans, Sparks, J. D. Smith, Bartz, Kooper. NTSU interviews with Pryor, Detre, Schwarz, Robinson, Gee, Douglas, Forsman, Stewart, Reese. Levitt's comments in his report in the University of Houston Library.

Madson's comments in his diary and manuscript, courtesy of Q. C. Madson. Winslow's comments in Winslow, *The Ghost of the Java Coast*, pp. 147–148. C. D. Smith's comments in his "Narrative," NHC. Hamlin's comments in his "Narrative," NHC, and his *Shipmate* article.

Battle report in Maher, "Action Report of the USS *Houston* (CA-30) in the Battle of Sunda Strait, 28 Febraury 1942," NHC.

Chapter 12. *The Japanese Put Them There to Die*

Author interviews with Gee, Fulton, Galbraith, Pryor, Sparks, Maher, Payne, Mrs. Galbraith, Schwarz, Bartz, Eddy, Rogers, Lamade, Willey. NTSU interviews with Gee, Pryor, Detre, Schwarz, Stewart, Robinson. Additional information from survivors Kooper and Rogers in the San Diego *Union*, November 11, 1982, and from Rogers in "Prisoner of War Log, 1 March 1942 to 16 August 1945," NHC.

Madson's comments in his manuscript, courtesy of Q. C. Madson. C. D. Smith's comments in his "Narrative," NHC.

U.S. Marine Corps prisoner-of-war reports from USS *Houston* survivors in the History and Museums Division, HQ, U.S. Marine Corps: John H. Wisecup, Pfc.; Charley L. Pryor, Sgt.; Marvin Earle Robinson, Pfc.; Eugene David Rochford, Cpl.; Howard Robert Charles, Cpl.; Walter L. Grice, Pfc.; Carl H. Williams, Pvt.

HMAS *Perth* survivors accounts in McKie, *The Survivors*.

Navy Department press releases; awards and citations, NHC.

Information on the launching of the USS *Houston* (CL-81) in *The New York Times* and the *Houston Chronicle;* also in the William A. Bernrieder Collection, University of Houston Library.

Japanese camp commander's speech to Allied prisoners at Thanbuyzat, Burma, in the University of Houston Library.

Additional information on the construction of the Burma railway in John Costello, *The Pacific War* (New York: Rawson, Wade, 1981), pp. 396–397; Wigmore, *The Japanese Thrust*, pp. 569–570, 588.

Bibliography

Books

Bergamini, David. *Japan's Imperial Conspiracy*, Vol. 2. New York: William Morrow, 1971.

Costello, John. *The Pacific War*. New York: Rawson, Wade, 1981.

Gill, G. Hermon. *Australia in the War of 1939–1945*, Vol. 1: *Royal Australian Navy, 1939–1942*. Canberra, Australia: Australian War Memorial, 1957.

Holbrook, Heber A. *USS* Houston: *The Last Flagship of the Asiatic Fleet*. Dixon, CA: Pacific Ship and Shore, 1981.

Hoyt, Edwin P. *The Lonely Ships*. New York: David McKay, 1976.

Ickes, Harold L. *The Secret Diary of Harold L. Ickes: The First Thousand Days*. New York: Simon & Schuster, 1953.

Karig, Walter, and Kelley, Welbourn. *Battle Report: Pearl Harbor to Coral Sea*, Vol. 1. New York: Rinehart, 1944.

Leutze, James. *A Different Kind of Victory: A Biography of Admiral Thomas C. Hart*. Annapolis, MD: Naval Institute Press, 1981.

Mason, Theodore C. *Battleship Sailor*. Annapolis, MD: Naval Institute Press, 1982.

McKie, Ronald. *The Survivors*. Indianapolis, IN: Bobbs-Merrill, 1953.

Messimer, Dwight R. *Pawns of War: The Loss of the USS* Langley *and the USS* Pecos. Annapolis, MD: Naval Institute Press, 1983.

261

Morison, Samuel Eliot. *The Battle of the Atlantic: September 1939–May 1943*, Vol. 1. Boston: Little, Brown, 1947.

———. *The Rising Sun in the Pacific: 1931–April 1942*, Vol. 3. Boston: Atlantic-Little, Brown, 1948.

Organization and Ship's Regulations of the United States Ship Houston. Washington, D.C.: US Department of the Navy, 1937.

Payne, Alan. *HMAS Perth.* Garden Island, NSW, Australia: Naval Historical Society of Australia, 1978.

Perry, George Sessions, and Leighton, Isabel. *Where Away: A Modern Odyssey.* New York: Whittlesey House, 1944.

Prange, Gordon W. *At Dawn We Slept: The Untold Story of Pearl Harbor.* New York: McGraw-Hill, 1981.

Preston, Antony. *The Ship*, Vol. 9: *Dreadnaught to Nuclear Submarine.* London, England: Her Majesty's Stationery Office, 1980.

Soule, C. C. *Naval Terms and Definitions.* New York: D. Van Nostrand, 1922.

Spurr, Russell. *A Glorious Way to Die: The Kamikaze Mission of the Battleship* Yamato, *April, 1945.* New York: Newmarket Press, 1981.

Thomas, David. *The Battle of the Java Sea.* New York: Stein & Day, 1969.

Toland, John. *But Not in Shame: The Six Months after Pearl Harbor.* New York: Random House, 1961.

Tolley, Kemp. *Yangtze Patrol: The U.S. Navy in China.* Annapolis, MD: Naval Institute Press, 1971.

———. *Cruise of the Lanikai.* Annapolis, MD: Naval Institute Press, 1973.

Van Oosten, F. C. *The Battle of the Java Sea.* Annapolis, MD: Naval Institute Press, 1976.

Wigmore, Lionel. *The Japanese Thrust.* Adelaide, Australia: Griffin Press, 1957.

Willmott, H. P. *Empires in the Balance: Japanese and Allied Pacific Strategies to April 1942.* Annapolis, MD: Naval Institute Press, 1982.

Winslow, W. G. *The Ghost of the Java Coast: Saga of the USS Houston.* Satellite Beach, FL: Coral Reef Publications, 1974.

———. *The Fleet the Gods Forgot: The U.S. Asiatic Fleet in World War II.* Annapolis, MD: Naval Institute Press, 1982.

Newspapers and Periodicals

Periodicals reviewed for the book include *The New York Times*, *The Washington Post*, the *Houston Post*, the *Houston Chronicle*, the *Chicago Daily Tribune*, the *Chicago Sun*, *Shipmate*, *Our Navy*, *U.S. Naval Institute Proceedings*, *Stars and Stripes*, and the *Blue Bonnet*. Specific articles are cited in the Chapter Notes.

Archives

History and Museums Division, U.S. Marine Corps: Survivor Reports (cited in Chapter Notes).

M. D. Anderson Library, University of Houston: Cruiser *Houston* Memorial Collection.

Navy and Old Army Branch, National Archives: Deck Logs.

North Texas State University Archives, Oral History Collection: interviews with survivors.

Operational Archives Branch, Naval Historical Center: Action reports prepared by A. L. Maher, senior survivor; A. H. Rooks's "Estimate of the Situation"; narratives prepared by T. C. Hart and W. A. Glassford; narrative prepared by A. C. Robinson, USS *Marblehead;* General Board Records (Cruisers); Asiatic Fleet Dispatches; Survivor Reports (cited in Chapter Notes).

U.S.S. *Houston* Survivors Association, 267 Forest Drive, Union, New Jersey 07083.

Index